The Geopolitics
of Real Estate

Geopolitical Bodies, Material Worlds

This series publishes studies that originate in a range of different fields that are nonetheless linked through their common foundation: a belief that the macro-scale of geopolitics is composed of trans-local relations between bodies and materials that are only understandable through empirical examination of those relations. It is the interaction of these elements that produces the forces that shape global politics, often with outcomes that differ from the predictions of macro-scaled theories. This world poses questions: how do materialities such as the built environment and the body reproduce global power structures, how are they caught up in violent transformations and how do they become sites of resistance? How do assemblages of human and non-human elements both fortify and transform political space? What possibilities for political change are latent within the present?

Series Editors
Jason Dittmer, Professor of Political Geography at University College London
Ian Klinke, Associate Professor in Human Geography and Tutorial Fellow at
   St John's College, Oxford

Titles in the Series
The Geopolitics of Real Estate: Reconfiguring Property, Capital and Rights,
   Dallas Rogers (Forthcoming)
Choreographies of Resistance: Mobilities, Bodies and Politics, Tarja Väyrynen,
   Eeva Puumala, Samu Pehkonen, Tiina Vaittinen, Anitta Kynsilehto
Moving Lives: Critical Reflections on Climate Change and Migration, Andrew Baldwin
   and Giovanni Bettin
Territory Beyond Terra, Kimberley Peters, Philip Steinberg, Elaine Stratford
The Politics of Bodies at Risk: The Human in the Body, Maria Boikova Struble

The Geopolitics of Real Estate

Reconfiguring Property, Capital, and Rights

Dallas Rogers

ROWMAN &
LITTLEFIELD
———— INTERNATIONAL
London • New York

Published by Rowman & Littlefield International, Ltd.
Unit A, Whitacre Mews, 26-34 Stannary Street, London SE11 4AB
www.rowmaninternational.com

Rowman & Littlefield International, Ltd. is an affiliate of Rowman & Littlefield
4501 Forbes Boulevard, Suite 200, Lanham, Maryland 20706, USA
With additional offices in Boulder, New York, Toronto (Canada), and Plymouth (UK)
www.rowman.com

Copyright © Dallas Rogers, 2017

All rights reserved. No part of this book may be reproduced in any form or by any electronic or mechanical means, including information storage and retrieval systems, without written permission from the publisher, except by a reviewer who may quote passages in a review.

British Library Cataloguing in Publication Data
A catalogue record for this book is available from the British Library

ISBN: HB 978-1-7834-8332-7
   PB 978-1-7834-8333-4

Library of Congress Cataloging-in-Publication Data
ISBN 978-1-78348-332-7 (cloth : alk. paper)
ISBN 978-1-78348-333-4 (pbk. : alk. paper)
ISBN 978-1-78348-334-1 (electronic)

♾️ ™ The paper used in this publication meets the minimum requirements of American National Standard for Information Sciences—Permanence of Paper for Printed Library Materials, ANSI/NISO Z39.48-1992.

Printed in the United States of America

Contents

Acknowledgements   vii

1. Global Real Estate Semblances   1
2. Organising Technics, Mediating Technologies, and Discursive Code   15
3. Technics of Land I: Orality, Inclosure, Revolution, Land   41
4. Technics of Land II: Colonialism, Company, Measurement, Ownership   65
5. Technologies of Real Estate I: States, Banks, Population, Citizenship   83
6. Technologies of Real Estate II: Policy, Books, Visas, Events   109
7. New Discursive Code: Internet, Libertarianism, Upload, Download   133
8. Global Real Estate Assemblages   153

References   165

Index   185

About the Author   195

Acknowledgements

Out of respect for Aboriginal cultural protocol I acknowledge this book was written on Western Sydney University campuses that occupy the traditional lands of the Darug, Tharawal, Gandangarra and Wiradjuri peoples. This will always be their land. But as I show in this book, it continues to be subjected to Euro-centric legal codes and notions of property. The legal coding of property is often concealed within the mundane practices of everyday life, the almost invisible acts that many of us overlook, like placing a copyright symbol and a few legal words on the copyright page of this book. Few people read the copyright page, but it is nonetheless a powerful act that turns ideas into defensible property. In some small way, I hope to further expose the everyday practices of foreign settlers that allow them to claim Aboriginal land.

Thank you to Jason Dittmer for asking me to write a book for the Geopolitical Bodies, Material Worlds book series, after what I thought was a casual coffee at the 2014 American Association of Geographers Conference. I had originally proposed *The Globalisation of Real Estate* as a title of the book. Jason suggested *The Geopolitics of Real Estate*, and I quickly claimed it as my own. The ideas within this book have a slightly longer history, and they can be traced back to a brief moment at the Australasian Housing Researchers Conference in Adelaide in 2012. As Chris Paris approached the podium to talk about the second homes of the super-rich, he paused, and said in passing, "All this talk about community housing and the poor! If you really want to address the housing issues that affect the poor, then don't look at what the poor are doing. Take a look at the rich and super-rich." At the time, I was in the final year of a 3-year Australian Housing and Urban Research Institute (AHURI)-funded study looking at the politics of Australian housing. The first year looked at local housing politics. The second year focused on state and territory housing politics. Then quite fortuitously in the final year, I was looking at national-level housing politics. I had been watching Chinese real estate investment increase in Australia's residential real estate since 2011. I started investigating the politics of Chinese investment in earnest in 2012. Soon after, I set up the *Global Real Estate Project* to secure funding for an ongoing project. This book would not have been possible without the initial funding from the AHURI and the three rounds of funding from Western Sydney University between 2013 and 2015. The *Global Real Estate Project* took me from housing auctions in Sydney and Melbourne, where Australians that looked "Chinese" were being called foreign investors; to interviewing the Mousetribe in their basement air-raid bunker dorms in Beijing; to foreign real estate investment events in Hong Kong; and to the super-rich enclave of Sentosa Cove in Singapore. However, this book is not about the contemporary fieldwork that was conducted for the *Global Real Estate Project*. This book emerged out of being *in the field* and feeling that the typical history of foreign real estate investment is inadequate. Indeed, it was silent on many important issues. As an Australian, the most important silence for me was the question of *whose* land is being traded when we talk about foreign real estate investment? Foreign real estate investment history is surprisingly silent on the question of Indigenous land. I felt that I needed to historicise foreign real estate investment before I could begin to understand the empirical data collected for the *Global Real Estate Project*. This book is the product of those historical ruminations. But like any scholarly endeavour, I could not have completed this project alone. I would like to thank the AHURI and Western Sydney University (WSU) for funding the empirical studies. Special thanks to the people who worked on *Global Real Estate Project* studies: Chyi Lin Lee (Western Sydney University), Shanthi Robertson (Western Sydney University), Alexandra Wong (Western Sydney University), Gulia Del Maso (Western Sydney University), Jingjing Zhang (Western Sydney University), Jacqueline Nelson (University of Technology Sydney), and Ding Yan (National University of Singapore). Many of these great scholars helped with cross-cultural fieldwork in China, Singapore, and Australia, quantitative data analysis, or the anti-racism and migration analyses. I was lucky enough to test out many of the ideas in this book at the following workshops, conferences, and seminars in Australia, Asia, and the United States. In 2013, I was invited to the Changing Economies: Chinese Change and Australia workshop hosted by the Centre for United States and Asian Policy Studies (Flinders University) and the Institute of National Academy of Economic Strategy Chinese Academy of Social Sciences (China). In 2014, Tim Bunnell organised a visiting fellowship at the National University of Singapore, which provided invaluable access to research assistants and fieldwork sites in Asia. I presented at a Cities Clusters Seminar at the National University of Singapore. In 2015, Ray Forrest, Bart Wissink, and Sin Yee Koh invited me along to their Workshop on the

Super-rich at the City University of Hong Kong. I also presented work from the *Global Real Estate Project* at the 2015 Australasian Housing Researchers Conference, the 2015 Institute of Australian Geographers Conference, and the 2015 Australian Cities; Urban Geographies Workshop. Megan Watkins, Chris Ho, and Rose Butler invited Shanthi Robertson and I to present at the 2015 Asian Migration and Education Cultures Workshop. Peter Phibbs asked me to organise a panel session for the 2015 Festival of Urbanism in Sydney on the *Global Real Estate Project*. And in 2016, I organised a session at the American Association of Geographers conference on the globalisation of Real Estate with David Ley and Sin Yee Koh. I also presented at the 2016 Institute of Australian Geographers Conference and the 2016 Housing Theory Symposium, and organised a workshop on Cities and the Super-rich with Ilan Vizel. Thank you to everyone who provided critical feedback at events.

I published several papers, some with colleagues, from the *Global Real Estate Project*. Each shaped my thinking in this book: Rogers, D., and Dufty-Jones, R. (2015) "21st-Century Australian housing: New frontiers in the Asia-Pacific" in (eds.) *Housing in Twenty-First Century Australia: People, Practices and Policies*, Aldershot: Ashgate; and Rogers, D., Lee, C. L. and Yan, D. (2015). "The politics of foreign investment in Australian housing: Chinese investors, translocal sales agents and local resistance", *Housing Studies*, vol. 30, no. 5, pp. 730–748; Rogers, D. (2016) "Uploading real estate: Home as a digital, global commodity" in Cook, N., Davison, A., and Crabtree. L. (eds.) *Housing and Home Unbound*. London: Routledge; Rogers, D. (2017) "Becoming a super-rich foreign real estate investor: Globalising real estate data, publications and events" in Forrest, R., Wissink, D., and Koh, S. Y., (eds.) *Cities and the Super-Rich: Real Estate, Elite Practices and Urban Political Economies*. Basingstoke: Palgrave Macmillan.

Finally, as I was researching and writing about gender discrimination in the industrial home for Chapter 6, my wife, Jacqueline Nelson, was caring for our new baby Louie Francis Rogers with very little help from me (by the way, Jacqueline managed the anti-racism analysis for the *Global Real Estate Project*). My daughter, Nissa Rogers, helped out with Louie too of course, but that only made the gender disparity worse. It seems that the discriminatory forces within academia are still very much at play within our home. Therefore, a huge thank you – and apology – goes to my family, who supported me through this very poorly timed book project as we welcomed our new little family member into the world. Nissa and Louie, this book is for you – read it, there will be a test!

Chapter 1

Global Real Estate Semblances

SETTLING ON THE LAND[1]

In 1939, John Steinbeck cast light into the darkness of the "Great American" project of settler-colonialist land claiming with some brilliant, if not profoundly demoralising, prose. In a 250-odd-word passage in his masterpiece *The Grapes of Wrath*, Steinbeck summarises the devastating consequences for one family of tenant farmers who are dually trapped within the Dust Bowl and the Great Depression in 1930s America. Steinbeck pulls together many of the central themes explored in this book. He talks about the expulsion of Indigenous peoples from their land through violence, and questions whether the application of labour to the land should set the condition of ownership. He contrasts the subjective lived experience of home with the financial commodification of real estate. He describes in minute detail how non-benevolent banks evicted the colonisers from their bank-owned land. But most importantly he showcases the power of mediating technologies, such as written title deeds on paper, or new industrial machinery, or the role of measurement and boundary making in the land revolutions, which reverberated around the world in the last four centuries. Steinbeck's prose cuts through the politics of land and real estate to get to the heart of the issue: the relationship between land and body. He writes:

> The tenant men looked up alarmed. But what'll happen to us? How'll we eat?
> You'll have to get off the land. The plows'll go through the dooryard.
> And now the squatting men stood up angrily. Grampa took up the land, and he had to kill the Indians and drive them away. And Pa was born here, and he killed weeds and snakes. Then a bad year came and he had to borrow a little money. An' we was born here. There in the door – our children born here. And

> Pa had to borrow money. The bank owned the land then, but we stayed and we got a little bit of what we raised.
> We know that – all that. It's not us, it's the bank. A bank isn't like a man. Or an owner with fifty thousand acres, he isn't like a man either. That's the monster.
> Sure, cried the tenant men, but it's our land. We measured it and broke it up. We were born on it, and we got killed on it, died on it. Even if it's no good, it's still ours. That's what makes it ours – being born on it, working it, dying on it. That makes ownership, not a paper with numbers on it.
> We're sorry. It's not us. It's the monster. The bank isn't like a man.
> Yes, but the bank is only made of men.
> No, you're wrong there – quite wrong there. The bank is something else than men. It happens that every man in a bank hates what the bank does, and yet the bank does it. The bank is something more than men, I tell you. It's the monster. Men made it, but they can't control it. The tenants cried. ... (Steinbeck, 1939: 22–23)

I read Steinbeck's writing from 1939 as a semblance of the globalisation of real estate that occurred through the European colonial projects throughout the nineteenth and twentieth centuries. I use the word semblance to draw attention to the way this seemingly contained event – a crisis within the American project of nation-building – is covering over a deeper reality about the geopolitical transfer of land, bodies, labour, and capital. Steinbeck's story is significant, not because of the explicit story it tells, but for the implicit narrative that lies beneath the surface of this fictional narrative about Americanness. Read in this way, there is at least a dual narrative in Steinbeck's book. There is the explicit story about the Joads, a poor tenant farming family who are expelled from the land and their livelihood. There is also an implicit story about the failure of settler-societies; the failure of colonialism more generally. We need to move beyond the superficial appearances of events like this, which cover over the deeper historical realities that sit beneath the explicit narratives about land and real estate crises. What are the hidden, historical realities of an event like the one described by Steinbeck?

For too long, and increasingly from the Second World War, the politics surrounding land and real estate have been thought of as occurring within the sovereign domains of nation states; bounded and contained within their borders; fixed to particular political eras; and controlled by the regulatory categories that governments create to build collective ideas around citizenship and nationhood. Landed property and real estate rights are shaped by culture, and "not by an immutable necessity" (Weaver, 2003: 29). They transcend regulatory, physical, temporal, and cultural boundaries. As Weaver (2003: 30) describes it in relation to the British colonial project, "One culture rich in ideas about landed property rights rolled across other cultures that formally had maintained [and maintain] different perceptions of the land." Looking forward, Andro Linklater (2014: 4) opens his expansive magnum opus, *Owning the Earth*, with an obvious but nonetheless stark reminder about what is at stake in twenty-first-century geopolitical real estate relations; "Any realistic scenario for 2050," he writes, "has to consider how the earth will be owned." Looking forward is an important and wholly under-performed task in housing and urban studies.

What can contemporary semblances of the geopolitical transfer of land, bodies, labour, and capital teach us about the past, present, and future? The actions of the aspiring politician and self-declared radical opponent of multiculturalism, Nick Folkes from Sydney, Australia, are telling. In 2015, Folkes attempted to launch a new political party with a contentious leaflet with the words "STOP THE CHINESE INVASION" overlaid a bright red Chinese flag and a menacing looking Asian soldier (McNally, 2015: 1). The "invasion," to which Folkes refers, is not a military invasion. It is rather the material claiming of land by foreign Chinese bodies that he is constructing as an invasion. He claims, "The new dispossessed or forgotten people will one day be remembered as the 'stolen generation' priced out of their [housing] market by invading Chinese foreigners" (McNally, 2015: 1). The tendency has been to ignore, to attempt to forget about, people like Folkes in Australia. They unsettle our dreams of harmony and sovereignty, they reminds us of our troubled past, present, and future. John Ajaka, the Australian multiculturalism minister, labelled Folkes an "idiot. ... I can't think of any other word to call him" (McNally, 2015: 1). In settler-societies, dispossessing Indigenous peoples of their land is in one sense complete, and in another it is never finished. As such, Folkes does not simply reject the reality of Indigenous dispossession in Australia, rather he appropriates it – he colonises their discourse. His reference to the "stolen generation" is an attempt to colonise the terms that has been used to describe the forced removal of children of Australian Aboriginal and Torres Strait Islander descent from their families between 1905 and 1969 in Australia (Langton, 2000).

Folkes is a pre-eminent settler; he is here to replace and to defend (Veracini, 2013: 313). As Edward Cavanagh and Lorenzo Veracini (2013: 1) show, "Settler colonialism is a resilient formation that rarely ends." Settlers come with their own sovereign political orders, and Folkes refuses to acknowledge past, present, or future Indigenous land practices; he also refuses to acknowledge the successive waves of Chinese migration and real estate investment in Australia (Anderson, 1990; Ang et al., 2015; Robertson, 2013). "[S]ettlers want Indigenous people to vanish" (Cavanagh and Veracini, 2013: 1), and Folkes wants Chinese investors to vanish too. "Settler colonialism is about turning a place and a specific human material into something else," where the "colonisers 'come to stay' and to establish new political orders for themselves, rather than to exploit native labour" (Veracini, 2013: 313). Settler-colonialism is about the geopolitics of claiming, regulating, and protecting land, and it is the present structure within which Folkes is caught, rather than a series of historical events that occurred in the past (Veracini, 2013: 314). Folkes is shoring up his tenuous position within the current geopolitics of land and real estate. He has the weight of history on one side and force of the future on the other. This moment – this crisis of real estate sovereignty that Folkes' proclaims is real – is but another semblance of the globalisation of real estate. It is useful only in its capacity to tell us something about what lies beneath this event; something about the structures embedded within this event that stretch across time and space. Folkes' story tells us much about the "story of an original dispossession, of the 'primitive accumulation' Marx diagnosed whereby the mass of people are expropriated from their land and from their control of land, thus heralding the capitalist mode of production" (Porter, 2014: 390). Bernard Bailyn writes that historical analyses should comprise "structural studies woven into narratives that explain the long-term processes of change and the short-term accidents, decisions, and encounters which together changed the world from what it had been" (Bailyn, 1995; cited by Weaver, 2003: 30). What follows in this book, then, is a historical analysis of the geopolitics of real estate with settler-colonialism on the one side, and the rise of the über-wealthy and increasingly foreign elites (e.g., high-net-worth [HNW] and ultra-high-net-worth [UHNW] individuals) and Alpha Territories (e.g., the *territories* that the über-wealthy elites live in) on the other (Webber and Burrows, 2015: 2; Glucksberg, 2016).

LAND, LABOUR, CAPITAL

There is a long and rich history of critical reflection on the relations between territory, land, human labour, and capital. Take Sir William Petty's (1690) seminal idea that land has to be treated as capital, and only labour can release its value. Or Jean-Jacques Rousseau's (1750) disquiet about the feudal order giving way to private ownership, and his often-cited aphorism about "discovering land"; "The first man who, having enclosed a piece of land, ventured to say, 'This is mine' ...." Adam Smith (1776) famously floated the idea of the invisible hand, which neoclassical economists would later champion. And what about one of the first people to be known as a communist, François-Noël Babeuf? He advocated the confiscation and redistribution of land to create a more equitable society. Pierre-Joseph Proudhon coined the phrase "Property is theft," which Karl Marx and Frederick Engels (1848) ran with in *The Communist Manifesto*. Later, Friedrich von Hayek (1944) countered with his libertarianist proclamation about individual liberty and property in his best-selling book, *The Road to the Serfdom*, published in 1944. Over a lifetime, Edward Said's (1978; 1993; 1999; 2000) scholarship interrogated questions of land control, discourse, memory, culture, and exclusion. What makes the twenty-first-century different to the twentieth-century is not only the renewed scholarly focus on geopolitical questions about landed property and real estate, but also the broader public interest in these questions that has accompanied it. Two expansive scholarly manuscripts in particular encapsulate many of the questions and anxieties of the contemporary moment, but do so by looking to the past; these are Linklater's (2014) historical rewriting of land ownership and Stuart Elden's (2013) nod towards Michel Foucault's historical genealogy of institutional power, with his historical genealogy of territory. I draw heavily on these two accounts in this analysis, and their arguments implicitly underwrite much of the discussion that follows. Elden (2013: 8–9) writes:

> Genealogy [is] understood as a historical interrogation of the conditions of possibility of things being as they are ... There is a fundamental need to return to the texts that reveal the concepts that inform the practices. ... Territory should be seen as inherently related to, yet, ultimately distant from, two different concepts: land and terrain. Land is a relation of property [like real estate that sits upon it], a finite resource that is distributed, allocated, and owned – a political-economic question. Land can be bought, sold, and exchanged; it is a resource over which there is competition ... [a] three-way relation of 'land-capital-labor' ... Conflict over land is twofold: both over its possession and conducted on its terrain.

What is more surprising than Linklater and Elden's writings is the emerging corpus of popular books on the topic of global landgrabbers and the globalisation of real estate, which appeared on bookshelves in major capital cities around the world after 2010. While conceptually thin, these books tell us something important about the contemporary moment – something about the collective sociocultural anxieties of our time, which people like Folkes attempt to mobilise politically. There is, arguably, no greater litmus test for broad public interest in a social issue than the book titles at major international airports, and this is where I found two books that provide popular cultural counterpoints to Linklater and Elden's denser discussions, one dystopian and the other utopian. The first is Fred Pearce's (2012) dystopian *The Landgrabbers: The new fight over who owns the earth – How city financiers, Chinese billionaires, oil Sheikhs and agribusiness are buying up our hungry, crowded world*. The second is Martin Adams's (2015) cautiously utopian *Land: A New Paradigm for a Thriving World*. You can add to these books the wide-ranging media commentary on issues around individual and institutional foreign real estate investment in residential real estate and farm land in settler-societies (e.g., Australia, United States, and Canada) and former colonial states (e.g., United Kingdom) (Australia-China Council, 2012; Brumby, 2011; Calvert, 2015; Chancellor, 2012, 2013; Gottliebsen, 2012; Hyam and Janda, 2014; KPMG, 2012; Lang, 2011; Laurenceson, 2008; Mason, 2014; Nicholls, 2011; Schlesinger, 2013; Stanley, 2013; Stier, 2012; Sumption and Hooper, 2014; Taylor, 2012b; Trotman, 2013; Xiao, 2013; Zhou, 2013).

It is little wonder the New Zealand-based journalist Rakesh Krishnan Simha (2012: 1) used the popular catch phrase "Colonialism 2.0" to provocatively inquire, "Is the West reviving what was once a spectacularly successful Western strategy – colonisation?" (Simha, 2012: 1). It is a useful provocation, but one that is conceptually and historically problematic. Glen Coulthard's (2014) call-to-arms *Red Skins, White Masks: Rejecting the Colonial Politics of Recognition*, returns to one of the operative tensions in this debate, "Settler colonialism is territorially acquisitive in perpetuity ... an ongoing practice of dispossession that never ceases to structure capitalist and colonial social relations in the present" (pp. 150–151). Or as Patrick Wolfe (2006) puts it, "Whatever settlers may say – and they generally have a lot to say – the primary motive for elimination is not race (or religion, ethnicity, grade of civilisation, etc.) but access to territory. Territoriality is settler-colonialism's specific, irreducible element" (p. 338). Libby Porter (2014: 391) concludes, "A culture of land speculation, egged on by the promise of spectacular profits, all built off that original dispossession" is the context of all contexts, and it sits eerily beneath contemporary questions about the globalisation of land and real estate in settler-societies.

If dispossession is *the context*, then geopolitics is certainly one of the *many contexts* which it enframes. Geopolitics is used here both in a very limited sense, as relating to international relations, and in a broader sense to refer to the politics of geography (Dittmer and Sharp, 2014: more about the difference in the next section). While, foreign real estate investment in the United States, United Kingdom, Canada, Australia, and other countries is a long-standing cultural and geopolitical issue, there has certainly been a re-intensification of this geopolitics over the last decade (Baum and Hartzell, 2012; Buckley et al., 2010a; Dorling, 2014; Rogers et al., 2015). There is a substantial body of scholarship on East Asian investors in the settler-societies of Australia and Canada from the 1980 to 1990s and Western Anglophone investors in the former colonies and other comparatively more affordable European countries over the last three decades (Berry et al., 1999; Edgington, 1996; Javorcik et al., 2011; Paris, 2013; Ray et al., 1997). The increasing global real estate activity of the expanding middle class from Brazil, Russia, India, China, and South Africa (known collectively as the BRICS) and the Four Asian Tiger countries (Hong Kong, Singapore, South Korea, and Taiwan) have introduced new and revived some existing economic, cultural, and political sensitivities (Ley, 2011). The geopolitics relating to the history of non-white citizens purchasing real estate in settler-societies such as Canada, United States, and Australia remains highly contentious (Edgington, 1996; Javorcik et al., 2011; Ray et al., 1997). However, because the recent historical geography of the United Kingdom is enframed by the country's role as a colonial power, rather than as a settler-society, scholars from the United Kingdom are analysing the globalisation of real estate and its effects on cities, such as London, from a different ontological starting point (Glucksberg, 2016; Webber and Burrows, 2015). The ontological implications of who was dispossessed from their land is different, and as such this analysis is somewhat quiet on the effects of the globalisation of real estate within the former colonial state powers in Europe (although there is perhaps a fruitful comparative study to explore therein).

Furthermore, placing the settler-societies at the centre of this debate – as countries by which to measure the rise of Asia – rightly opens the discussion up to a charge of Euro-centrism (Said, 1978, 1993). Provocatively, Martin Jacques (2012) prompts a different type of regional and global imaginary in his book *When China Rules the World*. Jacques argues that while China is set to become the central economic, cultural and geopolitical player in the Asia-Pacific region and the world, the Chinese will not achieve this by becoming more "Western." Geopolitically, the rise of China may well challenge some of the settler-society's most cherished political, economic, and cultural ideals: the dominance of Western style nation states and democracy are chief among them. The shift in political and economic power from Europe and the United States towards China has facilitated changes in city formation and housing provision that are without precedent in human history (Jacques, 2012; Ren, 2013; Wu et al., 2007). When the Peoples' Republic of China was established in 1949, only 10 per cent of the national population lived in cities (Ren, 2013: xiii). By 1978, a time of major market reforms, that figure had only reached 20 per cent. In the last 35 years, China has implemented an uncompromising urbanisation process by adding more than 400 new cities with hundreds of millions of people moving from their historically agrarian communities into new urban environments (Ren, 2013: xiii). In 2010, it was estimated that 50 per cent of the national population now lived in cities (Ren, 2013: xiii). Subsequently, Chinese property developers have become experienced housing providers and Chinese nationals have quickly become experienced housing investors in national and international markets. Buckley et al. (2010b: 119) argue that China has been the focus of much inward foreign direct investment (FDI) research. But as of 2010, less empirical attention had been paid to China's outward FDI following the Global Financial Crisis and very little empirical attention was given to outward individual FDI from China into foreign residential real estate (Buckley et al., 2010a).

The scale and speed of the cultural, economic, and political rise of China has taken many local and global real estate professionals, government policy makers and urban scholars in settler-societies by surprise (Buckley et al., 2010b; Javorcik et al., 2011; Ley, 2011; 2015; Paris, 2013; Ray et al., 1997; Rogers, 2016a; Rogers and Dufty-Jones, 2015; Rogers et al., 2015; Webber and Burrows, 2015). For example, in Australia, the federal government's international relations commitments to Asia (Australian Government, 2012) is complicated by recent media discourse linking Chinese investors with increasing property prices and corruption (Rogers et al., 2015). In Canada, similar concerns forced the government to review their Immigrant Investment Visa, which allowed HNW and UHNW foreigners to acquire citizenship status through a real estate purchase. Hay (2013) defines individuals with asset holdings in excess of US$1M as HNW and those with more than US$30M as UHNW individuals (p. 4). Recently individuals from the Asia-Pacific region became the greatest contributors to these two cohorts (Hay, 2013: 5). Thus, international relations are central to contemporary global real estate practices, and, therefore the rise of China is a major geopolitical disruption.

There are similarities in the politics and practice of foreign real estate investment in the Asia-Pacific and Americas between 1980 and 1990s and the first two decades of the twenty-first-century, as I will show later in this book. However, there also are important differences, four of which I briefly outline here. First, large Asian financial and property development companies are increasingly providing capital and technical expertise in the United States, Australian, and Canadian housing sectors (Baum and Hartzell, 2012; Rogers et al., 2015). Second, the business relationships between Western Anglophone and Asian real estate professionals have intensified over the last decade. These relations are increasingly facilitated through advancements in electronic communication technologies (Rogers et al., 2015) and transnational intercultural networks (Baum and Hartzell, 2012; Javorcik et al., 2011). Ang et al. (2015) highlight that settler-societies are in a unique position in this respect, and Australia has a particular advantage because more "than 8% of Australia's population was born in Asia. This is a much higher percentage than in other Anglophone countries such as the United States (4%) and the United Kingdom (2%) … Asian Australians bring with them linguistic skills, social networks and cultural knowledge, which can enhance links between Australia and Asia. But their role and contribution is insufficiently recognised" (Ang et al., 2015: 16). Third, the local economic systems, housing policies, home-ownership rules, and taxation settings within the BRICS countries are reportedly motivating local investors to diversify their domestic investments, leading them to look for investment opportunities overseas. Equally, the housing, foreign investment visa, economic, and educational landscapes of several Anglo-settler countries are reportedly preparing for new HNW middle class and UHNW super-rich investors and capital to flow into local real estate. Collectively, these flows of human and financial capital are reshaping global real estate investment practice (Baum and Hartzell, 2012; Buckley et al., 2010a; Javorcik et al., 2011). Fourth, the early twenty-first-century has seen a shift in housing scholarship with a critical gaze being cast upon the global inequities perpetuated by the world's new middle class and super-rich (Dorling, 2014; Hay, 2013; Piketty, 2014). This enquiry has come from a range of epistemic positions, with recent studies showing that gaining access to the economic, social, and political spaces of the new middle class and super-rich can be a difficult task (Short, 2013: 26). Related to this, much of the contemporary data on global real estate investment are focused on financial capital flows into or out of nation states and collated from national or real estate industry quantitative data sets (some important exceptions include: Buckley et al., 2010a; Glucksberg, 2016; Hay, 2013; Paris, 2013; Ray et al., 1997; Rogers et al., 2015; Webber and Burrows, 2015).

Academic, industry, media, and policy discourse is now replete with sensational, and at time sensationalist, discourse about the type, scale, and scope of human and financial capital that is flowing into real estate and cities around the world (Australia-China Council, 2012; Brumby, 2011; Calvert, 2015; Chancellor, 2013; Hyam and Janda, 2014; KPMG, 2012; Schlesinger, 2013; Standing Committee on Economics, 2014). Mirjam Büdenbender and Oleg Golubchikov (2016: 2) describe the hyperbole, by drawing on the *Global Real Estate Project*, as follows; "newspapers write on almost a daily basis about the 'invasion' of global cities by foreign real estate investors." For example, in terms of local real estate politics, as one media observer in Australia put it, "Today, Chinese money makes up the fastest-growing segment of the real estate market in Australia" (Taylor, 2012a: 1). It is both a familiar narrative and a conceptual trap to describe the globalisation of real estate in this way, and I do not want to rehearse this foreign capital transfer discourse here in detail. Nevertheless, it would be remiss of me not to note the sheer scale and scope of human and financial capital flows that are involved in the contemporary wave of the globalisation of real estate. What follows, then, is a selection of statistics for Australia. Local variations of this narrative exist for the United Kingdom and Canada too, and to a lesser extent the United States and other European and African countries (Australian Government, 2012; Baum and Hartzell, 2012; Berry et al., 1999; Buckley et al., 2010a; Edgington, 1996; Macken, 2014; Paris, 2013; Sumption and Hooper, 2013, 2014; Webber and Burrows, 2015).

Over the last decade, the changing nationalities of the individual foreign nationals investing in residential real estate in Australia have garnered considerable political and media attention. Indeed this change has been both rapid and significant. After 2012, much of the attention has been focused on Chinese investors and has been negative in orientation. At the time of the Asian Financial Crisis in 1998, 24 per cent of global individual FDI from

China was in foreign real estate (Buckley et al., 2010a: 247). According to the Australian federal government's Foreign Investment Review Board (FIRB), which sits within Treasury, approved foreign investment in Australian real estate by Chinese investors was A$712 million in 2006–2007, A$4.2 billion in 2011–2012, A$5.9 billion in 2012–2013, and $12.4 billion in 2013–2014 (Australian Government, 2012, 2013, 2014, 2015). This is a substantial increase in foreign capital flows from China. However, total Chinese foreign investment into Australia across all sectors was only greater than the investment from the United States for the first time in the 2013–2014 reporting period, with the United States being pushed to second place. There are well-reported limitations with these FDI data sets (Gauder et al., 2014; Robertson and Rogers, in-press; Rogers and Dufty-Jones, 2015). There are also deeper conceptual issues with thinking about the globalisation of real estate as a set of contemporary human and financial capital flows that sit outside of the history of land claiming.

If settler-colonialism is about the geopolitics of claiming, regulating, and protecting land, and real estate is a mediating technology through which to claim land, then there is an entire history of land and real estate mediators and intermediaries that is herein largely unexamined by urban scholars (Ley, 2011; Rogers et al., 2015). In other words, there is a need to examine the role that human *bodies* play in lubricating the movement of human and financial capital around the world. Contemporary scholars are paying more attention to the mediating role that the global real estate industry plays. This industry is made up of transnational sales agents, international property developers, international real estate publishers, foreign home loan brokers, global investment lawyers, and immigration and visa consultants (hereafter, global real estate professionals) who are operating in the spaces between the cultural, political, and economic borders that are constructed by nation states (Mezzadra and Neilson, 2013). The same is true for the colonial period. During this period, committee members and lawyers within seventeenth-century joint-stock companies were also central to the movement of human and financial capital around the colonial world, as Philip Stern (2011) notes:

> As law and justice served to buttress the [joint-stock] company's authority within a settlement, it also reinforced a broader vision of a system of settlements, bound together in a network of exchange and movement (p. 29) ... the street names were themselves only systematised after 1688, in the hopes of reducing potential confusion during attack or siege as well as regularising property deeds and the assessment of ground rents and taxes (p. 31) ... population was also, a number of political economists including Company committee Josiah Child argued, the core source of a polity's wealth. Immigrants planted land and produced for the local economy (p. 37) ... true ownership and sovereignty could not lie in passive grants or first discovery but had to be maintained

through the use, occupation, possession, or improvement of the [landed] jurisdiction in question. (p. 56).

Today's global real estate professionals, much like the committee members and lawyers within seventeenth-century joint-stock companies, are busy shoring up their tenuous positions within the geopolitical landscapes of global land claiming and real estate they find themselves within. The ideas about the global real estate industry and joint-stock company – and more importantly, therefore, the narratives that are built solely from statistical data sets about Asian and other foreign investor capital flows – are nothing more than another set of semblances of the globalisation of real estate. They too are only useful for their capacity to show us what is common and dissimilar about what lies beneath these events; something about the structures that get embedded or set free as each new crisis in land or real estate stretches across time and space. Assembled together, they show how mobility, dispossession, improvement, use, occupation, or possession changes over time. What Saskia Sassen (2014) calls "*conceptual* subterranean trends" (p. 5), which can be "hard to see when we think with our familiar geopolitical, economic, and social" epistemological tools (p. 6). Searching for and assembling the subterranean conceptual trends – the organising logics of land and real estate – allows us to assess whether the contemporary geopolitics of real estate is an extreme version(s) of older geopolitical real estate structures and manifestations, or something entirely new.

GEOPOLITICS OF REAL ESTATE

A productive way forward is to study the spatialities and temporalities – the geography – of the politics of land claiming and real estate investment over an extended timeframe (Dittmer and Sharp, 2014: 3). Although there is a need for specificity; a specific emphasis on how the land claiming and real estate geographies contribute to and emerge from particular geographies of land and real estate politics. This is what is meant by a historical analysis of the geopolitics of real estate. It is spatial in a mathematical sense, in that the material parameters of space can be used to bracket off and conceptualise different "spaces" – the boundaries of a nation state, a plot of land, or the limits of privately owned property. It is also spatial in a more subjective sense, in that different people and institutions are engaged in endless struggles (i.e., politics) over setting the boundaries of, or validating their subjective experiences within, physical space. It is temporal in a rationalist mathematical sense too, because Western notions of calendar time are fundamental differentiators that shape and inform peoples' understanding and experience of the social, cultural, political, and material worlds. However, rationalist mathematical time, and particularly Gregorian calendar and early mechanical clock time, are problematic temporal frames for a historical analysis of the geopolitical land claiming events that involve Indigenous peoples.

Geopolitics should not, therefore, be understood in a narrow sense as international relations, global politics, or the political practice of statecraft (as I and others have previously described the geopolitics of real estate, e.g., Büdenbender and Golubchikov, 2016; Nozeman and Van der Vlist, 2014: 35; Rogers and Dufty-Jones, 2015: 223). Geopolitics should not be understood through "a narrow instrumental form of reason that is also a form of faith, a belief that there is a secret substratum and/or a permanent set of conflicts and interests that accounts for the course of world politics". Elizabeth Ermath (2011: 20) writes, "The construction of time as a neutral medium remains for most of us merely common sense, largely thanks to nineteenth-century historians in all fields from literature and social analysis to biology and geology." Following Ermath's (2010) critique of the temporal neutrality of modernity, "a value invented by the Renaissance" (p. 134), Louise Crabtree (2013: 100) argues that Western notions "progress, growth, and value increase are all deeply shaped by a model of linear time," which is indebted to Western knowledge systems and entirely incompatible with many Indigenous temporal frames as they relate to land. In fact, the temporal neutrality of modernity, expressed and regulated using Gregorian calendar and mechanical clock time, is a mediating technology the settler-colonists used, and continue to use, to restory particular people and places, as we will see. Hyatt (2005: 517) reminds us that Western notions of time have become a significant form of social control, which requires us to "consider again the hegemonic rule of the clock in western industrial society." The same could be said of the hegemonic rule of physical space, and Foucault (with Miskowiec 1986: 23) argues that physical space still needs to be "desanctified" in a similar way to which Ermath has done for time. This is true for a study of the geopolitics of real estate too; there is a need to de-colonise space in relation to the globalisation of real estate. But given my focus on history and temporality, I have not pursued this theoretical task in this analysis (although I have started this work in other places: Rogers, 2014).

It is well known in philosophy that mathematical, physical, and material conceptualisations of time and space are not a set of a priori conditions (Bachelard, 1969; Lefebvre, 1991; Massey, 1992, 2005; Osborne, 1995). Rather "reason" frames the conditions of possibility that set the political reasons for demarcating calendar time and physical space in particular ways. Geography is always, therefore, (geo-)political. Critical geopolitics is, as Gearóid Ó Tuathail (1999: 107) argues, a theoretical enterprise that problematises the geographical "structures of [the] power and knowledge in question." Critical geopolitical scholarship (Dittmer and Sharp, 2014), in contrast to so-called classical geopolitical scholarship (Kelly, 2006: 24), is recalibrating the empirical focus back towards the everyday lived experiences of people who are operating within the geopolitical structures of power and knowledge. Critical geopolitics involves much more than an analysis of the global-level practices of statecraft. The object of study is often local, particular, and embodied. Understood in this way, I conceive of Caroline Knowles' (2014) *ground level* study of the rubber sandal[3] as a work of critical geopolitics, although Knowles may not describe her work in these terms. In any case, I am following this *ground level* approach in this geopolitical analysis.

Colonial land claiming and foreign real estate investment are quintessentially geopolitical concerns, but they should not be solely viewed as events that are played out at the "global-level," or as events that solely involve global actors, corporations, and nation states. Feminist scholars such as Joanne Sharp (2007) and philosophers such as Jeff Malpas (2012) have deployed the concept of topology to productively do away with modular notions of scale. They provide a conceptual pathway that focuses on so-called "global scales of analysis without abandoning their attention to the importance of the embodied everyday experience of peoples in different locations in the world economy" (Sharp, 2007: 381; also see Pain, 2009). Jason Dittmer (2013) activates the relational ontology of a Deleuze–Guattarian-inspired assemblage theory to do away with the rigid markings of scale within his geopolitical scholarship. The emphasis is on how everyday life, and different topologies of power, work through a constantly changing set of translocal assemblages, including, but not limited to, different bodies, localities, regions, nation states, and global flows (Acuto and Curtis, 2013; Anderson et al., 2012; Dirlik, 2003; Dittmer, 2013; 2014; Dittmer and Gray, 2010; Harman, 2013; Kennedy et al., 2013; McFarlane, 2009; Pain, 2009; Robbins and Marks, 2010). The 'global' is still important within a critical geopolitical analysis, but the body is recentred. As Dittmer (2013: 6) argues, drawing on Bruno Latour (2005), this is "a 'bottom up' process."

For example, "settler societies built 'homelands' through the mass murder of Indigenous peoples, and many continue to deploy military force in ongoing land claims disputes ... 'red scares'" (Cowen and Smith, 2009: 31) – the fear of the invading Asian – continue to frame the local actions of people in settler-societies. Deborah Cowen and Neil Smith (2009) argue that "these changes are woven into a broader recasting of the form and meaning of territorial state boundaries" (p. 31), such that classical geopolitical spatial and temporal imaginaries are called into question. "The border" can no longer be viewed as a physical territorial frontier that can be secured with physical force, nor is it solely a political border that can be secured by political legitimacy. Foreign land claiming and real estate investment are made manifest precisely because of the impossibility of securing the physical and political border from the movement of human bodies. Crises in foreign land claiming and real estate demonstrate the *impossibility* of physical and geopolitical borders because of the geoeconomic movement of human and financial capital across these borders (Cowen and Smith, 2009: 32; the authors' emphasis). The nation state is forced into an ongoing negotiation between the territorial, political, and economic arrangement of their borders by what is happening to the bodies "on the ground." Deborah Cowen and Neil Smith (2009) describe the contemporary moment as displaying a "global economic logic that transcends geopolitical calculation, even if the system of national states remains intact and powerful." Nation states "have to renovate their modus operandi" from a politico-territorial to an economic register (p. 38).

This analysis explores, therefore, how the bodies on the ground interact with these types of negotiations from the bottom-up. Rather than the global driving the local, or the local shaping the global, the assemblage of bodies, technologies, land, real estate, events, history, and territory develop their own agency for action. For example, war creates a crisis that often solidifies the physical territorial borders of nation states and it changes the condition under which land and real estate might be claimed. However, it is the movement of a huge army of human bodies across the ground that is mobilised to claim the large sways of land under the changing politico-territorial conditions of war. Of course, large sways of land and human bodies are also lost. During peacetime, the physical territorial borders of nation states might slowly loosen up, and an entirely different set of politico-territorial and economic conditions is opened up alongside it. Land and real estate can be claimed under a new set of conditions by the movement of a single human body across a physical and political frontier. Think about how the settler-societies used the baby boomer *body* after the Second World War as a technology through which real estate investment could be mobilised to rebuild the nation state's consumer economy.

In the pages that follow, it is not a matter of determining causality, such as which part of the assemblage affected the other. Rather, the analytical tactic is to look for the emergence of a set of historical and contemporary land and real estate crises, to see how they take shape, how they are assembled, and if and how the subterranean conceptual trends, organising logics, and technologies of land and real estate claiming accumulate over time.

NOTES

1. This is the title of a poem by the nineteenth- and twentieth-century Australian poet Henry Lawson. Lawson H. (1940) "Settling on the land." In: Compiled by Angus and Robertson (ed.) Prose Works of Henry Lawson. Sydney: Halstead Press.

2. See the Acknowledgements for a description of the *Global Real Estate Project*.

3. The rubber sandal is colloquially known as the Flip-Flop in the United Kingdom, and comically, for the Britons, as a thong in Australia.

Chapter 2

Organising Technics, Mediating Technologies, and Discursive Code

MOMENTS OF REAL ESTATE CRISIS

The movement of human and financial capital into foreign land and real estate has long been a contentious cultural and geopolitical issue (Rogers et al., 2015). The reconfiguration of Asian geopolitical power has ruptured the conceptual landscape for understanding international real estate relations, and new methodologies are needed. This book is underwritten by an anticipatory historical methodology that de-essentialises and historicises the globalisation of real estate. The methodology is historical, but one that is not bound by the constraints of mapping causal events across calendar time. It is not a temporal analysis that is structured by a series of chronological events, as traditional historical methodologies might stipulate (Jenkins, 1991: 6). It is a historical analysis of the geopolitics of real estate, but one that is free of calendar time as the central organising frame. Ermarth (2011: xvi) argues that the assumption of temporal neutrality and causality is a discursive product of modernity. She claims, "Historical methods and assumptions govern to a significant degree the now common-sense definitions of identity, causality, time and sequence" (p. xvi), and that calendar time is not a reliable frame of reference for a historical analysis. (This is especially the case for understanding Indigenous land claiming; see Crabtree, 2013.) Thus, the focus is on mapping moments of real estate crisis over an extended timeline. The aim is to create an anticipatory – essomenic – analysis of the globalisation of real estate, but with a different chronological register than Elden's (2013: 322) Foucauldian-inspired genealogical analysis of "territory as political technology." I share with the twentieth century's finest theoretical portmantologist,[1] Michel Foucault, an interest in writing a counter-history. However, there is a historical linearity and a radicarianism to Foucault (1969: 5) and Elden's (2013: 8) work that this book does not share.

Chapter 2

Fairclough (1992: 230) advocates a focus on "moments of crisis" to expose hidden or obscure social, cultural, or economic struggles. Such moments of crisis make visible aspects of social practices that might be difficult to notice, because they have been normalised or forgotten. Moments of crisis can also reveal change in progress, the actual ways in which people work through social, cultural, or economic conflicts (Fairclough, 1992: 230), and how wider changes in society and culture manifest in the everyday practices of the people involved in particular events. For Judith Butler (1997: 97), these events include "citational practices" that have developed from the historical "sedimentation of prior institution and use." The citational practices of real estate, such as referring back to or citing the importance of private property or the loss of the commons, become "invested with the power to establish and maintain the subordination" of the next group of land and real estate claimers by cueing particular sociocultural histories and institutional practices (Butler, 1997: 97). These citational practices are always enacting broader cultural, financial, and legal values and norms. This approach, then, has an explicit focus on the encounter, but a focus that does not necessarily presuppose a *telos*, or a logical reason for action, or historical causality (Malabou, 2015: 49). Rather, it privileges an analysis of transformation in action, with *a moment crisis* as the operative node of enquiry; it uncovers and records the transformation of land and real estate knowledge systems, technologies, discourses, and events from within the moment of crisis. Thus, it is historical, in that it is recording historical events, without necessarily being confined to outlining how these events can be linked together causally or temporally.

Individual foreign investment in residential real estate in several Anglosphere and Asian countries have long, contested, and diverse histories, which arguably stretch back to the establishment of property in land in the respective countries (Elden, 2013). However, much of the recent scholarship on global real estate investment is focused on the ruptures and discontinuities that foreign investors and the super-rich bring upon cities with their investment practices (Dorling, 2014; Hay, 2013; Paris, 2013; Sassen, 2014). This emerging body of scholarship investigates the lives, investment practices, consumption patterns, and brokerage and discourse networks of the super-rich, and focuses quite tightly on the practices that surround the super-rich (Burrows and Savage, 2014; Dorling, 2014; Hay, 2013; Ley, 2011; Paris, 2013; Rogers et al., 2015). For example, in the quantitative sphere, studies about the foreign real estate investment practices of the super-rich, in cities such as Los Angeles, Melbourne, and London (Dorling, 2014; Hay, 2013; Javorcik et al., 2011; Jones Lang LaSalla, 2014a, 2014b), have often been limited to incoming or outgoing FDI data. A key concern is about the globalisation of local real estate, and claims that some super-rich investors are parking their capital in the residential real estate of foreign countries in ways that might negatively affect local house prices (Paris, 2013; Rogers et al., 2015). Paris (2013: 94) argues that the impact of super-rich overseas buyers of real estate in prime global city locations is "contributing to a de-coupling" of parts of the city from the general dynamics of local housing markets. The claim is that individual foreign real estate investment is leading to the expulsion and exclusion of some sections of the local community from emerging high-net-worth neighbourhoods in London and New York (Butler and Lees, 2006; Paris, 2013; Webber and Burrows, 2015).

While a line of enquiry about the ruptures and discontinuities is important, I approach the question of foreign investment, the super-rich, and cities from the opposite direction. Rather than focus on the de-coupling effects, I open up the temporal scope of the investigation to explore the resourcefulness of real estate actors across the last four centuries. A small body of scholarship has investigated the morphology of land claiming and real estate practices from the seventeenth, eighteenth, nineteenth, and twentieth centuries against those of the early twenty-first-century (Elden, 2013; Linklater, 2014; Sassen, 2014; Weaver, 2003). Assessed historically, there is a cumulative impact on the way in which land and real estate, as private property, has been mediated through different technologies by colonisers, investors, governments, and real estate professionals over this time frame.

This analysis takes a step back to show how some of the very people who are now affected by the practices of the super-rich were central to propagating, circulating, and normalising property investment discourses and practices. Indeed, some of the core ideals that underwrite foreign investment and super-rich real estate discourses and practices can also be found, albeit in different forms, in the historical practices of the increasingly marginalised local middle class, and before them, a whole host of land claiming and real estate actors. It is not only the political and discursive practices of the super-rich that we must critique, but the way in which property investment ideals and practices have subtly emerged out of and are integrated into the everyday political and discursive practices of successive waves of land claimers and real estate investors. At first these seemingly unrelated and non-causal land and real estate crises will appear to have little historical connectivity. However, by expanding the analytical borderland beyond one or two centuries, the cumulative impact of these moments of real estate crisis becomes more evident.

The moments of real estate crisis I discuss in Chapters 3–7 are organised into crises of landed property and real estate occurring at three conceptual registers. These are further organised under two meta-conceptual ideas, which bookend Chapters 1 and 8 of the book. The five analytical concepts are outlined in greater detail below, before being deployed to rewrite recent narratives about the globalisation of real estate throughout the book. The three conceptual registers are (1) organising technics, (2) mediating technologies, and (3) discursive codes; the two meta-concepts are (4) semblance and (5) assemblage.

SEMBLANCES AND ASSEMBLAGES

A tension in any analysis of the globalisation of real estate is between global real estate *semblances*, such as those outlined in Chapter 1, and the global real estate *assemblages* outlined in Chapter 8. It is an active tension I do not resolve in this analysis, nor did I set out to do so. A "semblance" is the apparent appearance of some form or event, especially when the reality is different from the apparent appearance. In Brian Massumi's (2011a: 176) book on *Semblances and Event*, he uses his event-oriented ontic framing to outline a concept of semblance that reveals the "content that lies beneath their surface. ... It is only significant for what lies behind it." A semblance is at once a superficial appearance that covers over the true content of an event, while at the same time it is the only tool available to us to access the hidden "truth" of that event. Michel Foucault (1966: 74–78), in drawing a link between (re)semblance and imagination, noted that a (re)semblance is most revealing at the precise moment that it is fading away. Semblances are, therefore, in Massumi's (2011a: 64) words, "World-fragments. Drops of experience. Little absolutes."

It should be clear by now that there is purposeful and explicit politics to the historical line of enquiry I am developing herein. At its most fundamental it is about challenging the claim that we can attribute blame for the collective effects of the globalisation of real estate to one set of actors, at one moment in time, over another set of actors at the same or a different moment in time. In other words, I set out here to problematise a suite of contemporary discourses which draw causal lines, or a set of causal relationships, between long-standing societal issues, such as housing affordability problems in so-called global cities, with particular and often highly essentialised cultural groups, such as "baby boomers" or "Asian foreign investors." The following headline, from the popular digital global real estate company *Homes Abroad* in the United Kingdom, is an exemplary case of what we might call a global real estate semblance: "Chinese Investors Drive Up Property Prices in Major World Cities" (Calvert, 2015: 1). This superficial discursive statement covers over the complex *reality* of contemporary global real estate practices – it is a semblance that covers over and contains the *truth*. It is important because, as a statement, it can assist us to access what lies beneath, which, in this case, involves complex geopolitics, cultural histories, local real estate practices, media discourse, and other factors that have led to this statement. Using this conceptualisation of semblance, as the title of Chapter 1 subtly eludes, much of what we know about the globalisation of real estate, such as the incoming and outgoing foreign investment data, the media commentary, the nation states' regulatory environments, is a mere semblance of the event that we might call the globalisation of real estate. But at the same time, these semblances provide us with a way of accessing the hidden realities, the complex real estate assemblages that lay beneath these global real estate semblances.

It is not possible to write a complete history of the geopolitics of real estate, which would need to cover the land politics and real estate histories of every continent over a time frame that stretches back to the first recordings of human history, although there have been some great attempts recently (Elden, 2013; Linklater, 2014). Thus, I have collected in the pages that follow a series of short historical vignettes – semblances, little absolutes, drops of experience, and world-fragments – of the land and real estate politics that might, when I assemble them together in Chapter 8, reveal more of the *truth* that lies beneath the geopolitics of real estate in the twenty-first-century. The idea for presenting a set of short historical vignettes comes from the organising schematic of Gilles Deleuze and Felix Guattari's (1987) book, *A Thousand Plateaus: Capitalism and Schizophrenia*. It is, therefore, indirectly inspired by their notion of assemblage (from the French: *agencement*) at this metalevel. Translator, Brian Massumi, summaries the organising schematic of *Plateaus* as follows:

> This book that speaks of many things. … It is difficult to know how to approach it … that presents itself as a network of "plateaus" that are precisely dated, but can be read in any order? That deploys a complex technical vocabulary drawn from a wide range of disciplines in the sciences, mathematics, and the humanities, but whose authors recommend that you read it as you would listen to a record? (Massumi, 2011b: ix)

This current project is not a work of philosophy, but like Deleuze and Guattari's book, I have organised the short historical vignettes with a clear schematic logic. Chapters 3–7 each contain three short historical vignettes, each of which covers a specific historical moment of land or real estate crisis. The vignettes can be read in any order, but once assembled together in Chapter 8, to use the language of Deleuze and Guattari, these *plateaus* present a network of historical geopolitical real estate events that can teach us something important about contemporary real estate moments of crisis. Thus, the first level at which I am putting assemblage theory to work is at the level of the organising schematic of the manuscript itself.

To be sure, the concept of assemblage can draw on a diverse range of assemblage theories and thinking, from Deleuze and Guattari (1987), Manuel

DeLanda (2006), and Bruno Latour's (2005) more philosophical works, through to the more applied assemblage analytical tactics of Saskia Sassen (2006, 2014) and Aihwa Ong (2006, 2011). Each notion of assemblage has its own ontic framing, and at the level of ontology, these diverse theories are in many cases not wholly compatible. DeLanda (2006), following on, and diverging in places, from Deleuze and Guattari's (1987) concept of *agencement*, does not include any essentialised generalities into his social-ontological framing of assemblage. This is a useful starting point for a study of the geopolitics of real estate because it does away with, as a basic principle of operation, essentialised categories such as, for example, "nation states," "the market," "race," or "private property."

DeLanda's (2006) concept of assemblage is useful for theorising beyond, say, the nation state–centrism that locates the power to manage foreign real estate investment with governments and government policy; the cultural profiling of "Eastern" and "Western" global real estate professionals and investors; or the instrumental rationalities that frame the analyses of "incoming and outgoing" foreign investment capital flows (also see Acuto and Curtis, 2013). Within this notion of assemblage, the dichotomy between "Eastern" and "Western" international real estate investors and professionals breaks down. Global real estate professionals and investors are freed from the conceptual categories that might limit how we think about their actions, and we can see how they are increasingly mobile and *free*, in a geopolitical, virtual, cultural, and physical sense. Under this notion of assemblage, the real estate knowledge systems these actors draw upon, their complicated cultural identities and nation state(s) allegiances, the multi-language electronic technologies they mobilise, and their international real estate practices become the explicit target of the investigation. This allows for a conceptualisation of the contemporary global real estate industry, for example, as a complex, non-essentialised assemblage that blends culture, class, industries, knowledges, and technologies to shape and reshape investment discourse, policy, and practice around the world. This means theorising the social and material worlds as transient and open (i.e., *becoming*: Deleuze and Guattari, 1987) and as a sociology of material and social relations (i.e., flat ontologies with blended agency: Anderson et al., 2012; 2014; DeLanda, 2006; Dittmer, 2013; Latour, 2005). It directs us to collect historical data in the often-opaque geopolitical spaces between the cultural, regulatory, and geographical spaces of different nation states and cities.

There is an emphasis on "emergence" within Deleuze–Guattarian-inspired assemblage theory (DeLanda, 2000; 2006). For example, under this notion of assemblage, the global real estate industry would be viewed as having a property all of its own; an emergent property that is irreducible to the individual properties of the constituent parts, such as the global sales agents, the real estate investment lawyer, the regulatory frameworks they work within, and the customers they engage with. While emergence is relevant here, in this book I also depart, quite radically, from DeLanda's (2006) notion of assemblage, with his unrelenting emphasis on "emergence," by placing some weight on the old Castellian (Castells, 1996; 1997; 1998) and Deleuzean (1971) notions of "flows," and particularly the Foucauldian (1969: 82)-inspired notion of "mediation." This would be, I suspect, wholly unsatisfactory for DeLanda (2006), who never uses the term "mediation" in his book *A New Philosophy of Society: Assemblage Theory and Social Complexity*. For DeLanda, it is the process of emergence – the "emergent effect of processes of gathering and dispersion" of constituent parts (Anderson et al., 2012: 177) – which interests him. DeLanda's (2006: 3) notion of emergence also attends to the "effect of the causal interactions between component parts," which I also depart with at the historical level of this analysis. Deleuze and Guattari (1987) use the concepts of territorialisation and deterritorialisation to analyse emergence, showing that the heterogeneous parts that form an assemblage can be stabilising or destabilising for that assemblage. While I am interested in emergence, my notion of assemblage does not strictly follow this Deleuze–Guattarian and DeLandian epistemology (for a useful alternative definition of territorialisation, see Elden, 2013).

Beyond the organising schematic of the book, the analysis of the historical vignette material draws on recent geographical thinking with assemblage (Acuto and Curtis, 2013; Anderson, 2014; Anderson et al., 2012; Dittmer, 2013; McFarlane, 2009). Kennedy et al. (2013: 46) refer to assemblages as "complex flows, connections and becomings that emerge and disperse relationally between bodies." Anderson et al. (2012: 180) ask us to "examine the difference that thinking with assemblages might make." Similarly, Sassen and Ong, have called their assemblage analytical tactics "assemblage thinking" (see, e.g., Acuto and Curtis, 2013), although they do so from a very different ontic register. Their assemblage thinking moves us closer to the establishment of a set of analytical tools with which to undertake an analysis.

Sassen (2014) sees a "foundational juxtaposition in our present ways of constituting economic space: a development of complex forms of knowledge and creativity that too often bring with them, besides robust profits, astoundingly elementary brutalities" (p. 220). For example, as eighteenth-century colonial land claimers or twenty-first-century global real estate professionals move across a range of systemic legal, territorial, and financial edges, they contribute to, create, and destroy an astounding array of real estate successes and failures. Sassen (2014: 8) draws attention to the contemporary "global market for land," which, with similarities and differences to the colonial past, is produced by transforming "sovereign national territory into a far more elementary condition – land for usufruct" (Sassen, 2014: 82). Ananya

Roy (2015) argues that Sassen's "story of territory becoming 'merely land' is [a] compelling" way to think about the "logics of expulsion" (Sassen, 2014: 1). Sassen develops the idea of a global territory that is increasingly "ungoverned" by, and deterritorialised from, nation states (see Sassen in Acuto and Curtis, 2013: 22), wherein we enter "a new phase of advanced capitalism … one with reinvented mechanisms for primitive accumulation" (Sassen, 2014: 8). Ong shows that while this so-called ungoverned territory is not necessarily governed by nation states, it is still governed (see Ong in Acuto and Curtis, 2013: 22). Ong's Foucauldian-inspired concept of a "global assemblage" is defined as a "space of enquiry, not a theory but a way to 'frame' [the] analysis … the space of problematization and intervention is the space of assemblage" (see Ong in Acuto and Curtis, 2013: 18 and 20). It is towards a geopolitical assemblage of land and real estate claiming practices that the analysis in the vignettes is directed. The networking of different local actors and physical sites creates a translocal space within which to locate a range of governance-subject-objects (Corry, 2013: 54); that is, people and objects that are essentialised as bodies and things with the aim of governing them (Foucault, 1980, 1997). I identify the colonial, and later the foreign real estate investor body, as a governance-subject, which is increasingly thought of as governable and is governed by their own and others actions (Foucault, 2011). Therefore, the idea of mediation is important because the *body*, which I conceptualise as a mediating technology below, is central to each vignette.

The body turns out to be an important technological form that is involved in the transmission of subjective ideas (mentalities) and material artefacts (materialities) within each vignette. I have, where I can, centred the body in each historical and contemporary vignette. Furthermore, the relations of exteriority mean that a component part, such as a subjective body, a mechanical device like a surveying instrument, or a real estate sales practice or event, can be detached from one assemblage and plugged into another. I pay particular attention to the relations of exteriority that traverse across the diverse vignettes. Having outlined the two meta-concepts of *semblance* and *assemblage* that broadly frame the organising schematic of this book, I will now move onto the three conceptual ideas that are employed for the purpose of vignette analysis. These three concepts are used with a little more focus on their epistemological utility.

...

The schematic for presenting the vignettes is organised in a way that emphasises either the organising technics, mediating technologies, or discursive codes of particular epochs. Chapters 3 and 4 emphasise organising technics and mediating technologies; Chapters 5 and 6 emphasise mediating technologies and discursive codes; and Chapter 7 emphasises the new digital discursive codes. The epistemological purpose of using the concept of organising technics instead of the concept of mediating technology or discursive code, and vice versa, is one of emphasis. Analysing through the notion of an organising technic places greater emphasis on showing that the actors involved in land and real estate claiming are acting according to the prevailing ideological enframing of land, property, or real estate of a given epoch. In addition, they put this organising technic into practice by using the mediating technologies that are available to them within that epoch. Analysing through the notion of a mediating technology places greater emphasis on showcasing the technologies that the actors used through their land and real estate claiming practices. Because a mediating technology is a part of the organising technic assemblage, the use of a particular mediating technology also occurs within the prevailing ideological enframing of land, property, or real estate of a given epoch. In addition, when the actors put this mediating technology into practice, they do so by mediating the discursive codes – through the mediating technologies – that are available within that epoch. Therefore, analysing through the notion of discursive codes places greater emphasis on showcasing that coding, decoding, and recoding that takes place through the mediating technologies that the actors used through their land and real estate claiming practices. Because discursive coding, decoding, and recoding is a part of the organising technic assemblage, each coding, decoding, and recoding act is conditioned by the prevailing ideological enframing of land, property, or real estate of a given epoch and the technologies that are available within that epoch.

Organising Technics

The concept of organising technics has two conceptual starting points, each relating to one of the two terms used within the concept. Let me start with the concept of technic. In a technological society, argues Jacques Ellul, technology is a mentality, a form of intentionality that is "embodied in the modern world after 1750" (Lovekin, 1991; paraphasing Ellul, 1954). For Ellul, a "technic" refers to the totality of the knowledge systems, methods and tools that, taken together, produce a certain reality (Ellul, 1954; 1981; Lovekin, 1991). Ellul suggests that from the mid-eighteenth-century, scientific rationality and technological progress were brought together in a way that produced a technical intention (i.e., *d'une intention technique*) from which social actors are unable to disengage. The knowledge systems and the technological tools create a technical consciousness (i.e., *la conscience technique*) and a technical state of mind (i.e., *l'état d'esprit technician*) (Ellul, 1954). To take charge of a technic after the Enlightenment required much more than a working knowledge of that technic, argues Lovekin (1991: 83), because the technics incorporate their own intentionality. Rather than a technic being a process that involved a set of methods and tools, in a technological society the technic becomes a mentality with an overarching knowledge system that is scientific, rationalist, or deployed in the pursuit of progress. In a posthumously published article on *Technical Mentality*, Simondon (2006) locates technic as a mentality that exists prior to the event. Massumi (2009: 17), summarising Simondon, argues, "The key point is that the moment of technical mentality – *the technicity of the technical object* – is always immanent to a material event of taking-form." The notion of a technical mentality developed here, and therefore the notion of "technic" I use hereafter, incorporates the rules of knowledge production and the technological tools that are employed within an embodied action, but positions the technical mentality as being always already present in the "cognitive schema" of the actor before the event (Simondon, 2006: 17). For example, private property is always already present in the cognitive schema of a real estate agent, and it is exerting an influence on the agent long before he or she employs any sales technologies to sell real estate.

It is important not to fetishise technic and technology. Philosophers of technology have long pondered the dangers of an unfettered commitment to the modern technological project (Cassirer, 1930; Giedion, 1948; Heidegger, 1977; Hoel and Tuin, 2012; Lovekin, 1991; Mitcham, 1994; Mumford, 1934; Spenglek, 1931). You can read a reserved optimism in the work of scholars such as Simondon (2006). Martin Heidegger (1977) is famously more critical. He rejects an instrumental view of technology, such as engineering that attempts to position technology as an applied science. Heidegger, who is not a technological determinist (Lovitt, 2013: xiii), argues that modern technologies are a "revealing" or "enframing" (*Ge-stell*), and an exploitation of nature and natural resources (*Bestand*) in the world. For Heidegger, modern technologies create a world of resources to be used and consumed, and this is premised on the objectification and quantification of the natural world, which leaves out the "thinghood" in things. This creates the conditions for producing and categorising objects, including land and real estate as private property. Technics are a "revealing" of a new way of being-in-the-world, the revealing of a technical mentality that, for Heidegger, obscures a relation to Being (Mitcham, 2013: 19). Heidegger (1977: 287) argues, the "Enframing means that way of revealing that holds sway in the essence of modern technology and that it is itself not technological." Jean-Jacques Rousseau (1750) calls into question the enlightenment idea that technological and scientific progress will necessarily lead to the advancement of society by unifying technological knowledge and wealth with a virtue ethics. For Rousseau and Heidegger, humanity, or what it means to be human, and our subjective realities are intricately bound up with technics and technological objects. In their respective seminal texts, Lewis Mumford (1934) and Ellul (1954) raise ethical and moral questions to warn that technologies could be used to exercise punitive forms of power over others, or to narrow human experience. Mumford (1934), in particular, argues that this should be challenged and guarded against.

With these warnings in mind, it is hard to avoid the allure of Ellul's (1954) neo-Marxist historical materialist study of technology, which, itself, was built from José Ortega y Gasset's (1939) survey of the historicity of thinking through the concept of technics in his *Meditation on Technics* from 1939. Like Simondon (2006), Ortega (1939) argues that cognition precedes event. Before scientific rationalities, Ortega argues, the technician engaged in a creative process of imagining a future desired world, before setting about bringing that world into being. However, scientific technics presented a uniquely modern problem for Ortega. Because the scientific technics include particular technical mentalities, the scientific technician gives up part of their imaginative and exploratory faculties, which had hereinto motivated earlier technics to solve certain social problems. "The technicity of modern technic is radically different from that which inspired all previous technics," argues Ortega, " a new way for the mind to operate that manifests itself both in technics and even more in pure theory" (Mitcham, 1994: 48 citing Ortega). The same is true for the organising technics of the real estate technicians. To be a real estate technician they must give up thinking about housing as anything other than private property, because this is part of the technical mentality implicit to this organising technic.

Ellul (1954), following Ortega, was careful not to restrict his notion of technic to a particular application or moment (Lovekin, 1991: 157). Friedrich Kittler (2002) would later show that it takes many actors to produce a technic, and this occurs through trial and error, or even by accident. Through repeated use, a technic becomes a conscious practice, and if successful, it might be handed down from one generation to another. If we are serious about resisting the urge to fetishise technology, then Ortega and Ellul's works contain a conceptual trap that must be addressed. The limitation with the early philosophers of technology, such as Ortega and Ellul, is that their work is profoundly determinist. Technological determinism, to paraphrase Kittler's (2002) famous claim, is the belief that technological media determine our human condition. While Kittler captures, at least intuitively, a part of the contemporary experience of modern communications technologies, determinist thinking, in all its forms, has been heavily critiqued for rupturing the agency of individuals and other social actors by predetermining human pasts, presents, and futures. Marxism, and particularly Marx's form of historical materialism, has also been accused of this type of teleology. However,

Winthrop-Young (2011) argues that Kittler's later work on media technologies is more indebted to the discursive scholarship of Michel Foucault than the determinist historical materialism of Karl Marx. Winthrop-Young (2011) argues that Kittler's statement, that technological "media determine our situation," is a highly qualified statement that does not presuppose a *telos*. Kittler (2002: 153) argues that "technological media are never the inventions of individual geniuses, but rather they are a chain of assemblages that are sometimes shot down and that sometimes crystallise."

Ortega (1939) and Ellul's (1954) conceptualisations of technics are useful for undertaking a historical analysis of the organising technics of the technicians of landed property and real estate, only if their determinist positioning is accounted for. Determinism is incomparable with the emphasis on emergence and blended agency within assemblage thinking. Ortega (1939) and Ellul's (1954) conceptualisations of technic was a part of the rationalist project of modernity, whereby a set of technological means would *produce,* or lead to, particular ends. An organising technic – as an assemblage of technical mentalities, mediating technologies, and actors – has its own emergent agency, which is not irreducible to its constituent parts. An organising technic is greater than the technical mentalities, mediating technologies, and actors involved. There is no place for technological determinism within assemblage thinking because the future is always open – "As Deleuze liked to say, the whole is not of the parts, but alongside them and in addition to them" (Massumi, 2009: 40). An organising technic is an emergent and relational concept, which includes the technical mentality, mediating technologies, and embodied actors. However, its conceptual utility and emphasis is on tracing and mapping the ideological enframing of land, property, and real estate at different points in time.

For example, Kittler and Paul Virillio show that the organising technic of war drives technological developments. Virillio (2008, 2009) argues that war drove the move from feudalism to capitalism, and Kittler (1995) shows how military research and development was implicated in the development of the Internet. In the context of geopolitical land claiming and real estate practices, national level mentalities about war and recovery, especially surrounding the two World Wars, was heavily implicated in the development of real estate mentalities in settler-societies like the United States and Australia (Veracini, 2015). Furthermore, conflicts over real estate business, conflicts over real estate as property, conflicts over territory, conflicts over citizenship, and conflicts over governance are always already present in contemporary real estate practice. These conflicts – one professional against another, one investor against another, local citizens against foreign investors – drive developments in the real estate mediating technologies.

This is where the notion of "organising" becomes important, which is used in a similar way to Saskia Sassen's (2006: 10) notion of "organising logics." However, Sassen uses the term logics in a way that abstracts the technical mentalities (e.g., private property) and essentialised categories (e.g., "national and global era: the state and the empire" (Sassen, 2006: 11)), to which the word logic refers, from the agency of the various actors and the events (i.e., embodied action). I have recentred the technical mentalities in this book so that I can directly expose the mentalities that are written into the bodies that are involved in various land claiming and real estate practices. Sassen (2006) also contends that older organising logics get subsumed into newer organising logics, and then these newly formulated logics can be redeployed in pursuit of new objectives. In doing so, Sassen (2006: 18) discusses "path dependencies" or shows how "medieval capabilities get relodged into a radically different assemblage articulated through an organisational logic that bears little resemblance to that of medieval times." This is too linear and deterministic for my purposes. In broad terms, an organising technic is an assemblage of technical mentalities and mediating technologies that are always immanent to an embodied action and event; hence, my focus on embodied action in the vignettes. The crises analysed in the next two chapters include: the rupturing of the storylines about people and place of Indigenous peoples; the redistribution of land through the Inclosure Acts from the seventeenth-century in the United Kingdom; the creation of the colonial joint-stock company to move financial and human capital around the world; restorying the lands of Indigenous peoples to facilitate the sale of colonised land to foreign buyers; and the land revolution in twentieth-century China. These organising technics include many of the heterogeneous parts that underwrite the various *capacities for* storying and restorying the land, measuring and enclosing the land, claiming and distributing the land, and creating local and global markets for global real estate; but they may not necessarily be causally related. The effect is cumulative at the level of technical mentalities, rather than historically causal.

Mediating Technologies

Mediating technologies reveal their latent capacities within the event – within the crisis. They are technologies of power and, therefore, have their own genealogies, interconnected histories, and geographies. Within the geopolitical history of land and real estate claiming, some mediating technologies appear, disappear, and reappear at different times and places. However, there is one mediating technology that is always present, and that is the human body. By locating the human body at the centre of each vignette, I'm following Foucault, who writes: "The body is also directly involved in a political field; power relations have an immediate hold upon it; they invest it, mark it, train it, torture it, force it to carry out tasks, to perform ceremonies, to emit signs

... the body becomes a useful force only if it is both a productive body and a subjected body" (Foucault, 1975: 25). By drawing attention to the mediating technologies that are in play within a given moment of land or real estate crisis, the emphasis is on the technologies that are used to mediate the flow of different landed property and real estate mentalities and material goods, models and methods, information and data, and political and discursive content. As noted above, the concept of technology should not be understood in the narrow common-sense notion of the term, as electronic technologies or digital media, but rather as anything that can be used in combination with the subjective, material body to facilitate the flow of information and resources. This expansive definition allows for many tangible and intangible, cerebral and corporeal, material and immaterial artefacts and processes to be included as technologies of power. There is no limit or boundary to what might be or become a mediating technology. The subjective human body is a mediating technology. A surveying instrument is a mediating technology. A real estate title deed is a mediating technology. Public policy is a mediating technology. A newspaper is a mediating technology. A home loan is a mediating technology. A website is a mediating technology. A mobile phone is a mediating technology.

However, these mediating technologies are not conceptualised as having finite *properties*, but rather as having infinite *capacities* that cannot be reduced to their unitary function within a particular assemblage. As Dittmer (2013: 3) argues, "They can be parts of multiple wholes at any given moment," or as Anderson (2014: 10) states, "What a body may be able to do in any given situation, in addition to what it currently is doing and has done." Anderson (2014: 10) is referring here to Deleuze's notion of a "body" that "can be anything." If these modern technologies represent new modes of human existence, as Heidegger suggests, then analysing the mediating technologies can reveal how real estate finance and capital flows, or information about colonial landed property or international real estate investment, are central to different geopolitical real estate assemblages. These technological assemblages act as a set of "techniques, or arts, of governance" (Elden, 2013: 13) and become "the way reality discloses itself to us in contemporary times" (Žižek, 2014: 31). Each assemblage of subject(ive)-body-object-event has its own agency, and creates a different landed property or real estate reality, if only for a moment.

Therefore, mediating technologies involve complex assemblages of material, embodied, and discursive technologies. Care needs to be given to investigating how different subjective bodies (e.g., foreign real estate investors or colonial land claimers), along with their guiding mentalities (e.g., private property as mentality), are assembled together with technological objects (e.g., surveying instruments and loan documents) and discursive codes (e.g., real estate data), within particular encounters (e.g., global real estate sales event). These encounters – of mind, body, object, and event – have an agency that is not reducible to the mind, body, object, or event.

Reconceptualising these encounters also requires a reformulation of subject–object agency, especially as it relates to foreign land claiming or global real estate practice. This is an ontological position that is strongly advocated by some post-humanist and post-anthropocentric scholars (Braidotti, 2013), but Fredrick Kittler and Marshall McLuhan (1967) are particularly useful in relation to media technologies. Kittler (2002: 31) starts with McLuhan's famous aphorism "the medium is the message" (McLuhan, 1967), which suggests that an analysis of media(ting) technologies should be directed towards the technological form (i.e., the medium) itself. This means *form* over *content*; or an emphasis on Kittler's "technological medium" over Foucault's "discursive content" at this level of analysis. Foucault's work on discourse is re-elevating and given greater weight in the analysis of discursive code (see the next section). The analysis that follows is broadly framed by a Kittlarian analysis of the media(ting) technologies and a Foucauldian analysis of the discursive coding. What makes Kittler's work different to McLuhan's, indeed more radical, is that he was interested in the materiality of the body in relation to communication software and hardware. Kittler argues that McLuhan put too much emphasis on the body and the subject. In other words, McLuhan thought that the technological software and hardware was an extension of the body. Kittler argues that McLuhan is too anthropocentric in his analysis, and that media(ting) technologies are more than an extension of the subject. Kittler argues that media(ting) technologies generate information and refer to each other in excess of the subject. Rather than thinking about Kittler as a techno-determinist, which he has been accused of being, and McLuhan as anthropocentric, I bring their very different forms of blended agency thinking into conversation with the flat ontologies of assemblage thinking. Rather than being a techno-determinist, Kittler (2002) was interested in showing how media(ting) technologies are developed to "strategically override" (p. 36) the senses to create a vision of reality – a mentality. But Kittler and McLuhan require us to conceive of this as an embodied process that involves integrating technological software and hardware, that is, media(ting) technologies, *into* the body. These subject–object technologies override, or at least interconnect with, the senses, shaping the mentalities of the person.

One of the key reasons for using an analytical framework that is informed by media technologies is because Mitchell (2004) describes the twenty-first-century urban condition as one of mediated connectivity. I am not proposing that we turn everything into a machine; that we conceptualise government, society, industry, and the virtual and material worlds as actually existing machines within machines. There is an anthropomorphic danger in reading philosophers like Deleuze, Guattari (2004), and Latour (2007) too literally when they use machine and coding metaphors to conceptualise human and social agents and agency. Whether or not Deleuze, Guattari (2004), or Latour (2007) are anthropomorphizing technologies and machines is a moot philosophical point in relation to the utility of the machine and coding conceptual metaphors for understanding how prior eras relate to the twenty-first-century condition. Since the turn of the last century, significant changes in technological form increased the speed with which the discursive content about real estate could be amassed, analysed, and transmitted (Manyika et al., 2011; Rose-Redwood, 2006), and ideas about machines and coding now wholly enframe almost every human activity. These changes are reshaping real estate investment practice at the global level. Foucault (1969) argued that to exercise power it is not enough to amass knowledge – such as real estate data – rather it is by controlling the analysis of data to produce knowledge that power is truly operationalised. Therein resides, for example, the politics of the new electronic real estate knowledge systems that is discussed in Chapter 7. By controlling the electronic knowledge systems you can create subjective realities to exercise power over others; you can integrate data with the subjects' real estate mentality. This diversification of technological forms and the way the real estate mentalities are circulated allow for a diversity of local real estate investment subjectivities, which are now common to both Anglo-sphere and Asian nation states, to be increasingly amalgamated and up-scaled into a global real estate investment space. Indeed, middle class real estate intermediaries from Anglo-sphere, Russian, Asian, and other countries are central to the globalisation of local real estate in their own and other countries.

As will become clear in Chapter 7, twenty-first-century real estate practices will increasingly be framed by digital technologies. The real estate sales agent with an Internet-enabled real estate sales software platform on their tablet, or a foreign real estate investor accessing global real estate sales information on their smartphone, represent the twenty-first-century real estate subject(ive)-body-object-event assemblage *pièce de résistance*. These new human-digital assemblages are reshaping the mentalities of not only the people who use them but also those who bear witness to these technological changes. These subject(ive)-body-object-events assemblages of blended agency are both governing and governable (Mitchell, 2004), in other words, they are governable and governing real estate cyborgs. This builds on the "the idea that one must put a technology of the self to work in order to have access to the truth" (Foucault, 2001: 46–47). An example of a governable real estate cyborg is a real estate investor who is networked into complex real estate and financial information systems by way of their smartphones, tablets, or computers. An example of a governing real estate cyborg is a real estate professional who sifts through and selects complex real estate, financial, and immigration information, and feeds this information to investors by way of their smartphones, notebooks, websites, real estate events, and investment products. These real estate cyborgs have foreign investment visions created for them through the process of circulating discursive codes through different subject(ive)-body-object-event assemblages. The mediating technologies and the discursive coding are necessary because they allow these actors to navigate the increasingly complex foreign investment, financial, immigration, and local and translocal real estate information systems. While this analysis does not draw as centrally on theories of affect, it nonetheless resonates with Anderson's (2014) concept of *bodily capacities* that "describes how greed becomes an embodied disposition that distorts and dominates an individual's relation to their life" (p. 12).

Rather than conceptualise these geopolitical real estate practices as occurring within a transnational space or as a global practice, these practices, which operate across nation states and cultural boundaries, are conceptualised as a global network of local actors working from different local sites. McFarlane (2009) and Featherstone (2011) use the concept of translocal assemblages to describe these types of "global" networks. Each vignette showcases how different tangible and intangible technologies are brought together. For example, the technologies include the embodied storylines of Indigenous peoples (i.e., the body as a mediating technology), or the legal Inclosure Acts and court documents written on paper in the United Kingdom (i.e., paper as a mediating technology), or the burning of title deeds during the land revolution in China (i.e., fire as mediating technology). The use of the terms technology and technic do not, therefore, refer to digital societies or digital technologies, although digital technologies (i.e., the Internet as a mediating technology) have a role to play within the history of the geopolitics of real estate that is presented in Chapter 7. The analysis is working towards capturing a twofold process. (1) How are different mediating technologies brought together? For example, how is a global real estate website linked into a real estate showcase event that potential real estate investors attend? (2) How do information and resources flow through different subject(ive)-body-object-event assemblages? For example, how, and by whom, does real estate, visa and education information flow from a policy document in Australia, through a global real estate agent's website in Hong Kong, and then through and between human bodies at a real estate showcase event in Singapore, and then back onto Chinese social media?

The emphasis in this book is on mapping the mediating technologies that link the social actors, nation states, cities, and cultural practices of different nation states together. They include technologies such as colonial land companies, colonial surveying practices, housing policy, home loans, foreign investment visas, and mobile human bodies. The concept of discursive code (elaborated below) places greater emphasis on the information and resources that have been disciplined by the organising technics and mediating technologies of a given epoch, as they flow through the different subject(ive)-body-object-event assemblages. This could be written code, diagrammatic code, arithmetic code, pictorial code, digital code, and embodied code (e.g., private property mentalities).

Discursive Code

Much like the way the concept of technology has been colonised by a discourse about the rise of digital machines, so too the concept of code has been colonised by a discourse about computer programming. Computer code is but one of many modalities of code, but it has been drawn into the discussions about cyber-utopianism and -dystopianism in ways that limit its conceptual efficacy. Like the term technology, there is a risk of digitomorphising[2] the term code, by linking it too centrally to the notion of machines and digital technologies. This digitomorphised notion is not how I use the concept of code in this book. Like a mediating technology, there is no limit or boundary to what might be or become a discursive code. Discursive code can be the logic of a machine. Discursive code can be an encrypted security system. Discursive code can be a cultural logic. Discursive code can be a structured feature of society. Discursive code can be the logic of a market or commodity. Discursive code can be the logic of an event. Discursive code can be a narrative, artistic, or poetic practice. Discursive code can be freedom creating or hegemonic. Discursive code can be a genre. As David Berry and Jo Pawlik (2005: 1) suggest, the notion of code is a defining feature of the contemporary moment, but Deleuze and Guattari (2004: 4–8) are not interested in setting a limit between societies and the coding schemes that regulate them. They ignore the "question of where code stops and the society starts, rather it forms a tracing of the code-society or the society-code" (Berry and Pawlik, 2005: 3). Discursive coding, decoding, and recording, as an action, involve conforming to the disciplinary functions of both form and content.

There is a relationship between "what is structurally possible and what actually happens" (Fairclough, 2003: 23), between the coding structures, discursive content, and the events. Fairclough argues that the relationships between form, content, and event are "mediated: there are intermediate entities [that] can be thought of as ways of controlling the selection of certain structural possibilities and the exclusion of others, as well as the retention of these selections over time …" (Fairclough, 2004: 115). Therefore, coding has a form. At its core it is about the art of inventing and fabricating structural possibilities. The coding practices have organising technics and distinctive mentalities built into their coding schemas, and they conform to these technics and mentalities. The coding schemas work to "displace subjectivity" and are "a reflection of the biases, norms, and values of the coding elite" (Berry and Pawlik, 2005: 2). The structures regulate and close off the generic to promote the particular. Coding also has discursive content, which is both created and consumed. The content is put to work on the target body, to which the coding is aimed, but it also works on the coder, decoder, and recoder. Each code is a component of, or built from, other coding forms and content. "In other words, this is the fundamental action of a society: to code the flows and to treat as an enemy anyone who presents himself, in relation to society, as an uncodable flow, because, once again, it challenges [*met en question*] the entire earth, the whole body of this society" (Deleuze, 1971).

Moving onto the concept of discourse, Foucault argues that social, institutional, and political objects of knowledge are constructed through processes of accepting and rejecting "the truth" about some essentialised category. The "truth" that is generated to represent a group of real estate investors, for instance, can be established by regulating the flow of information within different social, institutional, and political sites (Foucault, 1969). Foucault was particularly interested in institutional discursive formations and regulation. "Who, among the totality of speaking individuals, is accorded the right to use this sort of language (*langage*)?" writes Foucault (1969: 55), "What is the status of the individuals who – alone – have the right, sanctioned by law or tradition, juridical defined or spontaneously accepted, to proffer such a discourse?" Foucault is interested in the process by which institutions "authorise their activities by claiming to be speaking the truth" (Danaher et al., 2000: 40), and the link back to discourses which are understood as bodies of knowledge. O'Farrell (2005: 86) argues, "[i]deas and words have a material and historical existence and they can be analysed alongside other historical artifacts and events. People's very lives and whole existences have been, and are, at stake in these words and these ideas."

It is worth noting that Kittler's (1995) early works, and particularly his magnum opus *Discourse Networks 1800/1900*, are heavily Foucauldian. But he moves beyond Foucault in some important respects. Kittler is perhaps the bridge between Foucault and Elizabeth Ermarth's notion of the Discursive Condition, which she places in direct opposition to the Modern Condition. Ermarth (2011) argues, "The Discursive Condition requires experimental action: new terms, new languages, new tools of thought, and not for their own sake ... but precisely for finding practical new ways to deal adequately with practical problems" (p. xiv). Ermarth (2011: 20–29) moves well beyond Foucault's so-called representational theorisation of discourse and his genealogical analysis of governmentalities. Ermarth rejects many of the rationalist certainties of modernity, and she mounts a sustained attack on the way scientific rationalities intersect with questions about time and space (i.e., history), which is important for this historical analysis. She resists the allure of turning away from the concept of discourse, which some scholars have done under the instruction of more-than-representational theories (Thrift, 2008). Ermarth takes close aim at, what she calls, the assumption of temporal neutrality (i.e., calendar time) that was a creation of science, "the view of time as a neutral, homogeneous medium like the space of pictorial realism in painting; a time where mutually informative measurements can be made between past, present, and future, and where all relationships can be explained in terms of a common horizon" (p. 20).

Thus, discursive coding, decoding, and recoding occur in an Ermathian postmodern temporality that is disruptive. Where new atemporal relationships between past, present, and future are possible, and where yet hereinto configurations of bodies, technologies, and events are forming. There are interactions between linguistic and oral practices (e.g., the oral traditions of Indigenous peoples or statements by politicians), numerical data (e.g., quantitative FDI or real estate data), embodied action (e.g., non-representational interpersonal interactions at a global real estate sales event), and electronic data (e.g., foreign investment policy information that is passing through a global real estate website). These types of discursive interactions require specific coding practices and are more embodied, affective, transient, changeable, and ephemeral than Foucault's theorisation of discourse is assumed to allow. Although, Foucault's corpus does, in places, explicitly focus on how technologies of power have been brought to bear on the materiality of the body (see "The body of the condemned" in Foucault (1975: 3)).

In one sense these concepts represent a set of signifiers that can help us understand the changing conditions of social, political, financial, and material production, *vis-a-vis* Foucault. In another sense, Deleuze and Guattari argue that subject(ivity)-body-object-event assemblages are machines, and that these machines can be found within other machines *ad infinitum*. The metaphor of machines that *flow* into other machines, in ways that interrupt, subvert, colonise, and/or connect with other machines, resonates with Mitchell's (2004) idea of the governing/governable cyborg. Whereby the "human body itself is increasingly augmented, as it is technologically, surgically, chemically and electronically modified. With extended limbs and expanded memories, bodies are networked with the planet itself – by means of connections such as telephone and sewer lines – creating what Mitchell [(2004: 39)] terms a 'spatially extended cyborg'" (Nayar, 2004: 82). In quite a different way, the concept of discursive code can also be thought of in relation to Latour's (2007: 1) claim that "the slightest move in the virtual landscape has to be paid for in lines of code ... [but] the fancies of our brains have shifted so little from the real to the virtual." Latour is discussing more than computer code here too, he is pointing to the very dilemma that the twenty-first-century real estate cyborg must face; how to negotiate the spatiotemporal discontinuity that is opened up in the space between the *real* and the *virtual*. Thus the concept of discursive coding, decoding, and recoding, "serves as a translation between different discourses and spheres, DNA code, computer code, code as law, cultural code, aristocratic code, encrypted code" (Berry and Pawlik, 2005: 2).

HISTORY AND SILENCE

"Whereof one cannot speak, thereof one must be silent," writes Wittgenstein (1922: Proposition 7). Indeed, if every historical analysis is incomplete, then what we cannot write or speak about we must pass over into silence. The silent events and happenings are not, however, outside history. They have been simply relegated to a space of relative historical silence. This history of the geopolitics of land and real estate is a highly selective history, and much of the historical detail remains in the shadows. In this sense, it is a fractured and disconnected history. It does not make sense if it is viewed through the hegemonic rule of calendar time (Ermarth, 2011). I have gathered together in the chapters that follow 16 vignettes of land and real estate politics that unsettle contemporary ideas about the geopolitics of real estate. I will conclude this chapter by noting some of the major historical silences that are absent from this history of the geopolitics of land and real estate.

If there is one major silence in this book, an omission so large, in fact, that it screams out from between the pages, that is the land claiming and reframing mentalities that were born in Russia. This book is broadly focused on the geopolitics of settler-societies with a focus towards the end of the analysis on the contemporary geopolitics of real estate in the Asia-Pacific region. As such, there is little discussion of Russian practices and philosophical reflection. Without Russia as a historical case study, we would be without some of the most informative philosophical contributions of the nineteenth-century, Karl Marx being the most obvious example, with his reserved optimism in the *mir*. Indeed, an entire book could, and should, be devoted to a Russian historical geopolitical analysis of real estate, not least because Russian foreign real estate investors are very active in contemporary global real estate markets (Büdenbender and Golubchikov, 2016). The Russian story cannot be covered in a vignette; it is an expansive narrative across vast times and places. Some key moments include Peter the Great, Tsar of Russia 1682–1721, chastising landowners for their inhumane treatment of serfs, and only 60 years later Catherine II, Russian Empress 1762–1796, giving the landed gentry and nobility the freedom to use extreme violence on serfs, even to force a serf into exile. In 1861, serfdom was abolished at the Tsar's imperial command; at this time, property in land was central to the around forty-seven million serfs and four million slaves being set free (Easley, 2009).

There are also rich poetic and discursive texts and pictures to bring into the debate. Leo Tolstoy's astute short story, titled *How Much Land Does a Man Need?*, is a good example because it concludes with a fitting reminder of the end game of land claiming: "His servant picked up the spade and dug a grave long enough for Pahom to lie in, and buried him in it. Six feet from his head to his heels was all he needed" (Tolstoy, 1886). There are a whole suite of terms that require detailed reflection in relation to land claiming, commoning, and private property, such as peasants who avoided communal tasks (*miroyedi*), or the wealthier peasants (*kulaki*) who employed waged labour on their farms (Easley, 2009; Linklater, 2014; Tolstoy, 1886). In the twentieth-century a new image of the Soviet Union emerged, which is captured in the now infamous propagandist posters of young golden-haired people ploughing endless fields with new technological inventions such as tractors. By the 1930s, "90 per cent of the land was farmed by collectives, *kolkhozi*, measuring on average about six thousand acres, whose workers were either paid by the state or out of the farm's earnings" (Linklater, 2014: 318–319).

There are also radically different land and real estate mentalities that existed or exist in the Middle East and Asia that I have not covered in this book. Under the sixteenth-century edicts of Süleyman the Magnificent, there was a montage of different ways to take charge or own the land (Kunt and Woodhead, 1995: 34). For example, the grand vizier, Mehmed li Pasha, introduced the *Tanzimat*, an Ottoman Land Code in 1858. In Japan, the feudal rearrangements at the time of the Meiji emperor were reconfigured when the Japanese nobility expelled the Shogunate in 1868 (Ravina, 1999: 23–30). Shogunate had previously divided up the land among hundreds of lordships, known as *daimyo*. The *daimyo* divided up the land to their samurai warriors, who were the only class permitted to own land (Linklater, 2014: 306–307; Ravina, 1999: 136). "The samurai in turn authorised peasants to work the tiny plot – three quarters of the farms measured less than three acres – in exchange for payment in rice and labour" (Linklater, 2014: 307). More broadly, Wolf Isaac Ladejinsky was instrumental in reforming land in the first half of the twentieth-century in Japan, Mainland China, Taiwan, and South Vietnam, as well as in countries across Southeast Asia and the Indian subcontinent – the latter of which had seen five centuries of foreign domination of their land and peoples, first by the Mogul Empire and then by the British Empire. And let us not imagine for a moment that the question about claiming Indigenous land is an event or problem of the past. Settler-colonialism is always in the present and driving towards the future. Take, for example, the village of Madiangin in Sumatra, where, despite the Sultan of Siak granting formal title to the traditional custodians of the land in 1940, the logging company, Arara Abadi, began logging around their village. The traditional custodians of the land blocked the logging roads and cut the supply of logging equipment off from the forests (see Pearce, 2012: 202–203). Pearce (2012: 203) cites a Human Rights Watch report, "Hundreds of Arara Abadi enforcers armed with clubs attacked three villages with disputes against the company, beating scores of residents, injuring nine seriously, and abducting 63 … with the help of local police – who were no doubt grateful that the company had recently built them a new police station." In South America, Che Guevara was killed in 1967 while attempting to bring about revolution that involved land and farming practices in Bolivia. Linklater (2014: 326) argues, "Land reform could be said to have been the one constant in all the political convulsions of Latin American politics. Whether elected or not, almost every new government repeatedly promised to bring it about."

We sometimes forget that material territorial boundaries were initially required to fortify subjective and legal notions of private property in the minds of the population. The devil's rope, or barred wire, was also a contentious technology of enclosure (Krell, 2002), and it also links the claiming of land into the techno-industrial production of the machinery of war. Certainly, there are elaborate histories of the relationships between war and land covering many centuries. Even placing human or animal *bodies* on the land, to occupy, or to squat on the land ahead of the survey line was a productive way to claim land during the colonial period. In the 1800s in the United States, the cattle branding iron "was assumed to convey a right to use a more or less established territory" (Weaver, 2003: 287), and therefore the sale of a branding iron carried with it the right to territory. Improvement and speculation, as mentalities, are underwritten by the idea that by applying labour to land you can increase its value. This is evident within many of the land claiming narratives. However, there is another temporally mediated land claiming mentality that is closely associated with improvement that is not covered in explicit detail, and that is the holding mentality. From the feudal idea of holding land in perpetuity to the colonial idea of rapid improvement and sale, to possess and hold the land was intricately connected to the mentality of improvement (Weaver, 2003: 22).

Natural or man-made disasters are also important. Be it either the Great Fire of London in 1666, or the Chinatown fire and earthquake in San Francisco in 1906, fire has been a powerful technology of real estate reconfiguration. In the wake of natural disasters, old and new forms of political power assert or reassert themselves within the real estate landscapes of towns and cities. In the San Francisco case, the largely white political leadership tried to expel the Chinese community from their urban homeland after the fire (Lee, 2001), but were defeated by the Chinese community and the iconic and highly essentialised Chinatown that is a common feature of global cities around the world was born (Anderson, 1987, 1990, 1995; Ley, 2011). Access to, and the management of, water was also important to land claiming, and drainage and sewage technologies greatly increase the functionality of towns and cities and allowed for population increases. In nineteenth-century London, this contributed to increases in land and real estate values (Goodman and Chant, 1999). Even the discovery of gold drew people from the far side of the globe, and a history of real estate could easy be developed around the gold rushes in settler-states (Clarke, 2002).

The institution of the family is perhaps one of the most powerful motivators for claiming, enclosing, legally securing, and trading in land and real estate. In the mid-eighteenth-century, about half of England's estates were protected by various trusts that had been established to keep land and real estate within the family (Linklater, 2014: 176). The property mentality reached its most repulsive when human bodies were classified as slaves, rendered as property, and moved around the world in the service of white colonial notions of progress and development. In 1824, Thomas Jefferson, then in old age, highlighted the effects of linking human bodies with notions of commodified property that are authorised by legal codings. Jefferson writes, "For actual property has been lawfully vested in that form, and who can lawfully take it from the possessors?" (Jefferson cited in Kazanjian, 1967: 119).

Noting the silences listed above, and many more historical omissions that I have not mentioned, the remaining six chapters are organised as follows. Chapter 3 presents three organising technics: (1) the storylines of land that continue to be used by Indigenous peoples; (2) the enclosing of The Commons through the Inclosure Acts in the United Kingdom; and (3) the land revolution in China, whereby the rural peasantry sought to free themselves from the oppression of the feudal land system. Chapter 4 begins to shift the analysis from organising technics towards mediating technologies, by focusing on (4) restoring the lands of Indigenous peoples to facilitate the sale of colonised land to foreign buyers; (5) the creation of the joint-stock company as a technology of the British Empire; and (6) measurement and surveyor instruments as embodied technologies of land claiming. Chapter 5 is focused more centrally on role of mediating technologies, covering (7) the creation of the nation state, and its role in creating property-owning democracies; (8) the role of finance and banks in producing both housing security and insecurity; and (9) moving human and financial capital around the world to build the economies of settler-societies. Chapter 6 moves from the mediating technologies onto the role of the discursive coding practices of the twentieth and twenty-first centuries, showing (10) how public policy created the housing consumer after the Second World War; (11) the rise of real estate wealth creation "self-help" books; (12) the creation of global real estate visas and global real estate citizenship; and (13) the role of the property exhibition fair as a global real estate event. Chapter 7 is wholly focused on the new digital coding practices of the twenty-first-century, and (14) the role of Internet-enabled local and global real estate technologies; (15) the Libertarianism that is being built into the global real estate technologies; and the (16) uploading of twentieth-century real estate practices as the future for the twenty-first-century. Chapter 8 looks across the 16 vignettes in search of historical assemblages of the geopolitics of real estate.

NOTE

1. Foucault's portmanteau of Power/Knowledge is a good example.
2. To digitomorphise is to ascribe computer or digital technology form or attributes to a human, animal, plant, material object, or a process such as coding.

Chapter 3

Technics of Land I
Orality, Inclosure, Revolution, Land

ORALITY: STORYING PEOPLE AND PLACE

Edward Said (1993: xiii) captured a foundational, although oft-ignored, component of the politics of landed property when he wrote, "The main battle in imperialism is over land, of course; but when it came to who owned the land, who had the right to settle and work on it, who kept it going, who won it back, and who now plans its future – these issues were reflected, contested, and even for a time decided in narrative ... The power to narrate, or to block other narratives from forming and emerging, is very important ...." Regardless of the discursive form, the cyclical practices of reading and narrating the landscape frame how we understand our relationships to the land. Storytelling, songlines, narration, poem, performance, and art have been central to making sense of our relationship to land for centuries, perhaps even millennia (Elden, 2013; Linklater, 2014: 95). Stuart Elden (2013: 10) argues that questions about property in land stretch back as far as there is recorded human history.

One of the first philosophical attempts to question reality is attributed to Parmenides, an ancient Greek pre-Socratic philosopher who was alive early in the fifth-century BCE (Geldard, 2007; Vlastos, 1946). Parmenides' originally oral allegorical poem provides an account of a man's chariot journey through a set of gates towards a goddess. This journey across a territorial frontier – the gates – is used by Parmenides to represent the transition from ignorance (represented as darkness) to knowledge (represented as light) in the poem (Bowra, 1937: 98). Later, Hellenistic scholars claimed the ancient Athenian tyrant Peisistratos established a *Commission of Editors of Homer* to edit Homer's *Odyssey*, which was also most likely originally an oral poem. Peisistratos' editing of the *Odyssey* to ameliorate any inconsistencies was primarily a politico-discursive act that was underwritten by the politics of territorial storytelling (Graziosi, 2002: 207). Andro Linkater's (2014: 94) survey of the twelfth-century Irish epic, the *Táin Bó Cúailnge,* is replete with fabulous spatial commentary and territorial conflicts. Similarly, different spatial imaginaries and mythical territorial landscapes run through the sixteenth-century four-volume Ming Dynasty classic, *Journey to the West*.[1] Emerging literate societies continually orated and re-orated, and then later recorded in written and artistic form their relationship to subjective and objective space: the land.

There are many epic poems describing heroic journeys and territorial conflicts that I could draw on to analyse oral relationships to people and place. However, it seems appropriate, necessary even for an Australian author, to give the first word on the organising technics of land to Indigenous peoples. The Indigenous peoples of my colonised homeland, Australia, have used so-called preliterate linguistic and cultural technologies to read, document, and narrate the land and their relationships to it for centuries. Their linguistic and cultural practices include: painting and engraving on rock faces; painting on leaves and bark; carving wood; and creating songlines (Linklater, 2014: 95). These discursive practices are vastly different to the official documents and legal records the colonisers arrived with in 1788. For many preliterate societies, "the land *was* the story" (author's emphasis, Linklater, 2014: 98).

In the early twentieth-century, Anglophone anthropologists such as Adolphus Elkin (1932) and later William Stanner produced Darwinian accounts of Indigenous animist rock carvings and paintings. Their fieldwork and written texts were organised by a completely different set of organising technics to those of Indigenous peoples (Stanner, 1965). Their accounts were, problematically, based on western evolutionary logics and teleology. In Australia, Stanner coined the term the Dreamtime (*time out of time*), a naming process that itself was based on the Francophile scholarship of Lucien Lévy-Bruhl and a misunderstanding and mistranslation of the term *alcheringa* of the Arrente people. The Arrente people are the custodians of the Arrente lands at *Mparntwe* (an area surrounding Alice Springs in the Northern Territory, Australia). For the Arrente, the term *alcheringa* was the name of a spirit, and it signalled an entirely different set of spatiotemporal coordinates and fixtures than those envisioned by the early anthropologists. For many contemporary Indigenous peoples, The Dreaming also refers to the Creation time, and the Creation songs lay down the patterns of life. As the Australian feminist geographer Jane Jacobs (1996: 113–114) reminds us, there has long been a tension between the organising technics of Indigenous peoples and the settlers; the "Aboriginal sacred," she writes, "is deeply antagonistic to urban modernity's need to keep the sacred apart from the secular and to regulate it as if it were just another land use. … The Aboriginal sacred has a "nomadic" geography which is not derived from a premodern character but is reduced by the conditions of articulation established under modernity." These storylines are underwritten by dynamic Indigenous organising technics of people and place, rather being static stories from the past.

The Creation songs of Indigenous peoples are "subject to strict protocols of disclosure" (Jacobs, 1996: 113). Many of the physical sacred sites in the Australian landscape and the storylines that describe them are secret, and are only known by certain culturally authorised individuals. In their public form, some of which are familiar to the wider Australian public, these storylines discuss the relationships between different landscapes, animals, tribes, and nations. They explain how places and tribes were named during the Dreaming, in the *time before time*. Different features of the landscape are identified and labelled through, what anthropologists might call, mythology and magic. The origin of each tribe is outlined in relation to a totem animal, including ants, emus, kangaroos, and these totems and people are said to be part of the *country*. In their strictest private form, there are a set of cultural rules that dictate how, where, when, and by whom these storylines can be retold. The private, initiates only, versions of the songlines narrate and render the landscape in minute detail. The Australian continent is covered in songlines that can, supposedly, guide the singer spiritually and physically from the northern tips of Australia through the central desert core down to the southern states some three thousand kilometres away. In both their public and private forms, these storylines provide a template for Indigenous life. They showcase the intense lineage and relationships between preliterate people and land (Linklater, 2014: 94–95). Indigenous peoples in Australia embody the land so that the earth and bodies, past and present, are thought of symbiotic; the body, ancestors, and land are *country*. Marcia Langton (1999: 1) argues, turning the settler-colonialist discourse back onto itself, that Indigenous peoples in Australia "are born with an inchoate, inherited and transferable right to 'country.'"

There is always a danger of essentialising Indigenous oral practices of storytelling about people and place (Paradies, 2006) – to temporally suspend these oral storytelling practices *in time* as if they were from a bygone era. It is true that Indigenous technics of oral storytelling about country originated from an era passed, but they have also been in continual use in Australia since they were first sung thousands of years ago (Jacobs, 1996). It is equally problematic to conceptualise these practices as being untouched by colonial and other knowledge systems. Since first contact with Europeans in the eighteenth-century, these storytelling practices have repeatedly rubbed up against a whole host of settlers and their land-telling, management, and claiming technics. The oral organising technics of the Indigenous peoples of Australia, especially those relating to body, land, and country, have been and still are affected and shaped by their encounters with the organising technics of settlers.

We see this too in other settler-society countries around the world. In North America, the originally oral so-called Ojibwe and Chippewa "legends and myths" about Hiawatha, some collected by Henry Schoolcraft (1854) in the nineteenth-century, provide another example of detailed Creation storytelling that brings together in symbiotic fashion people, place, past and present within storylines. The organising technics of the British colonial empire, such as the scientific rationalities of evolutionary anthropology and the rational-legal forms of property rights, as we now know, were deployed in an attempt to overwrite a new set of people and land relationships across the British colonies. Attempting to restory or recode the landscape, and peoples' relationships to it, was a necessary discursive co-requisite alongside the settlers' actions in physical and legal space. Recoding the landscape with new stories was a way to challenge and at times change Indigenous relationships to land. As John Weaver (2003: 145) writes,

> "Although colonising governments conceded that first peoples theoretically held interests in land, they appropriated absolute sovereignty by one of three mechanisms: the right of discovery; the right of conquest, or the surrender of sovereignty by treaty. These rationalisations for sovereignty originated from convictions of cultural superiority – only one authority could govern, and it would be European." (p. 135) "… a requirement that indigenous peoples' interests in the land be cleared by formal acts became entrenched in the ideology of legality that survived on British colonial and American frontiers. Humanitarians would come and go; lawyers went on forever" (p. 145).

Australia's colonial history is bursting with examples of both the attempted colonisation of Indigenous storylines by the colonisers, and resistance to this colonial project by Indigenous peoples through storylines. Indigenous peoples shaped and influenced settler-colonialism everywhere because their storylines were embodied narratives, linking mythical and material landscapes with the past, present, and at times the future. The early colonial authorities, settlers, and land hunters needed local guides and translators, and at times Indigenous cultural allies, to help them to navigate the cultural and physical terrain. Some even used Indigenous peoples to help them to parley territory from others (Weaver, 2003: 123). Indigenous familiarity with the physical terrain and the ability of the Indigenous body to narrate and navigate the landscape was a form of power that the settlers sought to control and use.

For example, in the late eighteenth and early nineteenth centuries, the valleys of the Blue Mountains west of Sydney were a forbidding, and for a time an impenetrable, territorial barrier to colonial expansion. Indeed, the Blue Mountains became a symbolic and material frontier the settlers had to cross to further their colonial expansion. In 1813, an expedition led by Gregory Blaxland, William Lawson, and William Charles Wentworth found and followed a track used by the local Aboriginal people across the Blue Mountains.[2] West of the mountains was productive "farmland," another form of European recoding, that would support the establishment of Australia's first inland settlement at Bathurst, although unreliable water sources would challenge the settlers for decades. T.M. Perry's observations about using the embodied knowledge of Indigenous peoples as a technology within Australia's first project of colonial expansion from Sydney, argues Weaver (2003: 120), "holds true for frontier occupation in many other places around the world." A new colonial narrative about the Blue Mountains, which has since come to capture a part of the contemporary storytelling about this part of Western Sydney, began with the (re)naming of three points on the route over the mountains. The three physical sites were (re)named Blaxland, Wentworth, and Lawson. These names became a part of a colonial frontier narrative and were underwritten by the discourse of *terra nullius* on the one hand, and the discourses of exploration and discovery on the other (Buchan 2013; Heath, 2006; Crabtree, 2013; Tilley, 2012).

Blaxland, Wentworth, and Lawson's bodies were mediating technologies that recoded the Australian landscapes with rational-legal ideas of landed property. They each received 1000 acres for their colonial efforts. Years later, after honing his speculating skills and knowledge in Australia, Wentworth became a specular in Māori property deeds in New Zealand (Weaver, 2003: 211). Weaver writes, "William Charles Wentworth, Sydney lawyer and member of the council, defended the Māori's right to sell. He had been snapping up Māori deeds" (p. 138). Lawson – who put his body to work in the service of private property as well – trained as a surveyor in London. He claimed his 1000 acres and settled in Bathurst. In the case of Wentworth and Lawson, their bodies were mediating technologies through which an attempt to recode the Australian and New Zealand landscape with rational-legal ideas of European landed property was mobilised.

Indeed, the history of claiming land as property shows that the professional milieu of surveying, and the embodied practices of the transnationally mobile surveyor, is a colonial meditating technology of land claiming *par excellence*. A related activity was naming and renaming, and therefore, surveys simultaneously enabled and required place names. In this sense, surveying is both a discursive act and a performative enactment. In 1829, the surveyor-general of New South Wales instructed his surveyors to reduce or limit Aboriginal place names to a maximum of nine letters (Weaver, 2003: 301). Weaver (2003: 301) reports, the "great land rush involved enormous European naming exercises. Intriguingly, plenty of indigenous names endured, some because they assisted [settlers] to define boundaries." What is significant about the oral storytelling practice of the *country* is that not even the temporally significant eighteenth-century colonial contact points could completely fracture the lineage of Indigenous storylines about people and place into a hard systemic edge; with the so-called subjective and mythical storylines of Indigenous peoples' on the one hand and the "objective" and "rational" storylines of the colonisers' on the other. The latter Porter (2010: 62) labels "colonial Cartesian spaces produced by the explorer's gaze."

In a process of double displacement, the Indigenous "first" peoples of Australia were deterritorialised from the land when the first colonisers arrived, and then, it was only through this act of deterritorialisation that the first peoples came into being. In other words, the arrival of the colonisers provided the discursive referent – the second peoples, the "settlers" – that would later be deployed to imagine the "first peoples." The colonisers could not, however, fully recode the mythical storylines of the Indigenous peoples with their European organising technics, including their imported scientific rationalist stories about people and place. Rather, contact between the Indigenous peoples and settler-colonialists brought about a new assemblage of storylines about people and place. Over the next 200 years in Australia, Indigenous peoples and settler-colonialists would clash when they were forced to navigate this new and unstable storytelling assemblage, when two organising technics of land collided. One of the best examples is the famous 1992 *Mabo vs. Queensland* High Court of Australia case, the first to recognise Native Title in Australia. Eddie Mabo, a Torres Straits Islander, built a case relating to the ownership of a parcel of his people's traditional land against the Australian government with oral storytelling at its core. The case focused on the relationship between the songlines of the *Meriam* people and their place naming and land ownership customs.

As evidence, Mabo presented the Torres Straits Islander peoples' songlines and his legal team argued that these songs demonstrated the land ownership customs of his people. For a brief moment, the storylines of the *Meriam* people would be tested as evidence against the rational-legal colonialist narratives of the settlers, in a rational-legal court of law. This was significant, not least because historically the settlers had used their rational-legal colonial narratives, and their courts of law, in attempts to dismantle and recode Indigenous storytelling about people and place. The stakes were high, but in a landmark decision, the judge accepted as evidence the oral storylines on the *Meriam* people and found that Mabo's people had demonstrated a form of property ownership in their traditional lands, albeit a form of property ownership that was somewhat translatable into the coloniser's rational-legal terms. The term landmark might be used here with reference to its two definitions, as both an "object" of the landscape that is easily recognised and as an "event" marking an important turning point. The court ruled, "The common law recognizes a form of native title which, in cases where it has not been extinguished, reflects the entitlements of the indigenous inhabitants in accordance with their laws or customs to their traditional lands" (Porter, 2010: 31 citing, French 1994: 74). The judgement brought into sharp relief the tension between two competing organising technics of land, and therefore the different land mentalities of the people involved. Some settlers argued that the ruling appeared to "undermine the common law rights of Australia's stock farmers to almost half their land" (Linklater, 2014: 94–95). The centre-left Keating government enacted the Native Title Act 1993 and established the National Native Title Tribunal. But in 1998, the centre-right Howard government bolstered a political backlash against the Mabo ruling. The Howard government, it is worth recalling, famously refused to say "sorry" or "apologise" to the Indigenous peoples of Australia for their mistreatment at the hands of the settler-colonialists. Preferring a colonial-inspired narrative that was partly driven by parochial, perhaps even racist, ideas about White Australia's land claims, the Howard government introduced legislation to water down the *Native Title Act 1993* (see Porter, 2010: 31–33 for a more detailed discussion).

Weaver (2003: 145) was right; attempts for social justice will come and go but the lawyers will regulate these narratives forever. Linklater (2014: 94–95) shows, "the principle that these epic legends [and storylines] incorporate a sense of ownership remains intact in other common law jurisdictions. In 2007, the Supreme Court of British Columbia delivered judgement in favour of the land claims of a hunting group in British Columbia largely on the basis of what the judge called 'verbal messages from the past beyond the present generation.'" These cases highlight the central role of embodied storytelling as a mediating technology that sits between Indigenous peoples and the ground on which they live. The Mabo case in particular, like so much of Australian's recent land claiming history, turns on perhaps the single most important embodied territorial referent in Australia's colonial history, *terra nullius*. Ian Buchanan (2012: 120) argues, *terra nullius* not only denied prior ownership of land, but as the colonisers attempted to recode the land the discourse of *terra nullius* also established Indigenous peoples' relationship to the colony as one of exclusion. "Ultimately, then," argues Porter (2010: 32), "what the Mabo decision did was to recognise Indigenous people as landowners with unique property tenure rights" in excess of their status "as citizens of the Australian nation-state." Furthermore, the Mabo case shows that native title can co-exist alongside private property rights, at least for a time, but the Australian government reserves the right to revise these rights. While important, "[t]his is why the apparent overturning of *terra nullius* by the High Court judgement in *Mabo vs. Queensland* in June 1992," argues Buchanan (2012: 121), "did not change the excluded status of Indigenous people as much as might have been expected, or indeed as much as has been claimed." The centre-left Rudd government's "apology" to Indigenous peoples in Australia, when it did come in 2008, was a rare moment of national reflection on settler-colonial discourse and storytelling. It was an acknowledgement of the very real discrimination and suffering that colonial storytelling and practices had produced. It was an atypical national-level discussion, but as welcome and necessary as the apology was it did not change the contemporary material living conditions of Indigenous peoples, nor did it bring about a radical rethinking of the land claiming mentalities of contemporary settlers (Buchanan, 2012: 113).

This vignette demonstrates that there is no hard systemic edge that marks the end of the oral songlines and land-telling traditions of Indigenous people in Australia. The Cartesian-inspired colonial narratives about land continue to be produced by settler-colonialists. These oral traditions flow across time and space, and the land mentalities continue to flow through people and place. Settler-colonialism is not in the past, and the different organising technics and land mentalities of the colonial period continue to push up against each other at different times and in different places. However, as different organising technics and land mentalities come into contact, they change the modalities and politics of the oral land-telling practices. The narration of people and place represents a systemic flow across time and space, and these oral traditions have endured from as far back as there is recorded human history. The same cannot be said of the organising technics and land mentalities that framed peasant life across Europe and Asia for hundreds of years, an organising technic known as feudalism. As Linklater (2014: 105) shows, "[f]ew things divide the modern private world more completely from the past than the collegiate nature of tribal and peasant life." In the next section, I turn to the crisis in feudal land mentalities that emerged in the sixteenth-century to show how a land mentality can be radically reconfigured over a few centuries.

INCLOSURE: THE DECLINE OF FEUDALISM *EX POST FACTO*

Between 1537 and 1539, the notorious English lawyer and chief minister to King Henry VIII of England and Earl of Essex, Thomas Cromwell, bought more than 15 properties in the southeast of England at a cost of £38,000 (Linklater, 2014: 20). Linklater (2014: 20) reports that Cromwell sold most of them for a 9.5 per cent or £4,000 profit. When Cromwell was arrested in London in 1540 and beheaded soon after on Tower Hill, £7,000 in cash was found in his house (Linklater, 2014: 21). The profits were earned largely from property deals. It was the decline of feudalism in England, and in terms of the organising technics of land and property, the value of landed property was rising and along with it came an irresistible opportunity to profit from increasing land values. The temporal boundaries of this clash in land and real estate organising technics, if indeed temporal boundaries can be placed around the systemic edges of two organising technics, run from at least the English Reformation in the middle of the sixteenth-century until the start of the seventeenth-century. When Henry VIII rejected the papal supremacy in the early 1530s, he thus began the English Reformation and the dissolution of the monasteries in earnest. As the churches' taxation burden was shifted from Rome to England, Cromwell decided that the value of their extensive real estate and other assets should be established and recorded for taxation purposes. In 1535, the government surveyed the finances of all churches in England, Wales, and parts of Ireland, and produced the *Valor Ecclesiasticus* (the church valuation document). By the time Cromwell was executed, he had helped facilitated the transfer of one fifth of England's landed property wealth to the landed gentry. The landed gentry would now be beholden as taxpayers to the Crown. Cromwell emboldened the decline of the feudal land mentality to get behind the land mentality of private property. Cromwell had symbolically stepped out of the waning feudal land tenure order and into a new, soon to be market-centric, private property land order. In time, this organising technic of land and real estate would travel to the British colonies with the settlers.

A threshold had certainly been crossed, but the idea that feudalism might represent an organising technic is somewhat of a conceptual misnomer. Feudalism is a retroactive term that was formulated and developed *post facto* by scholars in an attempt to broadly capture the land tenure arrangements of different places within particular time periods (Elden, 2013). Yet, the power that was mobilised by assembling different people and land together, under what is now known as feudalism, contains some of the building blocks for later formations of property in land. In discussing the organising technics of feudalism, I accept that this organising technic is neither coherent nor uncontested; feudalism is, like most political economies, land tenure systems, and mentalities, a contested assemblage of many constituent parts that are shifting across time and space. In the mid-seventeenth century, the English Parliament passed acts to liberalise the *in capite* feudal tenurial system at home (MacMillan, 2006; Weaver, 2003: 188). The two central ideas that framed the legal debates and public discussions about land tenure related to the power and authority to "create or curtail property rights" and the "sources of revenue" that were enabled by these property rights and privileges (Weaver, 2003: 180–181). The *in capite* (tenants-in-chief) tenurial system allowed the upper gentry and nobility to hold land from their sovereign ruler and to further dispute (*enfeoff*) these lands to tenants (MacMillan, 2006: 90). Tenants were required to pay an inheritance and other fees to landlords. Another form of feudal tenurial system, *ut de manore*, attached fewer crown fees but those holding the land could not further distribute it, thus, they could not generate as much revenue from the land (MacMillan, 2006: 90). On several British colonial frontiers, the vestiges of these feudal land tenurial systems, which had been imported from Europe, lingered on (Weaver, 2003: 178). In some places, they lingered on well into the eighteenth-century.

Two specific political, legal, social, and economic assemblages of so-called feudalism, which faded away in Europe in the sixteenth-century and Asia in the twentieth-century, are of interest here. More specifically, the following is a search for some of the constituent parts that were later drawn into the colonial geopolitics of land claiming. While some dispute the exact dating of feudalism in England (Elden, 2013; Mackrell, 2007), there is broad agreement that it emerged around the tenth-century, after the Norman conquest of England in 1066. Soon after, King William the Conqueror ordered the great land survey of much of England and parts of Wales, and thus the creation of the Domesday Book. The Domesday Book allowed William the Conqueror to measure and catalogue the realm he had won (Elden, 2013: 115). This assemblage of an embodied surveyor, their surveying instruments, and the written text on sheepskin parchment (i.e., The Domesday Book) was a significant mediating technology for completing the great land survey. This technological assemblage allowed the King to establish and to enforce a land taxation system. Elden (2013: 154) warns against making generalisations about dating the rise and fall of feudalism, or seeking to uncover stable geographies of land tenure relations and ownership. He accepts, however, that feudalism in England began to decline in about the thirteenth and fourteenth centuries. For example, in the mid-fifteenth-century, about 60 per cent of England's 12 million acres of farmland was held by the Crown and nobility. At the beginning of the eighteenth-century, "the nobility, church, and crown together owned less than 30 per cent of the cultivated land" (Linklater, 2014: 36).

King Henry VIII's Tudor break-up of church estates was followed in the seventeenth-century with the further expansion of the English into Ireland and then the rapid *inclosure* of open fields and the commons around the eighteenth-century. Sir William Petty (1690) is often remembered as a seventeenth-century political philosopher, economist, and scientist. Three ideas were central to his political philosophy, ideas that he drew in part from the Dutch. First, land should be thought of and treated as capital. Second, only labour can release the land's value. Third, the supply of money is essential to release the value of capital in land, and therefore, he advocated for a reputable national bank. For Linklater (2014), in terms of political philosophy about land, labour, capital, and property, the seventeenth-century scholarship of Petty contains some of the political philosophy roots that can help describe our contemporary land and real estate realities. He claims, Petty, "[a]nticipating Milton Friedman's monetarist approach," delineates "the precise point at which capitalism and private property can be seen to have merged" (p. 58). In political philosophy, economic, and scientific terms, Petty was a pre-eminent surveyor and claimer of lands. However, Petty's story is perhaps more fascinating when you look at how his body was deployed as a technology of land claiming. Petty built into his *body* the cognitive and physical tools of land measurement, claiming, and commodification. In his late twenties, he mobilised, quite literally, this embodied mediating technology when he secured the contract to survey and map Ireland. The rationalist surveying *body as technology* would become a powerful tool of British colonial expansion, as we shall see.

Four major shifts were underway in England around this time period: (1) the enclosure of land, (2) a rapid increase in the population, (3) the movement of people into towns and cities and, (4) the detachment of land prices from agricultural production. The ambitious landed gentry sought to "possess and manipulate more land, at the expense of occupants" (Weaver, 2003: 22). The introduction of the initial *Inclosure Act 1773*, which is still in force in the United Kingdom, along with the many additional claims, is a decisive moment in the history of English land claiming. It coincided with the industrial revolution, which grew from the bottom-up in eighteenth-century England. Governments would later manage the industrial revolution as a top-down process across Europe and Asia, but in England, "the ambitions of innumerable individuals ... believed that by their own efforts they could own the hardware of machinery and the software of ideas, and make money from them" (Linklater, 2014: 175). Both the hardware of the new industrial machinery and the embodied software of ideas were mobilised and indeed were mobile across England and the British colonial world. The population grew from about seven million people at the start of the eighteenth-century to more than 11 million people by the end of the century (Linklater, 2014: 176). The increasing demand for agricultural commodities, due largely to population increases in towns and cities, should have pushed up the price of commodities such as wheat. Instead, the price for cereals and grains flattened out until the 1780s as the demand for land increased. "In other words, the value of the land was no longer dictated by its yield of crops and animal. What counted were the laws of supply and demand. More people wanted to buy land that there were owners prepared to sell" (Linklater, 2014: 176). During the eighteenth-century, the rising land prices enlivened the landed gentry into political action to enclose more land. Between the start of the eighteenth-century and the middle of the nineteenth-century, more than 4000 *Inclosure Acts* were passed, a testament to the power of the landed gentry in halls of power, both legal or Parliamentary.

Around this period, almost a quarter of England's farmland had been used for pasturing livestock under common usage rights or cultivated as open fields. The *Inclosure Acts* allowed the gentry and their supporters to use physical boundaries such as fences and hedgerows to enclose the common usage land as private *exclusive* property. The *Inclosure Acts* also worked to enshrine a set of legally enforceable land boundaries in the minds of the landed gentry (Linklater, 2014: 176); the laws helped to create a land claiming mentality. Part of the appeal for enclosing the commons with physical and legal boundaries had to do with the landed gentry being passionate about creating intergenerational wealth pathways for their property. Many set up various entails and property trusts to protect familial property interests. They also advocated for the wider use of *equity of redemption* to make it harder for lenders to foreclose on loans, and thus forcing the gentry to sell their land. "Where sales did take place, almost half were between existing landowners anxious to increase or consolidate their holdings" (Linklater, 2014: 176). The Tudor resistance to the enclosure of land, backed up by the anti-enclosure acts of 1489 and 1516, was but a fading memory in the eighteenth-century. The sixteenth-century agrarian land mentality that had underwritten the call for the restoration of the commons – as well as the material resistance to enclosing the commons, whereby peasants mounted stealth missions to down the fences and hedgerows – had failed. In the sixteenth-century, the landed gentry took aim at the Crown to protect their landed private property assets. They used their numbers in the House of Commons to create statutes that allowed them to avoid paying taxes on their property trusts, which were known at the time as "uses" (Linklater, 2014: 19). Henry VIII was furious and the Crown sued in Henry VIII's own courts of law to recover the forgone tax. He claimed that "uses" cost him two thirds of the tax revenues that would have been collected if the landed gentries' statutes had not passed. "In 1535, at the end of a two-year battle, the king was forced to accept a compromise that favoured the new property owners ... [This] represented the moment when one vital feature of the private property society became established, the landowners' use of political power to protect their own interests against the royal executive" (Linklater, 2014: 19). By the eighteenth-century in England, landed property was a source of capital, prestige, and a way to gain and exercise political power. The beginnings of the first free market land system were built on middle- and upper-class bodies protecting their landed interests. Privately enclosed land became an embodied mentality and a material manifestation of wealth and power. The landed gentry sought political positions and influence to safeguard their property interests. Ann Bermingham (1986: 10) reports, "In the first half of the eighteenth-century 74,000 acres of land were enclosed by act of Parliament, and in the second half of the century the figure swelled to 750,000 acres. Even these figures, which do not include acreage enclosed by private consensus among landholders, offer a conservative picture." On Linklater's assessment (2014: 177), "[a]ltogether, some seven million acres were transferred into private ownership through the enclosure orders, brutal testimony to the political power now wielded by landowners. In many cases compensation was paid, but the total value of enclosed land represented the transfer of about £175 million of assets from communal possession to the lawyers, merchants, and wealthy landowners who controlled Parliament."

This vignette demonstrates that enclosing the commons was a politico-legal act that was played out as much in the material landscapes of the countryside, as it was in the courtrooms of the Crown. More centrally, it was conflict between the agrarian land mentality of the commons and the private land mentality of the newly enfranchised landed gentry. In this case, the decline of the feudal order allowed the landed gentry, using their political and legal power, to stifle any resistance to the enclosure of land, and to reduce their taxation burden in the process. However, it is not a *fait accompli* that the rich and powerful, with their private property-mediated land mentalities, will necessarily maintain their power over the landless. Indeed, the decline of feudalism in China stands in stark contrast to the inclosing of the commons in the United Kingdom. In the next section, I turn to the crisis in feudal land mentalities that took place in twentieth-century China to show how a revolutionary communal land mentality was used to revolt against the old feudal order to radically reconfigure social life.

REVOLUTION: FROM FEUDALISM TO *FANSHEN*

Six years after the Communist Party began in China, Mao Tse-tung (1927) travelled throughout Hunan province to observe and report on the peasant movement. Reflecting on his fieldtrips, he wrote in 1927, "In a very short time, in China's central, southern and northern provinces, several hundred million peasants will rise like a mighty storm, like a hurricane, a force so swift and violent that no power, however great, will be able to hold it back. ... They will sweep all the imperialists, warlords, corrupt officials, local tyrants and evil gentry into their graves" (Tse-tung, 1927: 1). Mao believed he was standing on the edge of a radical change in the mentality of land ownership and management, and he wanted desperately to cross it. He was right, but while he would have to wait until 1949 to see this revolutionary land mentality fully implemented, the blood would start flowing before then. William Hinton's (1966) seminal *Fanshen: Documentary of the Revolution in a Chinese Village* showcases in extraordinary detail the everyday lived experience of the end of feudal landlordism in one village in northern China. It was an abrupt and bloody affair that was written into the minds and bodies of those involved. "Every revolution creates new worlds," writes Hinton. "The Chinese Revolution created a whole new vocabulary. A most important word in this vocabulary was *fanshen*" (Hinton, 1966: xx). This term means, quite literally, "to turn over," or "to turn over the body."

To the hundreds of millions of landless or land-poor peasants in twentieth-century China, the term was a call to put the body to work; "to stand up, to throw off the landlord yoke, to gain land, stock, implements, and houses" (Hinton, 1966: xx). In 1947, the Chinese Communist Party sketched out and then announced the Draft Agrarian Law on 23 December of that year. It reads, in part,

Article I – The agrarian system of feudal and semi-feudal exploitation is abolished. The agrarian system of "land-to-the-tiller" is to be realised.
Article II – Landownership rights of all landlords are abolished.
Article III – Landownership rights of all ancestral shrines, temples, monasteries, school, institutions, and organisations are abolished.
Article IV – All debts incurred in the countryside prior to the reform of the agrarian system are cancelled (cited in Hinton, 1966: 7).

These sixty-four words wholly capture the radical departure from landlordism that the Community Party was proposing. This simple speech act written on paper would, within one decade, completely restructure the relationships between people and place that had guided Chinese life for centuries (DeMare, 2007; Jacques, 2012). Village acting groups at the time performed plays and skits inside *yangko* dancing circles, and "drama troupes also performed for villages, teaching *yangge* dancing and putting on large-scale revolutionary operas" (DeMare, 2015: 187). These dramas, enacted in the everyday, retold stories about despot landlordism and land reform, with landlords portrayed as villainous oppressors and the peasantry as exploited (DeMare, 2015; Hinton, 1966: 11). Some more famous "land reform dramas" from The People's Drama Troupe include: *The Hatred of the Poor* "staring a local despot landlord villain"; *The Fanshen of Li Lanying* "about a female peasant who suffers from feudal exploitation"; *The Invisible Militia* "detailing a self-defence unit that battles reactionary landlords"; and *Wang Gui and Xiangxiang,* which focuses "on class conflict between a local despot landlord and his hired hand" (DeMare, 2007: fn. 21, p. 110). The most commonly known revolution performance is, of course, *The White-Haired Girl* about landlordism and peasant revolution (Clark, 2008; DeMare, 2015: 177). The body became the technology through which the land revolution would be mobilised, and storytelling about people and place would be the topic of discussion and re-education (DeMare, 2015; Jicai, 1996). In particular, the body was used as the technology and the site through which the manipulation of the peasants' land mentalities and thoughts about the landed gentry could be used to mobilise the land revolution (DeMare, 2015; Hinton, 1966). These dramatic performances were one of the sites of the revolution, storytelling events that were tasked with changing the land mentalities of the audience. Their purpose was to reconfigure land and body as a technological tool through which social change could be mediated.

Working on the subjective body with storytelling matters when it comes to struggles over land. Some contemporary scholars of Chinese history claim that a form of feudalism or *fengjian* was practised as far back as the 1046 BCE Chou Dynasty in China (Chan, 2009: 64; Feng, 2009). It is not insignificant that Feng (2009) translates *fengjian* as "to establish by means of boundaries" (p. 110), but Chan (2009: 64) questions the use of the term feudalism to describe land systems in China, claiming that naming it as such is a form of Orientalism. This form of mentality conditioning, using the body as a technology, is not unique to China, nor is it limited to this time period. Indeed, much has been written about the different revolutionary struggles that emerged out of the feudal orders of Europe (Elden, 2013; Linklater, 2014; Said, 1993) and Asia (DeMare, 2015; Hinton, 1966; Jacques, 2012; Jicai, 1996; Linklater, 2014), and the role of discourse and storytelling within these struggles. Elden's (2013) extended discussion of people and place relations across Europe between 500 BCE and the tenth-century is also an important contextual frame for European feudalism. Western philosophy scholars have paid particular attention to European and Russian transitions out of feudalism, including the Industrial Revolution in England discussed above. However, the stories from the early 1790s surrounding Jacques Roux and his followers in Paris, a group of revolutionaries known as *les enrages, against the rich*, constitute a good example of the embodied geopolitical actions that were occurring across Europe (Slavin, 1986). Following the signing of the Peace of Westphalia in 1648 and the developing discourse of co-existing European sovereign states, the French Revolution (1789–1799) further "sowed the seeds of a process of political revolution that has given rise to the modern nation-state" (Schurmann, 1968: xxxv). The first stage of the French Revolution, including the peasant revolt from August 1789, took aim at the *Ancien Régime* in general, and the abolition of feudalism more specifically.

In Europe and Asia alike, forms of Marxism (1818–1883) were central to the revolutionary struggles over land and property, as the countries attempted to build political identities around new national imaginaries and then the idea of a national economy, which was often underwritten by state-led industrial-technological developments in Europe. Many of the revolutionary struggles drew upon the historical materialism thinking of Karl Marx. A principle driver of historical change, argues Marx, is the assemblage of certain technologies and technics that are made available to particular groups, the productive forces that are produced by these technologies, technics, and groups, and the technical division of labour (Jones, 2003: 24–25). Marx's attention was not so much on the technologies themselves, but rather on tensions between different relations of production. Land relations were chief among Marx's

(1983: 52) concerns: "The landlords, like all other men, love to reap where they never sowed, and demand a rent even for the natural produce of the earth." Marx considered the division of intellectual production from physical production a major turning point in history, and the production of social inequality was the *product* of this division.

The contested spatiotemporal histories of declining feudal orders, which were analysed by Marx (1983) and others (Chan, 2009; Clark, 2008; DeMare, 2015; Elden, 2013; Linklater, 2014), remain important events in the history of geopolitical real estate relations. In the middle of the twentieth-century, Hinton (1966: xxv) wrote, "What happened in China yesterday may well happen in Brazil, Nigeria, or India tomorrow. Land reform is on the agenda of Mankind." By the end of the century, Hamilton (1996: 330) was arguing that Chinese capitalism was already hard to pin down, "because it is not readily confined to a time in history, to a place in the world, or even to what we might think of as a capitalist mode of production." The historical legacies and revolutionary struggles associated with Asian landlordism – and the rapid recent decline of feudalism in particular – are becoming increasingly important for understanding twenty-first-century global real estate relations. This is especially the case when considering the new foreign real estate investment relationships between Asia and settler-societies. "When the relations of production thwart the development of the forces of production, revolution has to result," argued Marx, and this occurred in the "transition from feudalism to capitalism" in China in the mid-twentieth-century (Jones, 2003: 25). Unlike the European decline of feudalism, in China, these events occurred relatively recently, and the memories of these revolutionary struggles are still shaping the land and real estate mentalities of some of the older Chinese (Jicai, 1996). Therefore, what was fascinating, and ultimately devastating, about the Chinese case is that the body was deployed as a revolutionary technology of land reform on a grand scale. This happened at a time when many of the settler-societies were using private property, in the form of real estate, to recover from the Second World War (as we will see in Chapter 6). In China, the body was mobilised as a central mediating technology for the various re-education programmes that started with the first acts of overthrowing the federal landlords and continued through the Cultural Revolution (Jacques, 2012; Jones, 2003).

At several times in China's long history, the peasantry has challenged the "emperor-ruled, landlord-tenant system" of dynastic governance (Hinton, 1966: 27). However, up until 1949, the feudal landlord-tenant system always returned. Part of the reason, argues Hinton (1966: 55), was that the social and productive relations of the feudal order were written into the bodies of all Chinese. The feudal land mentality was written into their bodies and their bodies needed to be un-storied before a land revolution could be sustained.

The peasants were unable to maintain their revolutionary projects because they had very little knowledge of other social orders or modes of land production. Any revolution would not only have to reconfigure "the material life of the people, but also their consciousness" (Hinton, 1966: xxiv). The land revolution was a revolution of the mind, a reconfiguration of a land mentality.

For example, in the village of Long Bow prior to 1949, under the feudal landlord-tenant system, 70–80 per cent of the land and other valuable property, such as farming implements and livestock, was owned by about 10 per cent of the population, which largely consisted of landlords and rich peasants (Hinton, 1966: 27). The two most exploited groups, the poor and middle peasantry, "owned less than a quarter of the land, and only five per cent of the draft animals," which were second only to land as the most valuable form of rural wealth (Hinton, 1966: 35). Life for these peasants was tough, and physical and sexual violence was common (Hinton, 1966: 35 and 51). With no banks and very little industry or village commerce, and with no land or livestock, the landless peasantry frequently could not marry. Those who could not pay their agrarian taxes were forced to take out loans, often from the landlords at high interest rates that many would never be able to pay back. Some were forced to sell their wives and children to pay their loans and other dues. Land was the safest investment, but it was easily confiscated from the poor in a village dominated by the landed gentry. Hinton (1966: 28) writes about a particularly ruthless landlord and village administrator named Ching-ho. "By far the largest source of Ching-ho's administration 'take' came from the cut he took of all taxes. If the county magistrate demanded two bushels of grain per family, he demanded five and kept three. He accepted no excuse for failure to pay. People had to deliver their tax grain even if they had to sell their children to do it. ... He was especially vigorous in taking other people's land and houses." Whether it was a male body working in the fields, or sexual violence inflicted on a female body, or the commodification of a child's body to pay an unpayable debt, the body was a technology of power within this land system. As if to make an explicit comment on the assemblage of bodies, land, labour, and capital, Hinton (1966: 32–45) states more generally about the landed gentry, "[c]hildren could be seized in lieu of property, but in a bad crop year teenaged girls sold for less than a hundredweight of grain, and they had to be fed (p. 32). ... The debts of the poor begin at birth. When a boy is a month old the family wishes to celebrate; but they have to borrow money in order to make dumplings and so, before the child can sit up, he is already in debt to the landlord. As he grows the interest mounts " (p. 44–45). Unlike the rural poor, the more wealthy rural landed gentry could afford to hire in-house educational tutors, and some even sent their children to a local or urban college. Educated siblings served to protect the landed gentry's interests by allowing these graduates to move into the higher levels of the central bureaucracy, the officer corps of the army, or into larger commercial or banking establishments in regional or urban centres (Hinton, 1966: 86). The idea that land ownership was the most important form of property and, therefore, the foundation for securing your families' future, was deeply embedded into the consciousness of every Chinese, rich and poor alike. Furthermore, there was a spiritual dimension to this narrative of land success. Those with landed property were thought of as being rewarded for their virtuous living, correct thinking, and spiritual purity, or at least the peasantry were encouraged to think of them in these ways (Feng, 2009; Hinton, 1966). Equally, the peasantry were taught to think that they were poor because of their contemptuous living and spiritual disharmony.

In the 1940s, about 90 per cent of China's population was rural and lived outside cities (Ren, 2013: xiii), and a large part of this population was poor and landless. Mao saw lying idle in the landless peasantry an untapped source of embodied power, and not for the first or last time would the strategy to claim land be a part of a strategy for war. During the Second Sino-Japanese War (1937–1945), land reform was central to the Communist Party's wartime strategy. In doing so, the Communist Party not only gave peasants a reason to help the Communist Eight Route Army fight the Japanese, and later the Kuomintang; it also provided a land mentality that demonstrated to the peasant population *how* land tenure relations could be reorganised (Magdoff, 2008: viii). The ruling Communist Party, headed by Mao, used the peasant body as an embodied technology for mobilising the land reform and moved the society across the systemic edge of two organising technics of land. "The principal technique for achieving and advancing the change in thinking on a mass level was the campaign or movement (*yundong*)," writes Jones (2003: 28). After the Japanese army surrender in late 1945, the Communist Party issued a directive on land reforms in 1946 and the civil war with the Nationalists began (or perhaps more accurately, resumed) soon after. At the local level, in the village of Long Bow, the Communist Eighth Route Army overthrew the collaborationist or "puppet" army of Chinese, who had collaborated with the Japanese army. As a Communist-dominated government was established in Long Bow, a mass education campaign was quickly established to recode how peasants collectively thought about land and property. Peasants were already confiscating land from the landed gentry in several Communist Party-controlled areas in north China, through social movements such as the Anti-Traitor Movement, the Settling of Accounts Movement, and The Gate. At a regional governance level, The Central Committee of the Communist Party was also about to issue the May 4 Directive on Land Reform (on 4 May) 1946, which formally authorised the confiscation of landlords' property (Jones, 2003: 29).

In the Anti-Traitor Movement, the members of the Communist resistance movement quickly established a government in Long Bow, which was "connected with the party even if not all involved were members of it" (Jones,

2003: 31). The old imperial order, which focused on the management of the internal bureaucracy from the top down to control the population, was stirring in the ranks of the Communist Party, and Mao would soon become the ruler of the party. Nonetheless, at the local level, the new government was drawing the peasant body, as a material and subjective asset, into the Anti-Traitor Movement. The government called a series of public meetings, which many of the villagers attended. They brought members of the collaborationist or "puppet" government before public meetings and accused them of collaboration with the Japanese army. In many cases, prior to the public meetings, representatives of the government would coach several villagers to publicly denounce those accused and to provide verbal testimony against them at the meetings. In addition to accusations of collaboration, the charges also related to landlord-tenant misdeeds. Numerous collaborators confessed to the accusations at the group meetings, and some were beaten to death on the spot. The results of these "public trials" were clearly orchestrated and predetermined by the government and there was never any question the accused would not be punished and have their land and property confiscated (Hinton, 1966; Jones, 2003: 31). The explicit aim of the Anti-Traitor Movement was to punish the traitors, but the implicit motivation of the new people's government was to get the villagers to participate, directly, in naming the crimes, accusing the perpetrators (called *speak bitterness*), and to find the accused guilty. Jones writes (2003: 31), "the whole community had to be mobilised to support the military (the civil war was in full force at the time) and to "settle accounts with the personnel of the puppet administration." Doubtless both of these aims were present, but a more important one seems to have been to begin the process of arousing the consciousness of the village to understand the revolutionary process that was under way and to realise they were a part of it."

The Settling of Accounts Movement was launched in Long Bow in January 1946 and was completed in a month (Jones, 2003: 29). If the Anti-Traitor Movement marked the beginning of mobilising the peasantry to end the feudal land tenure system in Long Bow, then the Settling of Accounts Campaign marked its zenith. In these two radical "movements" (campaigns) of land tenure and agrarian property reconfiguration, more than a quarter of the village's 375 hectares of land was seized, including over 85 hectares of land from "traitors" and "exploiters" of the poor peasantry and 22 hectares of land from religious and other institutions (Hinton, 1966: 146). Four hundred of the 8000 "sections" of houses were confiscated, over 1000 tonnes of grain were seized, 26 draft animals were confiscated, as was more than half of all the large farm animals in the village (Hinton, 1966: 146). The peasants were coached to think about the expropriated land and property as the fruits of struggle (*tou cheng kuo shih*), and "[o]n these fruits," argues Hinton (1966: 146), the peasants "based their hopes for a new life." The Settling of Accounts Movement was specifically designed to educate the poor peasantry about their exploitation at the hands of feudal property owners; it was working to reconfigure the organising technic of land in the village and the land mentalities of the peasants. It focused in particular on removing, or eliminating in some cases, the property owners by confiscating land and reducing the rents and interest payments (*chien-tsu, chien-his*) that property owners could charge.

The peasants' bodies, as a technology for implementing land tenure and political change, a political move, was also mobilised more generally throughout the Mao years. During the Anti-Traitor Movement, the young men who were leading the movement were called to meetings to be educated in the fundamentals of Marxism, including class and land relations and class-consciousness (Jones, 2003). This education process was about writing Marxist and anti-feudal ideals into the minds and bodies of these poorly educated or even illiterate young men, so that they could be mobilised as an embodied technology through which the land revolution could be achieved. Given the low education status of these Chinese, transforming the body into a revolutionary technology was achieved through group discussion of Communist policy and rural class structure. There was often "an idea" or a "form of thinking" that the group would attack. Mao Tse-tung's two 1933 articles on rural class relations, for example, were deployed as a part of the redemptive re-education strategy in the discussions. Simply having the material body in the place where the discussion was taking place was not enough; the subjective body was expected to understand the content of the discussion, and their understanding of the content was tested. Understanding was compulsory, and everyone had to prove, through discussion, that they understood what was "dangerous thinking" and how Marxism provided the remedy. "The most important part of the method," argues Jones (2003: 33), was directing the "discussion so that everyone agrees verbally with" and believed the information presented.

By 1948, the Communist Party was well established and the radical land reform, a locally driven initiative which was built on the 1947 Draft Agrarian Law and the new taxation system (*chien-tsu, chien-his*), was in full swing. Much like the old imperial days, the rising Communist Party did not see these local Chinese actors as individual rights-bearing subjects, but rather as subjective bodies that could be encoded with certain behaviours and beliefs that suited the central bureaucracy, and ultimately, at a later stage, the will of the Communist leader Mao Tse-tung. Hinton (1966) provides a vivid account of this process. He accompanied a work team made up of "educated" peasants and students from a local university that had been sent to the village of Long Bow to report on how the Draft Agrarian Law was being implemented on the ground. He found that much land and property had changed hands, but some of the organising technics of the old feudal system still lingered on;

they were still encoded into the bodies of the new landowners. The old feudal organising technic would be hard to transform, and some newly enfranchised landlords reverted to the kinds of behaviour they had rallied against, such as physical and sexual violence, extortion, and bribery. The Communist Party knew that more work needed to be done to recode these local Chinese actors to bring them in line with the central ideologies of revolutionary struggle. The Communist Party decided that the village had not undertaken the transfer of property in line with party dictates, and required the whole village to be reclassified according to two board criteria: (1) class (landlord, rich peasant, middle peasant, poor peasants); and (2) wealth (in land and agrarian equipment). However, much like the old imperial order, the central focus of this re-education programme, through a process called "The Gate" or "Party Rectification," was directed towards the Communist Party and its members. "The Gate" recoded or "purified" local members of the Communist Party through forced interrogation. At the local level, a group formed from non-party members that were made up of poor and landless peasants conducted the interrogations. Jones (2003: 33) states, "Arguably, the Cultural Revolution was simply a gigantic version of "The Gate" that was used in Long Bow to purge the local party. It seems to have been the feeling that the leaders' thinking needed special attention, and that an essential feature of these campaigns was an attack on them by the masses who are presumably not tainted by 'feudal' or bourgeois thinking." There is perhaps no better recent case of reconfiguring an organising technic of land through the explicit reformulation of the land mentalities of the people than the land revolution that took place in mid-twentieth-century China.

This vignette, therefore, demonstrates that the swift rupture of the feudal order in China was underwritten by an explicit strategy to re-educate the landless peasantry as a technology of power for the Communist Party, as Marx had suggested. It shows that it is not enough for the land-rich and politically powerful to acquire land as private property; they need to continually protect their landed assets in a physical and legal sense, but perhaps more importantly, they need to protect and maintain the land and private property mentalities that ultimately make their assets untouchable. The case of Long Bow shows that the private property mentalities were encoded so deeply into the bodies of the peasants that even when their bodies were freed from the legal and physical confines of the feudal order, the subjective effects lingered on. More recently, Jones (2003: 40) argued that most of the middle- to upper-level Communist Party members who are currently in power would have been "intensively indoctrinated" in Chinese Marxism through their participation in re-education campaigns, and that it is likely that these experiences would be working on their current real estate mentalities.

LAND: DISCURSIVE ACT/ENCODED PERFORMANCE

The three historical vignettes presented in this chapter outlined several organising technics of land that are enduring, rising, or fading away. The first was the storylines of *country* that continue to be used by Indigenous peoples in Australia. Drawing on the crisis of settler-colonial Indigenous land claiming in Australia, the vignette demonstrates that the oral songlines and land-telling traditions of Indigenous people are alive and well in Australia. This is despite the best efforts by successive waves of settlers, who, from the beginning of their colonial invasion, attempted to use their Cartesian-inspired colonial narratives about land to produce counter narratives about Australia. Settler-colonialism is as much in the present as it is in the past, and the land mentalities of Indigenous Australians are equally alive in the present as the symbiotic assemblage of the body, ancestors and land as *country*. What the Mabo case shows is that when different organising technics and land mentalities come into contact, the oral land-telling practices of Indigenous people can be assembled alongside the rational-legal organising technics of the settlers and used against them, if only for a brief moment. The second vignette highlights the power of putting into operation an organising technic that incorporates the rational-legal enclosing of the common land with a mentality about the supremacy of private exclusive property. In what has become a common practice in settler-societies around the world, the landed gentry in England used their political and legal power, which itself was built on their land-owning power, to defeat the land enclosure resistance movement, and later to reduce the tax they would pay to the Crown. However, the third vignette demonstrates that holding land as individual private property, and the rise of the rich and powerful more generally, is not a *fait accompli*. The crisis of feudalism in China provides a chilling reminder that land revolutions can seemingly come from the bottom-up. It also shows that the biggest challenge in a land revolution is not necessarily the physical claiming of land, but rather the more subjective task of recoding over the often well established and deeply embodied land mentality that existed prior to the land-claiming event. The three vignettes show that each organising technic of land is an assemblage of embodied discursive acts and performative enactments. The discursive acts, the stories we tell about land (and real estate), are heavily dependent on the prevailing organising technics of land (and real estate) that we are positioned within. However, the performative enactments of land are heavily dependent on the land mentalities that are encoded into our bodies. Furthermore, as the land mentality re-education programmes in China demonstrate, decoding and recoding land (and real estate) mentalities requires significant and sustained subjective work. This is important for thinking through not only what the current land and real estate mentalities might be that are shaping twenty-first-century geopolitical real estate relations. Arguably more importantly, it exposes the seemingly impenetrable task that would confront a political power that sought to amend, say, a political community's private property real estate mentality. The next chapter moves from organising technics towards mediating technologies, by focusing on: restorying the lands of Indigenous peoples to facilitate the sale of colonised land to foreign buyers; the creation of the joint stock company as a technology of the British Empire; and measurement and surveyor instruments as embodied technologies of land claiming.

NOTES

1. This allegorical tale is better known in the Europe, North America, and Australia by the English title of the dramatised television programme Monkey Magic.

2. You can read Lawson and Wentworth's diaries of the crossing at: Lawson, http://www.sl.nsw.gov.au/discover_collections/history_nation/exploration/blue_mountains/lawson/lawson.html; Wentworth, http://www.sl.nsw.gov.au/discover_collections/history_nation/exploration/blue_mountains/wentworth/index.html.

Chapter 4

Technics of Land II
Colonialism, Company, Measurement, Ownership

COLONIALISM: DISPLACE LOCALLY, SELL GLOBALLY

Any historical settler-society analysis of the geopolitics of real estate must consider how the organising technics of privately enclosed land that developed in Europe in the sixteenth to twentieth centuries were later globally mobilised through various colonial projects. From a geopolitical standpoint, the micro-colonial land claiming and redistributing events that took place in Europe, and particularly in Ireland in the seventeenth-century, provided a set of scalable schemas for the colonial conquests over the next three centuries (Linklater, 2014: 108; Weaver, 2003: 5). While each colonial project is unique, these new ways of claiming and distributing the earth eventually displaced millions of Indigenous peoples from their land. A central idea, constructed in different ways, which runs through Sir William Petty and John Locke's scholarship, is that ownership of property is created by the application of labour. Linklater (2014: 108) deploys John Locke's (1689) labour theory of property to argue, the "violence of expelling indigenous people and taking the territory that gave them identity as well as feeding them was an injustice that should invalidate the moral argument for private property." Karl Marx and Friedrich Engels (1848: as discussed in the previous chapters), and David Ricardo (1817) took up these ideas in their work on land, labour, rent, and use and exchange values. Ricardo stratified the three key components of industrial production into capital, machinery, and labour; and along with it land, or "The produce of the earth," as the foundation (Ricardo, 1817: 3). The division separated the "proprietor of the land" from the "owner of the stock or capital necessary for its cultivation" and the labour, or the "labourers by whose industry it is cultivated" (Ricardo, 1817: 3). Ricardo's analysis was wholly reflective of the geopolitical moment in Britain, which, on the eve of the Industrial Revolution, had a highly capitalised but sluggish land market (Linklater, 2014: 178). More recently, Libby Porter (2010: 53–57) and other Australian scholars have taken up Locke's arguments to critically review settler-society land mentalities. Their collective scholarship, from Petty to Porter, shows in different ways how the land revolution that created and then linked property interests and labour to capital creation between the sixteenth and twentieth centuries "brought into being a modern system which archaic societies organised on half-feudal, half-tribal lines were powerless to resist" (Linklater, 2014: 108). As the colonising Europeans travelled the world in search of new lands to conquer (Porter, 2010: 57), the Indigenous peoples they encountered were repeatedly evaluated "by European religion, laws, science, technology, political organisation, knack for warfare, and use of land" (Weaver, 2003: 5). Porter (2010: 57) writes, "Europe had long been fascinated by the lands it did not yet 'know'," that is, lands that "had not [been] drawn into production ownership in the way Locke came to identify."

Even the poetry of the "late nineteenth and early twentieth-century" colonial settlers is telling (Van Den Berg, 2002). Consider the Australian settler-poet Henry Lawson's poem *Settling on the Land*, which reads, "He selected on a run at Dry Hole Creek, and for months awaited the arrival of the government surveyors to fix his boundaries; but they didn't come, and, as he had no reason to believe they would turn up within the next ten years, he grubbed and fenced at a venture, and started farming operations" (Lawson, 1940: 1). Not only does this poem record the relational land claiming and boundary making practices of government surveyors and settlers, at the level of discursive practice, it also shows how important storytelling was to the settler-colonists. In his poem *The Old Australian Way* from the same era, Australian settler-poet Banjo Paterson (1902: 1) deploys the discourse of *terra nullius* to describe the land claiming of an outback adventurer named "Clancy," who "... drifted to the outer back, beyond the overflow ... he reached at last, oh lucky elf, the town of *come-and-help-yourself* ..." (Tilley, 2012: 260; Van Den Berg, 2002). Across the Pacific Ocean, the American poet Robert Frost waxes lyrical about how Americans claimed the land, and how the land simultaneously made and claimed the lives of Americans. In his settler land-claiming poem, *The Gift Outright*, Frost (1923: 1) rhymes, "but we were England's, still colonials ... to the land vaguely realising westward, but *still unstoried, artless, unenhanced* ..." (emphasis added by the author). These settler-poems are three of many striking examples of the storytelling of the early settler-colonialists, who ignored the land claims (e.g., *come-and-help-yourself*, or *he grubbed and fenced at a venture*) and storytelling (e.g., *still unstoried, artless*) of Indigenous peoples on the American and Australian continents, and beyond (Buchan and Heath, 2006; Crabtree, 2013; Tilley, 2012; Van Den Berg, 2002).

Assessed over a longer timeline, Indigenous peoples resisted settler-colonialist incursions into their physical space in the mid-nineteenth-century, but the storytelling about these events often turned into a politico-discursive project – a form of discursively mobilised power and resistance – in the twentieth-century. In Australia, the so-called history wars in general, and the Australian frontier wars in particular, are perhaps the most widely known examples whereby the settler-colonialist's incursions into Indigenous peoples' physical space were later reimagined, re-storied, and retold in a politico-discursive space. Many historians of settler-colonial Australia agree that a series of violent "encounters" took place between European settlers and Indigenous peoples between first contact in 1788 and the beginning of the nineteenth-century (Blainey, 1993; Linklater, 2014; MacIntyre and Clarke, 2004; Manne, 2003; Storey, 2016; Weaver, 2003; Windschuttle, 2002). Land politics was central to these events, and one of the first acts of violence in Sydney, in May 1788, was supposedly motivated by the clearing of land by the colonists soon after their arrival (Clune and Turner, 2009; Weaver, 2003). What contemporary historians (and politicians) cannot agree upon is whether these violent encounters were sporadic or organised. In short, whether they were isolated acts of frontier violence or a part of a broader conflict that can be thought of has having two distinct and organised sides, that is, Indigenous and settler. For example, some argue, the encounters between "isolated squatters" and Indigenous peoples, "though alarming ... did not amount to war" (Weaver, 2003: 147). Others contend that these conflicts did represent a war, at least in some sense. John Connor (2002: 35) argues that Captain David Collins (1798), who had been in the Sydney colony since 1788, certainly thought of "the outbreak of violence between British and Aborigines as 'war'" in 1795. In America, New Zealand, and Australia, as colonial ideas about individually titled and owned land overwhelmed the existing inhabitants, a series of raids and counter raids, attacks and retaliations, and full blown battles in some places, began to mottled the historical storytelling about these places (Blainey, 1993; Connor, 2002; Linklater, 2014; MacIntyre and Clarke, 2004; Manne, 2003; Weaver, 2003; Windschuttle, 2002).

Storytelling and discursively constructing land resistance narratives were important during the colonial land-claiming era. For example, Kenton Storey (2016: 3) cites the *Pacific Commercial Advertiser* from May 1861 making reference to an attack in Auckland, New Zealand:

> The Natives came down from the mountains in great numbers and surprised one of the settlements near Auckland, murdering in the most inhuman manner about 850 inhabitants. The most horrid barbarities were practiced by them in the attack, defenceless farmers butchered, women with children were cut open, and small innocent children had their hands and feet cut off, and in that miserable position left to perish. (Storey, 2016: citing the Pacific Commerical Advertiser)

Storey (2016: 4) argues that "the massacre described never actually occurred," and that the narrative may have been discursively mediated and reinterpreted from the "widely reported accounts of the 1857 Indian Rebellion." As described in the last chapter, each organising technic of land is an assemblage of embodied discursive acts and performative enactments. The discursive acts, the stories that are told about defenceless settler-colonialists, and the horrid, murdering Indigenous peoples are heavily dependent on the prevailing organising technics of land that these stories were created within. Furthermore, the performative enactments of land were heavily dependent on the land mentalities that were encoded into the bodies of the settlers and Indigenous peoples. The bodies were the technologies through which colonial land claiming was challenged, but perhaps not in the way that was recorded in the public discourse of the time (Storey, 2016; Weaver, 2003). The land was both "at stake" and "the terrain" on which the raids, attacks, retaliations, and battles was fought, but it was the organising technic and land mentalities of the settler-colonialists and Indigenous peoples that were at play in these encounters. Nowhere is this more apparent than in the clash between the organising technics of colonial land claiming that was mobilised through the mediating technology of the surveyors' instruments, against the organising technics of Indigenous land that were used to defend people and place, which included the mediating technology of the human body that intimately understands the land or *country*. Weaver (2003: 229) writes, "Some [Indigenous] peoples disrupted surveyors on frontiers, because they correctly distrusted crews as harbingers of a new order or because crews encroached without permissions or backing of a treaty or found themselves in the midst of inter-tribal disputes about land cessions." For example, in Australia, writes Weaver, "the surveyor-general issued a circular letter, advising all [surveying] crews to advance in a flank formation with flintlocks at-the-ready"; in other words, the colonisers were to walk into Indigenous lands with their guns loaded and ready to shoot (Weaver, 2003: 230). This directive followed the killing of two members of a government-contracted surveying party in 1840 by the Aboriginal people living in the Port Phillip District of New South Wales (Weaver, 2003: 230).

In the settler-colony of New Zealand, the settler-colonialists had attempted to use their politico-legal power to parley power from various Māori chiefs via the Treaty of Waitangi (Storey, 2016: 293). The colonisers quickly realised that rational-legal mediating technologies would not be enough to recode the landscape and the land mentalities of the Māori. Much like the Indigenous peoples of Australia, Māoris begrudged seeing the settlers' surveyors dividing up the land before their land negotiations with the settler-colonialists were even finished (Weaver, 2003: 230). For example, "The burning of surveyors' huts near Nelson in 1843 provoked a rash white response that escalated into an affray at Wairau that left four Māori and twenty-two Europeans dead"

(Weaver, 2003: 230). The response from the government was to warn "the New Zealand Company against showing survey instruments before the completion of land sales" (Weaver, 2003: 230). On many settler-colonial frontiers, teams of land surveyors encountered resistance from Indigenous peoples, all the while regularly enclosing and claiming more land than they were authorised by their land grants (Weaver, 2003: 231).

Moreover, physical violence was only one modality for exercising power and resistance on the land-claiming frontier. In 1763, in what is now the Great Lakes region of the United States, one of the first loosely allied resistance campaigns by several Native American Tribes was led, some suggest (Linklater, 2014: 185), by the Ojibwe chief Obwandiyag (Pontiac). Following Britain's victory in the Seven Years War (and the French and Indian War between 1754 and 1763 in the United States), and the signing of the Treaty of Paris in 1763, the physical resistance exerted by the tribes loosely united under Pontiac played a role in encouraging the British government to take geopolitical action in relation to land disputes. King Georges III issued a proclamation, The Royal Proclamation of 1763, which created a legal boundary, the proclamation line, between the British colonies on the Atlantic coast and American Indian lands to the west of the Appalachian Mountains. The Royal Proclamation of 1763 exposed the complex ways in which the embodied settler-colonial frontier people were coming into contact with the embodied resistance of Indigenous peoples. These events, however, were not only mediated by embodied physical or violent confrontations, they were also mediated through rational-legal documents that were created by fading monarch power structures in faraway lands. The proclamation defined the jurisdictional limits of colonial territorial expansion in what is now Canada, and prohibited the colonial governors from granting land to speculators beyond this boundary. The proclamation reads,

> Essential to Our Interest and the Security of Our Colonies, that the several Nations or Tribes of Indians with whom We are connected, and who live under Our Protection should not be molested or disturbed ... no Governor ... in any of Our other Colonies or Plantations in America, do presume for the present ... to grant Warrants of Survey, or pass Patents for any Lands. (King George III, 1763: 1)

The proclamation is an important document for Canada's Indigenous peoples even today, especially with regard to land claims, although its symbolic validity and legal weight have been continually tested since 1763. This case shows that the mediating technologies that are used by Indigenous and settlers alike, to measure, enclose, and separate, take many forms. They can be legal technologies written on paper, which assemble parcels of land, within

70   Chapter 4

legal documents alongside the rational-legal mentalities that are needed to decipher and police the legal texts. They also include the embodied technologies that assemble human bodies with surveying tools and surveying mentalities, of which George Washington is a great example.

Most people remember George Washington as the first president of the United States, or earlier, as a leader of the Continental Army in the American Revolution. Within the context of the settler-colonial land claiming that would soon underwrite the rise of the property-owning democracy in America (Ferguson, 2008), Washington was more importantly a colonial geographer – he was a surveyor and a cartographer. Like the geographically mobile William Petty in the seventeenth-century (England and Ireland) and William Lawson in the eighteenth and nineteenth-century (England and Australia), Washington's body was a technology that was used to decode and recode the American landscape with rational-legal ideas of landed property (Lengel, 2011). Washington had a lifelong interest in land claiming and speculation, and the proclamation line was an inconvenience for his plans to secure land that was promised to the veterans of the Virginia Regiment, who fought under Washington in the French and Indian War (Anderson, 2006). Washington forged ahead despite the proclamation line, and in an often-cited letter to Pennsylvania surveyor William Crawford on the subject of land claiming in 1767 he writes,

> I can never look upon the Proclamation in any other light … than as a temporary expedient to quiet the minds of the Indians. It must fall, of course, in a few years, especially when those Indians consent to our occupying those lands. Any person who neglects hunting out good lands, and in some measure marking and distinguishing them for his own, in order to keep others from settling them will never regain it. If you will be at the trouble of seeking out the lands, I will take upon me the part of securing them, as soon as there is a possibility of doing it and will, moreover, be at all the cost and charges surveying and patenting the same. (Washington et al., 1877)

This vignette demonstrates that the surveying colonial body is a recurring technology of power in the history of Indigenous dispossession of their land. This surveying mentality, that directs the body to search, to measure, to claim, and to enclose, is still evident today, as we will see in the coming chapters. However, it is a mistake to think that we should reterritorialise Indigenous peoples, in a Deleuze–Guattarian sense (1987), into the current settler-colonial assemblage of people, land, and property relations. That would be to reterritorialise Indigenous peoples into an existing discriminatory assemblage – to confirm their place within this discriminatory settler-colonial assemblage. Rather, we should attempt to deterritorialise Indigenous peoples from the discriminatory settler-colonial assemblage of people, land, and property relations. To do so requires an understanding of the organising technics and mediating technologies that have been moved, removed, or altered across past and present people, land, and property assemblages. Some of the settler-colonial technics and technologies for measuring, dividing, enclosing, and claiming land remain deeply embedded into people, land, and property relations in settler-colonial countries, and in the minds of the settlers. Colonial land claiming framed the rise of property rights in the emerging American republican democracy and the self-governing British settlement colonies, but the participants acted according to local conditions and geopolitical regulations. These geopolitical conditions included, as we will see in the next section, open up these lands to foreign capital and labour.

COMPANY: SELLING LAND, LABOUR, AND EMIGRATION

In 1905, John Davis (1905: 88) wrote, "[t]he point in history at which a study of English corporations (except those of the Church) must be begun is that of the dominance of feudalism. In the structure of an ideal feudal system there could have been no place for corporate forms: they would have been out of harmony with it." In seventeenth-century colonial America, the geopolitical project of colonial expansion and land claiming was mobilised through the colonial joint-stock company. *The Charter*[1] *of the Virginia Company of London*, otherwise known as the *London Company*, was an English joint-stock company established in 1606 by Royal Charter by King James I. It was a modern technology that brought capital raising and lending, land claiming, and international migration together, but it was not the first attempt to form a colonial joint-stock company. *The Mystery, Company, and Fellowship of Merchant Adventurers for the Discovery of Regions, Dominions, Islands, and Places Unknown, also known as the Company of Merchant Adventurers to New Lands*, was established in London in the mid-sixteenth-century. The company's first expedition was aiming for China. They made it no further than Russia. Despite the discursive claims in the company's title about adventure and the discovery of unknown lands, the company developed into an international importing and exporting business, with a particular focus on textiles rather than foreign land sales or immigration.

Sir Thomas Smythe, former governor of the East India Company, arranged the first chapter for the *London Company*. The expressed purpose of the company was to establish colonial settlements in North America. Much like the *Plymouth Company*, also established in 1906, the colonialist merchants used these companies to draw foreign skills and labour into the new settler-colonies through an international migration programme. The companies financed the settlers' travel to the new colonies, for example, through the *Plymouth Company and the London Company*.[2] In North America, the rising mercantilism of European colonial powers was written across the landscape as the land companies were permitted to establish colonies within a set of borders that were authorised by Royal Charter. *The Plymouth Company* was granted the rights to settle an area between the 38th parallel and the 45th parallel, an area approximately between the upper reaches of the Chesapeake Bay in the United States and the current United States–Canada border. *The London Company* was granted the rights to settle an area between the 34th parallel and the 41st parallel, an area approximately between Cape Fear and Long Island Sound. The word "parallel" refers to a circle of latitude around the earth, and signifies the globalising scale and imaginary of the colonial intervention. For example, the 38th parallel is 38 degrees north of the Earth's equatorial plane. The companies financed the settlers' global mobility to the settler-colonial outposts, by offering to finance their travel. The conditions of the agreement required the settlers to repay their travel costs, plus interest, with the profits they would make in the new settler-colony. By contrast, the globalising mercantilism of the Dutch meant that they were far less interested in ascribing value to their colonised lands. Securing trade routes, articles, and vessels was far more important, and indeed considered a more valuable investment in "property" than land (Weaver, 2003: 189). Like the French, they did not value land as a commodity that should be individually traded without substantial government oversight.

Philip Stern (2011) argues that we should not consider these global settler-colonial entities as joint-stock companies in the modern sense of the term, as a corporate-economic entity. He argues, rather, that the capacities of the East India Company better reflect "what early modern governments did: erect and administer law; collect taxes; provide protection; inflict punishment; perform stateliness; regulate economic, religious, and civic life; conduct diplomacy and wage war; make claims to jurisdiction over land and sea; cultivate authority over and obedience from those people subject to its command" (Stern, 2011: 5–6). Stern calls these joint-stock companies *Company-States* to highlight their governance and regulatory functions, and to prove his point, he shows how they rebelled against the governance and regulatory arrangements of the Crown (Stern, 2011: 8). The human body was central to the functionality of the colonial company-state, and was "conditioned by an institutional culture defined and constantly reinforced by ritual, procedure, and ceremony. Even seemingly pragmatic exercises, like letter writing, were imbued with political significance" (Stern, 2011: 11). The act of writing on paper, the keeping of ledgers and records, was a key mediating technology of settler-colonialism; and "Superiors scrutinise subordinates' writing … orderly letters signalled obedient behaviour. Writing was also the backbone of a global network, crucial to imagining such a geographically dispersed political system as coherent and to supervising and governing it" (Stern, 2011: 11).

Writing was a way to tame geography, but it also inculcated the organising technics of the company-state into the bodies of those in the service of the company. But more importantly, it was the geopolitical conditions that the company leadership found themselves within, the "opportunities, challenges, and problems that Company leaders confronted," that shaped the mentalities of the leadership (Stern, 2011: 14).

The early colonial company-states, especially the company-states that were operating on settler-colonial frontiers, set trade and migration and therefore the movement of goods and people to consume them as their objective (Davis, 1905; Stern, 2011). When it came to petitioning and negotiating Royal Charters and colonial grants, land tenure became a geopolitical issue; a mixture of local land politics and colonial charters that were managed through royal regulatory systems in Europe (Stern, 2011). Weaver (2003: 180–181) shows that the corporations and their supporters "weighed the advantages and disadvantages of two available forms of tenure" when advocating for charters, the *in capite* and *ut de manore* feudal tenurial systems (see the discussion of feudal tenurial systems in Chapter 3). Because trade and migration were the key objectives of these company-states, "extracting rents from tenants initially seemed unimportant, and so tenure *ut de manore* was favoured. Under charters with this tenure, land could be granted to colonists whose value to the company[-state] was not rent, but rather ability to produce supplies for trading posts and vessels" (Weaver, 2003: 181). Later, in New France (an area colonised by France in North America), which was managed by the *Company of the West Indies* between 1664 and 1674 and the Crown between 1674 and the Treaty of Paris, land was granted under *seigneurial tenure*. The *seigneurial* semi-feudal land tenurial system in New France allowed a *seigneur*, someone who had been granted a *fief* (heritable property or rights) by the Crown to rent most of the land to the *censitaire* (i.e., tenants). The *censitaires* cleared the land and farmed it. They also built houses and farm buildings, often around a central mill and they expected the estate to be well managed and the lands to be evenly distributed (Weaver, 2003: 186–187). "Many *seigneurs* from the 1670s to the 1740s transferred portions of their estates to discharge obligations, from family alliances, arrange inheritances, or endow religious orders … within French law and elite values there was scope for the use of estates in private economic plans. Yet transactions – for example, the creation of *les arrierefief* – should not be seen as evidence of a land market where participates sought capital appreciation" (Weaver, 2003: 187).

In Australia, land was allocated and granted according to the directive of the government, or even by "favour" (Weaver, 2003: 178). After defining the geographical spaces in Australia as *terra nullius*, the colonial power "instilled" Governor Phillip, with the power to grant land to "emancipists" in April 1787, at an allocation of 30 acres for each male, with additional entitlements if married (Butlin, 1994). In 1789, these entitlements were expanded to include military personnel (Butlin, 1994). By 1825, the sale of land by private tender had begun, and in 1831 Viscount Goderich II discontinued land grants in Australia to facilitate land sales by public and private interests (Butlin, 1994: 23). Mohr (2003: 2) shows that: "The project of developing a common law of the land (known in Roman law as a *'lex terrae'*), which might apply throughout the nation rather than to individuals as group members, was introduced as the law of the Norman Kings in England. It was to become one of the hallmarks of the modern state" and a key constituent, along with *terra nullius*, in discursively constructing land in Australia as a colonial asset. Embodied aristocratic desires and social legacies travelled over to the colonies with the ruling class. In the colonies, social class and rank, or even loyalty at times of political turmoil, provided a value system through which land could be allocated. Unlike the United States republic, these aristocratic legacies and value systems kept free market land allocation at bay, at least for a time, in the British settler-state. The movement of the aristocracy and the ruling class between Europe and the colonies opened up a politico-discursive space that would increasingly lubricate the flow and movement of land and real estate mentalities.

Edward Gibbon Wakefield (1796–1862) is the embodiment of European aristocracy values with settler-colonial ideas about land claiming and international migration (Mills, 1915: ch. 5; Temple, 2002). Wakefield was known as an educated (Westminster School and Edinburgh High School) but devious man. He is well known for using marriage (to Ward in Chancery, Eliza Ann Frances Pattle in 1816) and abduction (15-year-old heiress, Ellen Turner in 1826), for which he was later convicted and imprisoned (in 1827), to secure an income (for a detailed biographay and family tree, see Temple, 2002: 6). While imprisoned in London's Newgate Prison, he turned his attention to a systemic analysis of colonisation, which pivoted on immigration, labour supply, and the capitalisation of claimed land. His anonymous *Sketch of a Proposal for Colonizing Australasia* was printed in June 1829, and was later reprinted in London's Morning Chronicle (Wakefield, 1829b). His *A Letter from Sydney, the Principal Town of Australasia* was published in December with the name of Robert Gouger as editor (Wakefield, 1829a). Wakefield's ideas "caused some stir in Sydney," argues Graeme Petty (1967: 1). Wakefield had three primary technologies for mediating his ideas – the publication of written texts (letters, newspapers, pamphlets and books); the establishment of aristocratic societies; and using his body as a mobile-mediating technology throughout the British colonies (South Australia, Canada, and New Zealand). He certainly refined his ideas about "systematic colonisation" over the next 20 years, but the central thrust of his argument remained consistent. He argued that land in the settler-colonies should be sold, not "granted" or given away, at a price high enough to incentivise the new owner to: (1) pay the emigration costs associated with transporting poor immigrants to supply the labour for their properties and therefore, (2) to use their landed properties to produce a profit. As Linklater (2014: 236) notes, it "was not an egalitarian society Wakefield proposed," but a global capitalist economy comprised of capitalists and workers, and in this case, employers and employees who were globally mobile. Wakefield supposed that, initially, only the middle classes would be able to afford to purchase the settler-colonial land. But with abundant land and a shortage of labour in the colonies, the wages paid to immigrant labourers would be high. In a few years, the high wages would allow the immigrant labourers to purchase their own land, and they would then recruit and employ a new wave of immigrant labourers. Marx (1894: 839) later remarked in passing, in *Capital: A critique of political economy,* that Wakefield "discovered in the Colonies the truth as to the condition of capitalist production in the mother-country" (also see Linklater, 2014: 236; Temple, 2002: 132).

Much like the American colonial frontier, private joint-stock companies in Britain were looking towards Australian land as a source of profit. *The Australian Agricultural Company* was founded in 1824 and then floated in London. The company "raised $2.5 million to invest in buying land in New South Wales, and the *Van Diemen's Land Company* put more than one million dollars into property and harbour-building in Tasmania" (Linklater, 2014: 236). Wakefieldian ideas about globalising the scale at which the mobile settler-colonial body could be reconceptualised opened up new ways of thinking about global markets for land and sources of labour. It reveals something important about settler-colonial ideas about labour and land, and how these could be redistributed around the world. It is as relevant today as it was for Marx in 1894. Indeed, *The Australian Agricultural Company* remains a publicly listed company on the Australian Stock Exchange, one that was built on convict labour and colonial land grants. *The New Zealand Company* was formally established in 1837 and was explicitly founded to colonise New Zealand using Wakefieldian ideas about "systematic colonisation"; the company's name had been in use from an earlier attempt to colonise New Zealand in 1825. Along with the Earl of Durham, a landowning advocate named John Lambton who had the nickname "Radical Jack," Wakefield persuaded the Whig prime minister of the United Kingdom, William Lamb II (also known as "Lord Melbourne") to let their *New Zealand Company* acquire one million acres in New Zealand. The company was offered a Royal Charter to take legislative, judicial, military, and financial control of the New Zealand colony, but only if the company became a joint-stock company. After initially rejecting this condition, they eventually accepted and split the company into the *New Zealand Colonisation Company* and the *New Zealand Land Company* in August 1838, and further merged both of these entities with the *New Zealand Company* in May 1839. They formed the *New Zealand Land Company*, and then renamed the company the *New Zealand Company*. The company's stated aim, from this point, was to send emigrants to New Zealand under Wakefieldian ideas about labour, land, and immigration. The objective was to move human and financial capital around the world as part of their plan for the systematic colonisation of New Zealand's land and people.

Of course, the land claiming and migration strategy often met with resistance, and at times this even came from within the colonial governance structure itself. For example, as stories about the plight of Australia's Indigenous peoples travelled back to the United Kingdom, and opposition mounted in New Zealand, Lord Melbourne, who was "never enthusiastic about the new form of colonisation" (Linklater, 2014: 236), withdrew government support for the *New Zealand Company*. Richard Mills recounts an exchange between Lord Melbourne, the colonial administrator Henry George Ward, and English Lawyer James Stephen, citing opposition to what was happening in New Zealand as twofold: "First, it proposes the acquisition of a sovereignty in New Zealand which would infallibly issue in the conquest and the extermination of the present inhabitants. Secondly, these suggestions are so vague and so obscure as to defy all interpretation. The writers are plainly the victims of Mr. Ward's monomania ..." (Mills, 1915: fn. 18, citing Memorandum, 16 June 1837). Wakefield had become the embodiment of his own notion of systematic colonisation, and he went off to become the lands commissioner in Canada. Marx (1894: 839) understood, with exquisite conceptual clarity, the importance of this moment. It was a powerful geopolitical assemblage of labour, technology, land, and capital; "Wakefield discovered that in the Colonies, property in money, means of subsistence, machines, and other means of production, does not as yet stamp a man as a capitalist if there be wanting the correlative — the wage-worker, the other man who is compelled to sell himself of his own free will. *He discovered that capital is not a thing, but a social relation between persons*, established by the instrumentality of things" (Marx 1894: 839; emphasis added by the author).

This vignette begins to show how different subjects, objects, and mentalities are assembled together at particular moments. For example, the mentality and actions of someone within a joint-company was shaped by their relationship to the ritual, procedure, and ceremony of the joint-stock company, which itself was underwritten by the organising logics of systematic colonialism (i.e., to claim land and to move labour). The organising technics and mediating technologies of the company-state were always working on the body; working on the land and real estate mentalities of those within the joint-stock company. A key mediating technology explored in this vignette was the act of writing on paper, whether it was keeping ledgers or records, or receiving Royal Charters or land grants, or creating legal documents for courts of law. This form of colonial storytelling was not only useful for keeping the expansive political machinery of the joint-stock company functioning, but perhaps more importantly, it was useful for conceptualising the company and their activities itself. The ritualised practices that were performed by settler bodies led to the taming of geography and inculcated the colonialist mentality into the minds of the settlers. In the two vignettes outlined above, boundary making has been used as a form of power and resistance, and I turn to this question in the next section.

MEASUREMENT: LAND AS COMMODITY

In every location where individually owned land has been constructed as a form of private property there has been a change in the way land is measured, both objectively and subjectively (Linklater, 2014: 37). It should be clear by now that the measuring and surveying colonial body was a key technology in the colonial appropriation of land (Bennett, 1988: 194). From the formal surveying practices of William Petty and Charles Wentworth to the informal squatting practices of Jack Redgrave in Rolf Boldrewood's (1890) novel *The Squatter's Dream: A Story of Australian Life* (Hoorn, 2007: 148), boundary making often marks the beginning of the physical act of claiming land. In seventeenth-century Ireland, William Petty developed a Fordist-style assembly-line method to survey Irish land. Petty divided up each aspect of the surveying process into a set of simple and repeatable tasks (Linklater, 2014: 59). He then set up a team of managers to oversee the surveying process within the institutional demarcations of *The Office of Surveyor General of Ireland*. Later on colonial settler frontier after frontier, local or remote governments and authorities set up surveyor-general or public lands offices to install surveyors in their new colonial settlements. These institutional and embodied technologies of land measurement were set up to manage the growing demand and market for land. As Jeremy Adelman and Stephen Aron (1999) show, the importance of measurement, borders and emplacement were central to the shift from borderlands and frontiers (which resembled cultural and physical *lines* in the sand) to the enclosing of bordered states (which better resembled cultural and physical *containers*). The frontiers were fluid places where Indigenous peoples and settlers came into cultural and physical contact. Weaver (2003) asks us to consider the multitude of borderlands and frontiers from the sixteenth to the nineteenth-century as "areas where coloniser's regime of property rights had not been firmly installed, but where [settlers] were already marking out places in anticipation of that condition … (p. 18) In mapping and defining the landscape, colonising governments improved the flow of capital" (p. 216).

Linklater (2014: 33) argues that one of the most distinctive indicators that demonstrated an individualised market for land had developed in the settler-colonies was the appearance of the surveyor, who was always accompanied by their surveying tools of the trade and their surveying mentality. To enable Wakefield's globalising land market to develop, the sales agents in the colonial settlements – which included international trading companies, governments, and entrepreneurial individuals – needed to link buyers and sellers across expansive geographical, cultural, and financial frontiers. The colonial settlers brought with them a set of mediating technologies that would shape how land and then real estate would be conceptualised hereinto the colonies. Because of the globalising nature of these land markets, many of the buyers and sellers of colonial land had limited knowledge of local land markets, and the new suite of land measurement technologies provided a set of rationalist, that is "objective", tools through which specific mathematical and financial demarcations of lands could be compared across large geographical distances. They allowed the buyers and sellers to compare the location, size, and comparative value of land in terms that matched the prevailing intellectual fascination with rationalism and legal process. In addition to the body as a mediating technology, the colonial projects included the reappropriation of old instruments and technologies or the development of new instruments and technologies to speed up the land-claiming process.

The new and old technologies included: surveying instruments (e.g., compass or a *circumferenter*, transit or *theodolite*, the plane table, and the Gunter's chain); the creation of the professional land surveyor (e.g., professional identification and accreditation); and therefore paper-based technologies more broadly (from the professional surveying training publications and field notebooks to legal documents that recorded, in material and mobile form, the new rational-legal demarcations of land and property) (Bennett, 1988: 146; Linklater, 2014: 244; Weaver, 2003: 255). On many of the colonial frontiers, these technologies provided financial certainty and were initially used to divide up and sell crown land through the local governing authority's surveying or land office, albeit often to private parties. However, in the long term, these technologies would be largely privatised to manage the transfer and sale of landed property between private parties. Ideas about surveying and regulating the sale of land – surveying mentalities – were mobile throughout the colonies. Various administrators and legislators kept in contact with each other via letter writing, with the explicit aim of keeping up to date with or copying each other's "market-friendly alterations" to land law and measurement (Weaver, 2003: 216–217). For example, Weaver (2003: 216–217) writes, when the government of Manitoba in Canada "contemplated establishing a new system for land titles in 1884, it consulted

Australian colonies, which had tried a major revision ..." and as such, in the nineteenth-century the land systems "resembled one another."

What the surveyor was measuring and how value was ascribed to it were important (Bennett, 1988). Conceptions of both *measurement* and *value* had intellectual schemas that linked back to the politics of land in Europe. Much like the land politics in Britain, in eighteenth-century France the enclosure of common land removed the peasantries' traditional rights of access, while simultaneously creating a market for feudal estates within the wealthy aristocratic and merchant classes (Linklater, 2014: 200–201). While there had been tensions over how the land should be used by the peasantry and aristocracy in earlier periods, the eighteenth-century solidified a dramatic shift in the way the land was measured. No longer would the traditional unit, that is, "agricultural productive capacity," be used to measure and value a loosely defined geographical parcel of land. Rather, the new land market required a process through which an accurate measurement of a specific geographically defined parcel of land could be ascribed a financial value (Bennett, 1988). Land surveyors were central to shifting the value schema from the "agricultural productive capacity" of land to a "physical geographical demarcation" of land (Linklater, 2014: 200–201). In France from the 1750s, like the surveying geopolitics of other European countries, these land politics became embodied practices (Mackrell, 2007), and it is from France that we get the noun *géomètre*, a fantastically revealing name for the land surveyor. It is revealing because the term points firmly to the geographical containment, while it is silent about the productive capacity of land. The *arpenteur-géomètre* created invariable, objective measurements of land that were recorded on plans and official surveying documents, often using the Ancient Roman spatial unit of land measurement, the *perch*. Similarly, the enclosures and the break-up of church property through The Reformation in early-modern England helped create not only the embodied practices of the surveyor, but also the demand for their services, that is, surveying. Along with the professionalisation of the surveyor came the loose formulation of quasi-professional practices, standards, and terms, and then a bourgeoning trade in surveyor handbooks and manuals (Bennett, 1988; Weaver, 2003).

However, on almost every colonial frontier the surveyor-general was unable to stay ahead of the landhunters and spectators, with the exception perhaps of the well-funded surveyors on the Canadian prairies who managed to stay ahead of the landhunters (Weaver, 2003: 255). Surveyors and surveyor-generals squabbled about which methods and units of geographical measurement were more accurate, or faster to implement. Some measured out land parcels using abstract modalities of mathematical calculation, such as triangulation. Others literally took to the land with a Gunter's measuring chain and measured it out by hand and on foot. Professional qualifications for land surveyors were introduced by the government of Ontario Province, in former British Canada in the 1840s. This is where the now infamous American square township grid system of surveying land before sale was introduced in an attempt to keep up with the growing land market (Linklater, 2014: 244). Writing these standards, terms and practices down on paper allowed for mobility and uniformity, and Weaver (2003: 226) lists surveyor handbooks with titles such as *The Exact Surveyor*, *The Faithful Surveyor*, and *The Country Survey Book*. Adam Martindale published the latter handbook in 1682. This handbook captures a shift from the more abstract mathematical calculation of land parcels through triangulation to the physical measurement of land using the lengths of *metes and bounds*, which were suggested to be more accurate. The grid system allowed for greater scrutiny of surveyors because the physical measurements could be checked against written, often legal documents.

Interestingly, many of the surveyors in the American frontiers were employed as private contractors rather than public servants, and there was "fierce competition for surveying jobs" (Rohrbough, 1968: 96). Rohrbough (1968: 96) and Weaver (2003: 232) argue that across the vast American frontier lands no-one could navigate the geographical and legal geopolitics of land claiming better than the surveyors. It is therefore, "not surprising that most surveyors connected themselves in one way or another with the buying and selling of lands" (Rohrbough, 1968: 96). While surveyors and governing authorities debated which measuring modalities were more effective, what these surveyors and governing authorities were measuring and the purpose of that project of measurement was solidifying – the accurate measurement of land allowed the colonial governments to sell the land with increasing legal certainty. The aim was to increase the land sale revenues for the colonial settlements. As noted earlier, in-migration would provide the labour force for the colonies and this labour could be turned into capital for land purchases; land sales would fund the colonial project, and rationalist measurement was key to this process. In the short term, a speedy survey that resulted in pegs in the ground or other markings in the landscape took precedence over "plans in the registry office" (Weaver, 2003: 234). But assessed over a longer timeline, Linklater (2014: 34) outlines the relationship between paper, law, and property more succinctly; "the hidden weapon of private property [was] paper. Everything was written down. The deeds described how the property had been created and come into the owner's hands, and any incursion upon it brought the whole panoply of the law against the perpetrator. Paper recruited the power of government to the side of the property owner." Or as Weaver (2003: 92) puts it, "Land was measured and marked, but landed property rights were then abstracted into statements on documents, reduced to ciphers, and these texts or codes travelled, enabling interests in land to be traded or pledged for security against loans."

This vignette provides another example of how different subjects, objects, and mentalities are assembled together in pursuit of land-claiming endeavours. In this case, the land measurement mentality and actions of the surveyor were shaped by their relationship to the ritual, procedure, and ceremony of the emerging professional field of surveying. This, itself, was underwritten by the organising technics such as those that William Petty was working with as he charted Ireland in 1654. Later, settler-colonial governments and foreign landhunters alike would copy the rational-legal surveying technics of the Europeans. Although, as Weaver (2003: 134) notes, the written artefacts they produced "occasionally exposed their deeds to questioning by scrupulous people and subsequent generations," this remains true today. Thus reflecting on the thinking of the so-called founders of the American republic, Linklater (2014: 50) suggests that John Adam drew upon James Harrington's philosophy to create the pithy phrase, "Power follows property." I am tempted to go further with a Foucauldian twist to argue that *power follows the property that is written on paper in Western rational-legal terms.*

OWNERSHIP: IMPROVEMENT AS IDEOLOGY

The three historical vignettes presented in this chapter outline several mediating technologies and the resultant land and real estate mentalities that are now normatively accepted as rationalist ideas for the modern world. Many of us have long forgotten the radical changes to conceptions of land that surveying practices help to introduce. The most significant was a move from thinking about land as having fluid borders that could shrink in or stretch out in line with the "agricultural productive capacity" of the land, to a measurement of a clearly defined and mathematically stable parcel of land. The surveying mentality directs the body to search, to measure, to claim, and to enclose, and this mentality was in conflict with many Indigenous notions of land. Surveying was, therefore, a recurring technology of power in the history of dispossessing Indigenous peoples of their land, and it opened up the settler-colonial lands to foreign capital and labour. The surveying mentality was also compatible with the rationalist rituals, procedures, and ceremonies that were taking place in the joint-stock company. Within the joint-stock company, paper emerges as a key mediating technology through which power can be mobilised – by keeping ledgers or recording legal Royal Charters or land grants. Paper was used as a geopolitical strategy, to keep track of and to monitor how the joint-stock company was functioning on the global stage, and for conceptualising the company's role and function on that stage. In all of the practices the idea of improvement was the central mentality for the colonial-settlers. At each point of the colonial process the colonisers assumed that they were working towards betterment (Weaver, 2003: 5). With their rational-legal mentalities about measuring and claiming land, they justified, to themselves, many schemas and processes that would take the land from Indigenous peoples and sell it on, or give it away, to foreign European bodies (Crabtree, 2013). In the next chapter, I focus more centrally on the role of mediating technologies, covering: the creation of the nation state, and its role in creating property-owning democracies; the role of finance and banks in producing both housing security and insecurity; and moving human and financial capital around the world to build the economies of settler-societies.

NOTES

1. A royal charter is a formal document issued by a monarch as *letters patent*. A charter grants a right or power to an individual or a body corporate.

2. Also, see the *Newfoundland Company* (1906) and the *Bermuda Company* (1915).

Chapter 5

Technologies of Real Estate I
States, Banks, Population, Citizenship

STATES: *CUJUS REGIO, EIUS RELIGIO*

As much as his authorship of the Declaration of Independence and the purchase of the Louisiana Territory, Jefferson's plan for the physical and political structure of the future United States earns him his place as the single most important influence in the nation's beginnings. That the Founding Father most hostile to the concept of private landed property should have been the architect of its greatest triumph must be reckoned as one of the stranger quirks of history. (Linklater, 2014: 209–210)

To build a property-owning democracy – a society where between 65 and 85 per cent of households own the home they live in – requires two interrelated tasks (Ferguson, 2008: 234). The first is largely an instrumental task associated with claiming, measuring, quantifying, and distributing the land ready for the introduction of real estate. The second is a more subjective task associated with creating a real estate mentality that will function within the property-owning democracy, especially as the vision for this type of market-oriented society changes over time. I want to start moving the discussion onto the latter process, onto the creation and maintenance of real estate mentalities, although it is important to note that these two processes are intricately intertwined. It can be hard, perhaps even foolish, to separate them, but it will be useful for the discussion on digital real estate mentalities that follows in Chapter 7.

A defining moment for this discussion was the establishment of the Peace of Westphalia (1648), a precedent that developed into the idea that the world, or at least Europe, could be divided up into a set of co-existing sovereign territorial states (Croxton, 1999; Osiander, 2001). We are now familiar with what was once a new form of geopolitical reasoning in central Europe – an idea that was only later referred to using terms such as "Westphalian sovereignty" and the "nation state" (Dittmer and Sharp, 2014). Westphalia was originally created and understood as a geopolitical system, whereby inter-territorial state aggression could supposedly be held in check by a set of legal-moral norms that protected one sovereign state's "domestic" affairs from being interfered with by another or other sovereign states (Osiander, 2001). The rise of Europe brought with it the promotion of Westphalian ideals and especially the concept of sovereign territorial states, which became central to international law and the global division of state territory (Croxton, 1999). The ability to better record, regulate, and tax the revenues that were generated within the physical boundaries of a ruler's realm gave that ruler an advantage over those who could not command this economic authority (Osiander, 2001). These revenues could be put to work in the ruler's interests in very diverse ways. Maintaining security through the funding of military equipment was a common activity. So too was the funding of scientific endeavours that would later facilitate different European colonial projects, such as Britain's £20,000 prize for discovering a method of working out longitude (Sobel, 1995). Indeed, working out different cartographic problems has long been a concern of the rulers of realms and nation states, because it allows them to map, explore, and conquer other peoples and places. Linklater (2014: 128) reminds us, in 1747, that King Louis XV of France ordered the cartographer César-François Cassini de Thury, from the Cassini family of cartographers, to draw a map of France. Through the mediating technology of cartography, César-François Cassini de Thury used a then revolutionary technique called geodesic triangulation (Hewitt, 2010).

In relation to real estate as a sovereign government-driven political project that intensified from the eighteenth-century, Westphalian ideas about sovereign territorial states played a central role in enabling different sovereign states to own and distribute landed property. The idea of the nation state created the political and territorial demarcations within which sovereign governments could acquire, buy, and sell landed property, and thereby cultivate different real estate mentalities. Linklater (2014: 128) argues that the differences between the three ways of owning the land in the eighteenth-century – which I discussed in Chapters 3 and 4 as serfdom, peasantry, and private property – "were exaggerated by a unique concept enshrined in the Peace of Westphalia that ended the religious bloodletting." It "can be summed up in the phrase *Cujus regio, eius religio*, literally 'whose kingdom, his religion,' meaning that within a state's boundaries a ruler's authority ranked above any external power" (p. 128). While some have questioned the veracity of Westphalia in creating nation states (Osiander, 2001), Elden (2013: 317) makes a simple point – what was at stake in the wake of Westphalia "was effectively that of sovereignty."

What is striking about the birth of private real estate markets in the settler-colonies and the bringing together of real estate mentalities and government policy to create the property-owning democracies in the nineteenth-century is how much the real estate markets owe to government direction and intervention. This is certainly true for what would become the sovereign territorial states of Australia, the United States, and Canada. As the territorial and subjective nation state boundaries tightened up, the respective and often fluid governments set about building property-owning democracies, at least in these three settler-societies (Ferguson, 2008). As aristocratic mentalities about the landed gentries "worthiness" and "entitlement" to land were slowly displaced with ideas about a new market-based system, and its operative discourse of "market value" (Weaver, 2003: 217), a key issue and colonial task that emerged was how to allocate and distribute land within this emerging market-based system. A new set of ideas about land, property, and real estate would have to be written into the minds of the settler-colonialists. Cultivating and nurturing a real estate mentality within the population occurred thereafter, but it was premised on the idea of private property. Building and maintaining a real estate mentality within the population is a fundamental component of the state's maintenance of a property-owning democracy. Shedding the aristocratic value of "entitlement" allowed the new colonial and then sovereign governments to introduce and advocate for a schema of new values, which were driven by economic categories and individualist ideas about freedom and rights – not least of which was, of course, the freedom and right to own private property. Thus, a suite of new value schemas underwrote the instrumental practices of dividing up and selling off land. A new legal value system that saw "revenue" as an important operative term was supplementing the new guiding moral value system, which promoted "freedom" and "rights to property" as foundational components of this new social order (Cullen, 2004). Governments are still entangled in the processes that support and promote these legal and moral value systems today.

As demonstrated by revolutionary American governments in the eighteenth-century, greater control of land allocation and distribution could only be achieved if governments could establish "national" sovereignty and independence. Weaver (2003: 190) puts it more simply: "Step 1 – independence – eliminate dealing with London." The new governments, while still forming their own political and national identities and firming up their borders, and often still negotiating or fighting for their independence, took the lead from their colonial forebears and used landed private property as a technology to raise state funds or to retire their war and other debts. Weaver (2003: 95) argues that the idea that you could sell land to finance a colonial or sovereign state's past debts or future infrastructure commitments "in the name of a common good" originated in the new American "republic and flourished there first in the 1820s." These ideas then travelled to other settler-colonies and sovereign states. Weaver (2003: 218) discusses this type of financial manoeuvring in detail, showing how governments sought to pay off war debt in: The United States, under the Articles of Confederation; or Upper Canada, after the War of 1812; and in Argentina after its Indian wars in the 1870s. In the United States after the War of 1812 and in the Australian settler-colonies after 1850, governments used the private land market to fund and provide large public infrastructure projects. Similar to their European colonial predecessors, they used landed private property as a technology through which emigration to the settler-society could be mediated and enabled. Weaver (2003: 218) shows these schemes were often informed by egalitarian ideas – such as the "fund to rescue the poor of the United Kingdom (the initial plan for both South Australia and parts of New Zealand)" – which is a long-standing irony of these real estate markets.

The famous French political historian Alexis de Tocqueville (1835) found in the short term, at least in the mid-nineteenth-century Midwest America, that the freedom bestowed by private property rights was not leading to greater inequality. de Tocqueville's analysis was underwritten, as we now know, by a geographical short-sightedness in relation to the supply of land. Holding inequality at bay would last only as long as there was ready supply of land, and some on the Midwest American frontier even believed that American land was inexhaustible (Weaver, 2003). It was not. But while the land supply delusion of the revolutionary land market de Tocqueville observed was alive, America did develop along what could be called egalitarian lines (Linklater, 2014: 211). Over time, the revenue approach attracted periodic criticism. Some protested that while the profits had been privatised, the costs and governance of enforcing private property rights were being socialised (Weaver, 2003: 68). In Weaver's (2003: 73) words, "[p]rivate parties profited from the transformation, because the cost of securing and organising resources had been socialised." The old anti-*inclosure* arguments were resurfacing in these debates, and there was no guarantee that the new United States would universally adopt the private property system of land distribution and ownership. The ruling governments had many opportunities to adopt leasehold or other tenure arrangements. For example, when the war ended with Britain in 1783 and the ink had dried on the Treaty of Paris, the land between the Appalachians and the Mississippi was conferred and transferred to the "nation state" (i.e., the United States). The new republic government was bestowed with the legal authority to distribute the land and set the terms of ownership in any way it saw fit (Linklater, 2014: 196). In fact, some within the United States continued to question the private property-driven democracy the nation was building all the way up to the end of the nineteenth century. "In 1990, when President Mikhail Gorbachev started to introduce a market economy to the

Soviet Union, thirty of America's most distinguished economists wrote an open letter strongly recommending him not to sell the state's land, because in the long term it was more economically efficient to rent or lease it" (Linklater, 2014: 196). The economists' argument, writes Linklater (2014: 196), mirrored that of Thomas Jefferson many years earlier – that "leasing the land would allow future generations to enjoy a rising income from its growing value, while the sale of it would give a small gain but allow speculators to make the largest profit."

The notion of individual private entitlement, which was justified by drawing on the ideology of improvement, was regularly challenged by claims that citizens (as the subjects of sovereign territorial states) had a right to access public assets and resources (Weaver, 2003: 218), and this argument has its roots in the ideology of the commons. In the new United States, the birth of free market capitalism owes much to the way the newly nationalised land was distributed as private property, but there was resistance and an active tension between competing land mentalities. What is undeniable and less contentious is the centrality of embodied subjects – citizens – to the political project of private property and democracy. The federal government allocated millions of acres to enable the mobility and the employment of new Americans. There were railway projects that required large sways of land, and mining and lumber companies that needed land to build new industries as sites of employment. Most fundamentally, at least for their project of democratic citizen-building, they allocated land to promote education. For example, a "policy that began in Ohio, of reserving one square mile section in every range for education, would finance every kind of schooling from elementary schools through universities, and in particular the unrivalled system of 108 land-grants colleges and universities, stretching from Florida to California, that provided American industry with the largest well-educated workforce in the world" (Linklater, 2014: 233).

Following the turbulent wars that had plagued the eighteenth century, the first decades of the nineteenth century gave rise to a different political order. A suite of trade tariffs and other protective mechanisms encouraged local textile and machinery manufacturing in North America (Morris, 2014). This new geopolitics sought to marginalise Europe, and particularly English textiles from the American market (Morris, 2014; Stearns, 1993). Thus American industrialisation was underwritten by a protective geopolitics and an aggressive approach to international trade relations (Stearns, 1993). A key omission in debates about the geopolitics of industrialisation from this period, argues Linklater (2014: 333), is the "role played by the wide distribution of land ownership." As de Tocqueville (1835) shows, although this was not necessarily his aim, the state's industrialising market economy was partly built on the sale of land on the private market. However, this land, that had thus far underwritten American equality, was a finite resource. During this period of rapid industrialisation in the nineteenth century, much of the local politics in the colonial settlements and frontier towns concerned the measurement, distribution, ownership, and management of land (Weaver, 2003: 64–65). At the local level, American industrialisation was developing over the top of complex land settlement and legislation practices, and local authorities often struggled to keep up. Free settlers and squatters often jumped ahead of the frontier lines to lay claim to unsurveyed land, with governments either unprepared or incapable of overseeing and regulating this activity in many jurisdictions (Linklater, 2014; Weaver, 2003) – which has surprising similarities, in some respects, to the management of foreign real estate investment today (Ley, 2011; Rogers et al., 2015). Weaver (2003: 64–65) argues, in "all jurisdictions, authorities responded to administrative problems, shifting ideals, pressure groups, bribery, new environments, and evolving modes of exploitation." Linklater (2014: 257) adds, through a poetic reading of *Oceana*, "the creation of landed property spawned a host of property owner's associations to lobby for their interests and to acquire political power" (Linklater, 2014: 257). A discourse of democracy and freedom was worked into the language that the squatters, landhunters, and speculators used on many colonial frontiers, as they attempted to justify their land claims to the authorities and to themselves. Many frontiers people had a blatant disregard for authority and government, and many of the land regulations were "undermined by slick manoeuvring lubricated by bribes" (Weaver, 2003: 65).

Summarising the remarkable accomplishment known as the Public Land Survey of America, Linklater (2014: 230) concludes, "What had been measured out was unmistakably a democracy, and quite clearly a republic, but its foundation was undeniably imperial. And the structure that had made it possible was to be the model for the greatest territorial empire the world had ever seen." It was a paradoxical assemblage in so many ways. These early property-owning democracies, at least for a time, seemed to be able to balance the demands of an individualised system of private ownership, which promoted self-interest, with a seemingly altruistic motive to promote collective fairness and equality (to the exclusion of Indigenous peoples of course) (Linklater, 2014: 87). Thus, as de Tocqueville's analysis of the American property-owning democracy developed stress fractures, another paradox became clear. Despite governments' key role in kick starting the property-owning democracies in the settler-colonies, libertarianist thinking was emerging as a recurring theme. The colonial frontier towns were awash with early quasi-libertarianist thinking about the role that government should play – or not play – in distributing and regulating land; that is, a minimal one. It is a tradition that has continued and become more sophisticated over time. Scholars from the United States, many following the Austrian project of economic liberalism (Peck, 2010), have been vocal proponents of libertarianist government in relation to private property.

There are many ways of approaching libertarianism. A common political philosophy approach is to springboard Robert Nozick's (1974) ideas in *Anarchy, State, and Utopia* off John Rawls' (1971) opposing and prior argument in *A Theory of Justice*. Rawls sought to revive the social contract tradition to argue for a more redistributive form of government intervention. Nozick countered by deploying a somewhat intuitive libertarian call-to-arms; people should be able to reap the rewards of their labour and a Rawlsian-style interventionist, redistributive government would impinge on the freedom of individuals. Different schools of liberal thought championed these ideas much earlier. Most notable is the individualism advocated by a school of Austrian economists associated with Ludwig von Mises (1912), Joseph Schumpeter (1927), and Friedrich von Hayek, who championed a discourse of state apathy and the redemptive capacities of private property. This is the economic theorising, in part a manifestation of the Austrian project, put forward by the so-called Chicago School (Friedman, 1963), and the normalisation of so-called neoliberal rationalities by the Washington Consensus (Harvey, 2005; Peck, 2010; Peck and Tickell, 2002). Using the term "neoliberalism" to classify this amalgam of political philosophies loosely organised around the idea of minimal government and maximum private property, David Harvey (2005: 2) summarised the central thrust of the theory as follows: it is "a theory of political economic practices that proposes that human well-being can best be advanced by liberating individual entrepreneurial freedoms and skills within an institutional framework characterised by strong private property rights, free markets, and free trade." What had started as a radical and marginal economic project at the beginning of the twentieth century – a form of libertarian reasoning that positions government intervention as antithetical to individual liberty and freedom – had, by the end of the century, become a popular idea with some measure of intuitive appeal. The Austrian ideas had sidelined Karl Marx. Their ideas had reconfigured questions about labour and capital. Adam Smith's (1776) vision for a free market system where it was incumbent on the government to regulate the free market so that everyone, rich and poor alike, would have an equal opportunity to profit from their labour was distant.

Peck (2010: 380) suggests that "what began as a starkly utopian intellectual movement" was aggressively politicised between the 1970s and the 1990s. This was achieved by working ideas around free markets and individualism into the *bodies* of the next wave of economic leaders in countries in Latin America, including Chile, Mexico, and Argentina, and the settler-states of Canada, New Zealand, and Australia (for a detailed analysis, see Larner, 2009; Peck, 2010). A range of new technologies of government was rolled out in these countries to drive dramatic state-sector reform. This was achieved, quite literally, by changing the governance and economic mentalities of the current political leaders or the future economic advisers in select countries. From the 1970s, the more abstract intellectual projects that were developed by the Chicago School of Economics – including the contributions of Hayek (1948) and Friedman (1963) – were transformed into state-authored restructuring programmes, which were aggressively politicised throughout the 1980s. Much scholarship has focused on the roles that Ronald Reagan in the United States and Margaret Thatcher in the United Kingdom played in inculcating a politicised form of free market liberalism into the social and political spheres; and their collective projects are typical of what is now known as Thatcherism and Reaganomics (Harvey, 2005; Larner, 2009; Peck, 2010; Peck and Tickell, 2002). But what is important to note about these radical state-authored restructuring programmes is that they started as a political project that was directed at changing the minds of political and financial leaders around the world, and only after the free market and radically individualist mentalities had been established in the minds of the leaders was the political project of restructuring rolled out (Harvey, 2005; Larner, 2009; Peck, 2010; Peck and Tickell, 2002). By the beginning of the twenty-first century, the full effects of the Austrian project became clear – freedom had become the privilege of the rich. "To the rest of the world, the beacon of liberty had become a lighthouse warning of the greedy rock beneath" (Linklater, 2014: 371–372).

On reflection, therefore, there was more to Adam Smith than his discourse on the morality of the liberal state (Fitzgibbons, 1995: 15), because his rejection of mercantilism had a moral basis. Smith's economic reasoning was fortified by a moral philosophy that stands in contrast to the neoclassical economists of the twentieth century. Smith understood the role that banks and credit played in activating the "value" in landed property in eighteenth-century Scotland,

> They invented, therefore, another method of issuing promissory notes; by granting what they call cash accounts, that is, by giving credit, to the extent of a certain sum (two of three thousand pounds for example), to any individual who could procure two persons of undoubted credit and good landed estate to become surety for him, that whatever money should be advanced to him, within the sum for which the credit had been given, should be repaid upon demand, together with the legal interest. (Smith, 1776: 191)

By the second half of the twentieth century, the free market ideologue Alan Greenspan, who became the Chairman of the Federal Reserve of the United States in 1987, was championing small governments, big business, unfettered markets (Madrick, 2012: 225) and claiming that "economic liberty was synonymous with individual liberty" (Linklater, 2014: 361). The starkly utopian intellectual movement of free market liberalism had taken root in the minds of the financial leadership in the United States, and it was being draw upon to reshape the future of the nation.

This vignette shows, therefore, that a radically new organising technic – the nation state – allowed the settler body to become a technology of the state, that could be used to build a citizenry, a national identity, but most importantly for this discussion, to build a property-owning democracy in the settler-society. By the end of the twentieth century, not only was free market individualism, the right to own private property and a libertarian distrust of government written into the bodies of many of the citizens of the settler-property-owning democracies, they were written into the minds of the leaders in many countries around the world. Banks and bankers also played a major role in building the property-owning democracies and the real estate and private property mentality in the setter-societies, as we will see in the next section.

BANKS: NOT MEN; THE MONSTER

Economic historian Niall Ferguson's (2008: 42–65) concise survey of the birth of banking draws a causal lineage between today's banking sector all the way back to the famous family of Italian bankers, the Medici family. The Medici family were the owners of the largest bank in Europe during the fifteenth century. It is true that the history of banking starts much earlier than the eighteenth century, when, for example, Smith was writing about the relationship between bank credit and landed property in Scotland. Smith's (1776) scholarship highlights the essential role that banks played in creating and actuating "value" in landed property. William Petty also put forward, during the time of Oliver Cromwell, the idea of a national bank that could make available twice as much "credit" as their vaults held as hard cash or gold (Linklater, 2014: 65). The aim of this type of "national" bank was to keep the "market" stable by regulating the flow of money. There is also a voluminous literature showing how the London financial sector was later involved in providing financial services to the British settler-colonies (Belich, 2009; Cain and Hopkins, 1993; Ferguson, 2008; Linklater, 2014; Storey, 2016; Weaver, 2003). The temporal shadow from the intersection of land, banking, borrowed capital, and property is long and dark. So dark, in fact, that Ferguson (2008) suggests that there is disagreement among scholars over certain periods.

I want to return to the opening quote in Chapter 1 of this book, the quote from John Steinbeck's *The Grapes of Wrath*, as the starting point for this discussion about banks and bodies. Steinbeck shows how the land mentalities of the ruling class were changing at the beginning of the nineteenth century in the United States. In this fictional account, it did not matter if you worked the land, or if you were born or died on the land; the application of labour to land was no longer a productive way of claiming land ownership. A new technology of power, a technology that was many years in the making, was now the defining article of land ownership, as the tenant farmers found out in dusty Oklahoma during Steinbeck's portrayal of the Great Depression. The land technology was devastatingly simple, pieces of paper with words and numbers on them (Steinbeck, 1939: 22–23). In other words, loan documents or land title deeds. Before the Great Depression, as we have seen, rational-legal paper documents were a formidable technology of settler-colonial land claiming on various settler-colonial frontiers. Weaver (2003: 125) maps, for example, how rational-legal paper documents codified land through: "petitions for bringing occupied land under freehold" in southern Africa in the 1820s; "grazing licences" in colonial United States, Canada, and New Zealand. In other places "deeds, registered mortgages, unregistered mortgages … entitlements such as dower rights and the equity of redemption (second mortgages)" were powerful legal technologies of colonial power (Weaver, 2003: 125). The rational-legal paper documents that were produced through these banking and legal processes improved the security of tenure of the land-claimers and -owners. Landowners lobbied government for improvements to land conveyancing and land registration processes in the settler-societies. They also lobbied for changes to the way property documents were storied and the rules about who could access them. Increasing public access to these documents changed the way people engaged in real estate transactions, because "[a]nyone could examine the documents and find the essential chapters in the transaction story of particular properties, but registration itself failed to cure defects in the documents" (Weaver, 2003: 242).

Therefore, looking back on Steinbeck's discussion of the "bank," particularly with the benefit of hindsight of the 2007 Global Financial Crisis, which I return to below, his prose provides a revealing warning about the contemporary banking sector. He writes,

> And all of them [the land owners] were caught in something larger than themselves. Some of them hated the mathematics that drove them, and some were afraid, and some worshipped the mathematics because it provided a refuge from thought and from feeling. If a bank or a finance company owned the land, the owner man said, The Bank – or the Company – needs – wants – insists – must have – as though the Bank or the Company were a monster, with thought and feeling, which had ensnared them. (Steinbeck, 1939: 33).

Banks have an alarming history in the United States of being one of the recurring technologies (there are others, such as housing policy) through which the mass eviction of poor citizens from their land and homes has been facilitated (Bennett et al., 2006; Ferguson, 2008). Banking practices during the Great Depression marks one such event, and the Global Financial Crisis is another such event. I discuss each in turn below. What makes Steinbeck's banking *monster* so dangerous is that it is not intrinsically *evil*. In fact, the banking sector is often thought of as a benevolent institution. As the early Australian and American colonial frontier towns developed into settlements and the sale of public land picked up pace, the banking industry was developing an efficient method for legally recording the sale and ownership of land. The connection between banks and the allocation of land is striking around the turn of the eighteenth and nineteenth century in America. In 1803, the United States acquired 1,332,536 square kilometres of territory through the so-called Louisiana Purchase. The purchase from the French involved a cash settlement and the writing down of French debt to the United States. Linklater (2014: 182) shows that between 1811 and 1818 the number of banks in the United States jumped from 88 to 392, and in 1819 there were 27 banks in the state of Ohio alone. Of course, banks did not solely develop at this time to provide the capital for the purchase of public land. The industrial revolution was ramping up and the banks were lending money to people to invest in their land in other ways. Long before the Great Depression, the rising value of land allowed farmers to borrow money to mechanise their farming practices (Stearns, 1993). The money was used to invest in European cotton mill machinery, dairy farm equipment, "and to buy shares in turnpikes, bridges, insurance companies, and even in the banks that lent them money" (Linklater, 2014: 182).

Diamond Douglas and Philip Dybvig (1983: 401) argue that "[b]ank runs are a common feature of the extreme crises that have played a prominent role in monetary history." Confidence started to decline in the paper money that was being issued by the banks around this time, and the financial burden on government from the Louisiana Purchase did not help (Linklater, 2014: 222). The central bank, in what is now regarded as a misguided move, called in the silver from its branches just as a run on the banks was starting (Douglas and Dybvig, 1983; Stearns, 1993). In an interesting move, at least when viewed from the first decades of the twentieth-first century, the James Monroe administration did not become the lender of last resort and bail out the banks (Ashcraft et al., 2010). The banks crashed, and along with them the sale of public land. The Monroe administration moved to protect the capital investments in public land, much of which had been bought on credit. Under Monroe, "[e]ither the terms were eased, notably by extending the period of payment, or buyers were allowed to keep what land they had paid for and write off the rest" (Linklater, 2014: 222). The land economy kick started again, and the United States government earned almost half its revenue in 1835 from a boom in public land sales (Linklater, 2014: 222). A cycle of real estate boom and bust would plague the rest of the nineteenth century, but a narrative about landed property and real estate was being built into the minds of the settler-Americans and the employees within the new banking sector. One 1835 publication from the New York Agricultural Society points straight to the subjective – real estate mentality – aims of the writing on real estate investment of this time ("A," 1835: 155). In a short two-paragraph piece, entitled *Real Estate as an Investment*, one keen advocate of real estate investment, a writer known only as "A," argues,

> Perhaps at no period of our history, as in the last year, has there been so great a demand for money [i.e., credit], or greater facilities for obtaining it [i.e., from the banks]. ... Still, for an active man, an investment of money in real estate, where the products are taken instead of interest, and where, by good management, the farm is rendered more productive, is, all things considered, probably the best investment of money he can make. As a security, it partakes of the nature of a mortgage, while as a property, it is subject to his immediate control. The question may be asked, can he realize the legal interest from the products? I answer, at this time of day, with the advance of the art, it must be miserable farming indeed that will not do that. If I should rate the products of farming at ten per cent, upon the present price of land, after deducting all expenses, I am satisfied, from my own expense, and that of my neighbours, it will not be putting it too high. Were this a proper place, I could give many instances in which these profits have been nearly doubled; but it is not necessary at this time to substantiate this statement by facts – these, if necessary, can be subsequently made – yet, thus far, we have only a part of the profits. Who ever heard of a man buying and selling a farm at the same or a lessened price? It is so well understood that the seller is to have more than he gave, that it has almost become a settled principle in the purchase of real estate. This percentage is sometimes very high, but in almost all cases, it adds materially to the profits of the investment. ("A," 1835: 155)

Both the title of this agricultural publication, *The Cultivator, a monthly publication designed to improve the soil and the mind*, and the title of A's article, *Real Estate as an Investment*, show that a discursive relationship between real estate as an investment and the "facilities for obtaining" money, in this case the bank, has a long association in the United States. A slither of the discursive roots that would later link the financial prosperity of real estate investors with the property-owning democracy is visible in these marvellous statements by A. It is these types of ruminations that subsequent advocates of real estate investment internalised as real estate mentalities and built upon, and which eventually contributed to building the local, national, and then global real estate mentalities that are evident today. However, as I noted in Chapter 2, the emergence of a real estate mentality does not have a clear temporal or spatial origin, nor does it have a clear causal temporal trajectory, and it certainly does not have a single unifying geographical site of germination. In geopolitical terms, it has a diverse history that is in no way confined to the eighteenth or nineteenth century in the United States or any other settler-society. Nonetheless, several important changes occurred and intensified within settler-societies in the first half of the nineteenth century that certainly contributed to building the real estate mentalities that are evident today.

Weaver (2003: 125) shows how the governing powers and legislators in many of the settler jurisdictions introduced and amended laws with the explicit aim of "increasing the velocity" of land and real estate transactions, and many of the new laws or legislative changes intersected with emergent banking practices. Weaver (2003: e.g., 125 and 249) provides detailed examples, including: the establishment of land offices that sought to improve the legal registration and documentation of the ownership of land; reductions and even the elimination of interest-rate restrictions on mortgages; public offices to manage mortgage foreclosures; and "abolishing a wife's dower rights in a husband's property" (p. 125). Several high profile court cases from mid-nineteenth-century Australia are also insightful. One example is the case between MacDonald and Levy from 8 March 1833 relating to usury laws (Weaver, 2003: 249–250). Usury laws are legal regulations or rules that limit the amount of interest that can be charged on a loan. In Australia (as in other British colonial settlements), the governing authorities held on to the usury laws, albeit loosely, that they had inherited from their colonial forebears. These laws have their legal roots in the English and Roman-Dutch legal systems. A "medieval fusion of canon and civil law," writes Weaver (2003: 249), "usury measures held it unlawful for Christians to take any kind of excessive interests on loans." While morally outdated, legislators in Australia were less than willing to overturn local usury laws because they did not want to be seen to be snubbing the English and their legal statutes. In Sydney, the first bank was opened in 1817 and the usury laws officially fixed the interest that could be charged on a (bank or private) loan at around 5 or 6 per cent. However, it became common to charge 8 per cent or more in the colony at this time, argues Weaver (2003: 249). This discrepancy came to a head in the case of *MacDonald v. Levy*, which, as the legal documents recount, "was an action on a promissory note, a question arose as to what was the legal rate of interest in this colony – whether, in fact, the usury laws applied here. ... Whether there be in this colony any legal limitation to the rate of interest which may be taken of the forbearance of money" (Supreme Court of New South Wales, 1833: 1). The court ruling shows that the rate of interest being charged on loans in the Australian settler-colony was largely unregulated, and it certainly did not follow the 5 or 6 per cent rule that was mandated by the usury laws of England. Drawing on the cases of *Robert Jenkins, Esquire, v. William Kelly* (1810) and *John M'Arthur v. Henry Kable* (1811), the judge showed that 8 per cent interest on private loans was common (Supreme Court of New South Wales, 1833: 4).

These types of rulings were expressed in legal terms, but they were driven by the changing experiences and attitudes of the colonisers. In other words, they were legal in substance, but subjective in practice – they were being regulated by the organising technics of the settler-colony. In this sense, these colonial legal ruling documents symbolise the subjective changes in the bodies of the colonisers, just as much as they recount any changing legal doctrines or geopolitical negotiations between the old colonial powers and the new settler-colonial government. The reforms that followed "unclogged markets in important technical ways that involved adjustments to traditional English property law" (Weaver, 2003: 125). Purely techno-legal analyses do not show how these ideas were written into the bodies and minds of the new settler-colonists. Indeed, the subjective effects are not always clear within the ebb and flow of daily life. However, at times of real estate and banking crisis, such as the Great Depression and the Global Financial Crisis, the subtle ways that real estate has been written into the bodies of settler-colonialists or citizens, into their very subjectivity, are brutally exposed. As the American economy slowed at the beginning of the first decade of the twentieth century, in the lead up to the Great Depression, the relationship between bank credit and landed property was pushed to the surface.

In 1931, the Herbert Hoover Administration called on the loosely allied banking sector to set up a National Credit Corporation (Olson, 1977; Wicker, 1996). As a skilled engineer, Hoover strongly advocated for a rationalist, technocratic government (Smyth, 1919). He organised his ideas for such a government under the discursive title of the *Efficiency Movement*. Like some more recent ideologies that call for highly rationalist, technocratic governments (Peck, 2010; Peck and Tickell, 2002), Hoover argued that the government in the United States was plagued by inefficiency and waste, and that a supposedly more efficient expert workforce was the solution (Olson, 1977; Smyth, 1919). It was perhaps an easy and obvious choice for an engineer to come up with, but with the benefit of the critique of the Chicago School from the middle of the twentieth century (Shook, 2001), his approach was too functionalist. The biggest problem was that his ideas did not pay enough attention to the bankers as embodied subjects; he misread their individualist economic mentalities (Wicker, 1996: 92–96). Hoover assumed that these bankers were rational expert citizens who could be called upon to serve the state, but he had misunderstood their subjective motivations for trading in capital and land (Wicker, 1996: 96). Hoover wanted the big banks to act collegially and philanthropically through the National Credit Corporation to help the smaller failing banks (Olson, 1977; Wicker, 1996: 95). The bankers were indeed rational actors but they were not guided by collegial or philanthropic economic mentalities. They had no desire to invest in the failing banks, and the National Credit Corporation had almost no impact on the mass failure of banks (Wicker, 1996). By 1932, more than 5,000 banks had failed and unemployment had reached 23.6 per cent. In early 1933 unemployment peaked at 25 per cent (Swanson and Williamson, 1972). Record numbers of businesses and families defaulted on their loans across the United States at this time, and hundreds of thousands of Americans were forced into homelessness. Before the 1930s, only about two fifths of American households were mortgage owner-occupiers. Ferguson (2008: 242) shows that although few Americans borrowed money before the 1930s to purchase housing, those that did were in "deep difficulties" when the Great Depression hit. "In 1932 and 1933 there were over half a million foreclosures. By mid 1933, over a thousand mortgages were being foreclosed every day. House prices plummeted by more than a fifth" (Ferguson, 2008: 243).

If the act of evicting someone from his or her home is a battlefield, then the banking sector was on the frontline. Cue and enter Steinbeck's discussion of the "bank as a monster," and his vivid portrayal of the poor tenant farmers being forced off the land in the Dust Bowl in the Midwest, as they take to Route 66 to chase a false promise of employment. "The bank – the monster has to have profits all the time," writes Steinbeck (1939: 34), "It can't wait. It'll die. No, taxes go on. When the monster stops growing, it dies. It can't stay one size." Of course, many banks and businesses failed, but people and families suffered along with them. Many of them ended up in so-called Hoovervilles, the makeshift shantytowns that appeared in the cities across the country, and that filled up with Americans the United States could no longer provide for (Olson, 1977). One of the key problems for the banks and all those who owned or worked the land, a point Weaver (2003: 125) outlines very precisely, was that in "depressions, one great imperfection with landed property and its derivatives was universal – namely, inadequate liquidity." "Liquidity" refers to the degree to which real estate can be quickly bought or sold in the real estate market without affecting the price of the real estate asset (Dufty-Jones and Rogers, 2015). If nothing else, land and real estate crises are a lesson in the importance of liquidity.

In a now familiar tale of state intervention at times of banking crisis, President Hoover and Congress approved the Federal Home Loan Bank Act (Ashcraft et al., 2010). The aim of the act has broad similarities to the "economic stimulus" interventions of contemporary governments (Ashcraft et al., 2010; Ruming, 2015); it aimed to stimulate new housing construction and to reduce foreclosures (Ashcraft et al., 2010). Similarly, in a final attempt to stimulate the economy, the Hoover Administration pushed through the Emergency Relief and Construction Act (Williams and Williams, 1940). Again, with broad similarities to contemporary interventions (Ruming, 2015), in 1932 the administration attempted to use the funding and construction of public infrastructure (i.e., dams) to save the economy through the Reconstruction Finance

Corporation (Olson, 1998). The Federal level Reconstruction Finance Corporation also had the authority and a mandate to save the banks, and although they had up to $2 billion at their disposal, the bank runs and bank failures continued (Olson, 1998). In 1933, the new Roosevelt administration made changes to the banking sector. The now infamous 1933 Glass-Steagall Act – due in part to its failed revival after the Global Financial Crisis – separated commercial banking and mortgage lending from investment banking (Benston and Harland, 1990).

Linklater (2014: 359) argues that the Glass-Steagall Act "kept house prices roughly in line with incomes from the 1940s to 1970s." I return to the eudemonism of the property-owning democracy in Chapter 6, which is an important contextual frame for this discussion. Additionally, for detailed analyses of housing and bank crises across some of these time periods also see, for example: Carmen Reinhart and Kenneth Rogoff (2008), George Glaster (2012), Keith Jacobs (in-press), Ferguson (2008: 231–283), Rae Dufty-Jones (2016), Ruming (2015: 190), and Hulse and Burke (2015). I make a more focused point about housing and bank practices at the time of the Global Financial Crisis, an event Ferguson (2008: 265) has dubbed "subprimia" (see the body of work above for more detailed and broader scoped analyses). Ferguson argues that the 2007 Global Financial Crisis had less to do with the traditional banking practices that emerged out of the twentieth century, and more to do with the rise and fall of securitised lending that was developed for the bond market (Ferguson, 2008: 65). "Securitisation," as it applies to bank loans, is a banking practice whereby a bank is allowed to originate loans and then repackage and sell them on to another lender (Ferguson, 2008: 65 and 262). Subprimia is a catchall term that is used to describe the devastating process whereby local mortgage brokers targeted low-income, poor, and often black neighbourhoods with low-documentation and NINJA (no-income–no-job–or–asset) home loans in America. The families that were explicitly targeted by these lenders often had poor credit histories, or worse (Shiller, 2008). The Bush Administration "signed off on legislation to force Fannie Mae and Freddie Mac to make sure that 30 per cent of their loans went to borrowers with low and moderate incomes" (Lanchester, 2010: 99). Related to this, Jacobs (in-press: citing Lanchester 2010) argues that the "long-standing precautionary settings such as the 1933 Glass-Steagall Act were repealed, and all this 'freeing up' of the property market was tied together by the determination among legislators that banks were 'too big to fail.'" As Lanchester (2010: 100) shows, the aim of expanding the property-owning democracy was heavily implicated in the subprime mortgage objectives of the United States government.

Not only did the strategy have a "racial edge" (Lanchester, 2010: 101), it relied on the old ideological mentality of private property and real estate, and the assumption that life would be better for poor families if they could get onto the first ladder of the real estate market. Loan restrictions were loosened, credit histories were given less gravitas in loan assessments, and full-time jobs and deposits were viewed as a luxury rather than a necessity (Shiller, 2008). If a poor renter can cover their rental and housing costs, the prevailing logic of private property suggested that they might be able to cover mortgage and housing costs, although each loan application would need to be individually assessed (Lanchester, 2010). On the surface, the strategy seemed to be having the desired effect, at least in the short term. "American home ownership increased to an historic high of 68.9 per cent, and the gap between ethnic minorities and the white ... population narrowed: between 1994 and 2005 white home ownership increased by 8.3 per cent, African American by 13.6 per cent, and Hispanic by 20.1 per cent" (Lanchester, 2010: 101). Underneath, the programme was not functioning as intended. Many of the loans were interest only and large numbers of borrowers had limited means to pay back the principle. Introductory low interest rates caught others off guard as higher interest rates kicked in (Shiller, 2008). Furthermore, in some cities, such as Detroit, only a minority of borrowers were first homebuyers, and many new loans were subprime refinancing loans. This allowed, argues Ferguson (2008), "borrowers to treat their homes as cash machines, converting their existing equity into cash" (p. 266), and between "1997 and 2006, US consumers withdrew an estimated $9 trillion in cash from the equity in their homes. By the first quarter of 2006 home equity extraction accounted for nearly 10 per cent of disposable personal income" (fn. on p. 267).

The root of the "problem," the subprime crisis and then the Global Financial Crisis, when it did emerge, does not lie in the poor families that took out these loans. They were sold a repackaged and financially turbocharged version of the Great American property-owning dream, which at its core, is a real estate mentality. The monster – the banks and the bankers – must take a large part of the blame for the subprime meltdown and the Global Financial Crisis. "[J]ust like in space," writes Ferguson (2008), no one could hear the poor scream, when these often marginal families were caught up in the unfolding securitised subprime crisis, because the interest they were paying (or failing to pay) on their mortgages was "ultimately going to someone who has no idea" they existed (p. 262). As surprising as it might be, there is an even more sinister outcome of the subprimia crisis. Repossessing the *homes* (i.e., not real estate) from low-income households, many who should never have been given home loans in the first place, was just the first step in the bust and boom of real estate markets. The dispossession of the poor from their homes, and in some cases their cities, following the Global Financial Crisis was soon reimagined by the real estate and banking sectors not as a crisis but as an opportunity. The "crisis" narrative quickly turned into a discourse of "opportunity," which, as it turns out, encapsulates one of the very problems with bringing globalising market-centric real estate systems together with global capital (Darcy and Rogers, 2014; Rogers and Darcy, 2014; Rogers and Dufty-Jones, 2015).

As I show in the next chapter, the emerging global real estate industry mobilised this real estate "crisis" by pitching it to global real estate investors as an "opportunity" they could capitalise on. For example, an Australian book entitled *Real estate riches down under: How to make a fortune investing in the Australian property market* is handed out for free at international real estate events in Asia. In this book the author says, "having made her fortune in Australian real estate" she now "teaches to the Asian market so that others can benefit from the enormous wealth to be made in the Australian property market' [sic] (Grubisa, 2014b: ii). The discursive twist in this book is located in the way a narrative, which is borrowed from the United States, is used to reimagine "repossessed" real estate as "distressed" real estate and promoting it as a great way to "profit in real estate in the new [post GFC] economy" (Grubisa, 2014a: 85). The Australian real estate self-help educator Stuart Zadel (2014) describes this strategy more bluntly in *The new way to make money in property fast!*: "Australia's Debt Expert and barrister, Dominique Grubisa … has developed a system to buy 'distress real estate' at substantial discounts directly from the banks" (p. 7).

This vignette shows that neither the banking sector, the various real estate industries, nor the government are benevolent actors when it comes to real estate. Keith Jacobs (2015: 53) calls on critical housing scholars to "cast aside a view of the State as a benevolent agency whose primary objective is to ameliorate the conditions of the disadvantaged." Jacobs' "myth of the benevolent state" could equally be levelled at the myth of the benevolent banking and real estate industries, although fewer people are convinced of their benevolence after the Global Financial Crisis. The banks that formed around the time of the mass public land sales in the United States in the early nineteenth century were a key mediating technology that expelled often poor and marginal Americans from their homes time and time again. As we will see in the coming chapters, the assumption that life would be better if you can get into the real estate market is a mentality that would go on to underwrite the Great American and Great Australian Dreams. But to build these dreams the ruling authorities not only needed a sovereign nation state to build it within; they also needed bodies that they could inculcate with a real estate mentality. As we will see in the next section, if the ruling authorities did not have the embodied labour and capital in their country, they could always import it.

POPULATION: MIGRATING LABOUR-CAPITAL-LAND

It is a misnomer to talk of an increasingly globalised world of connected labour, capital, and land as a recent mid- to late-twentieth-century development (Crafts, 2000; Elden, 2013; Ferguson, 2008; Lanchester, 2010; Weaver, 2003). It is equally misguided to theorise the intensification of economic, political, social, and cultural relations that developed between nation states after the Second World War as a wholly new phenomenon (Baldwin and Martin, 1999; Crafts, 2000; Ferguson, 2008). In the late 1990s, at least in the economic realm, economists Richard Baldwin and Philippe Martin (1999: 1) called the fixity of the term "globalisation" with mid- to late-twentieth-century global trade "glo-baloney." They argued, the "world has seen two waves of globalisation in the past 150 years, and in some ways," the world of the early twentieth century "was more tightly integrated" than the world of the early twenty-first century (Baldwin and Martin, 1999: 1). In purely economic terms (Dowd and Timberlake, 1998; Rosensweig, 2010), in the three decades between 1885 and 1914 the global trade of goods "reached almost as large a proportion of global output" as the decades between 1985 and 2015 (Ferguson, 2008: 285). Tim Butler and Loretta Lees (2006: 469) argue, "There is little to no detailed empirical research that 'fixes' globalisation at the local/neighbourhood level – most work focuses on global nodes or networks or undertakes ethnographies within the space of global flows." John Maynard Keynes (1919) captured the tail end of the so-called first wave of globalisation well by focusing on the way a body in London might have experienced the globalising colonial world in 1919. He wrote reflectively not long after the end of the First World War, what

> an extraordinary episode in the economic progress of man that age was which came to an end in August, 1914! [i.e., the beginning of the First World War] The inhabitant of London could order by telephone, sipping his morning tea in bed, the various products of the whole earth, in such quantity as he might see fit, and reasonably expect their early delivery upon his doorstep; he could at the same moment and by the same means adventure his wealth in the natural resources and new enterprises of any quarter of the world, and share, without exertion or even trouble, in their prospective fruits and advantages; or he could decide to couple the security of his fortunes with the good faith of the townspeople of any substantial municipality in any continent that fancy or information might recommend. *He could secure forthwith, if he wished it, cheap and comfortable means of transit to any country or climate without passport or other formality*, could despatch his servant to the neighbouring office of a bank for such supply of the precious metals as might seem convenient, and *could then proceed abroad to foreign quarters*, without knowledge of their religion, language, or customs, bearing coined wealth upon his person, and would consider himself

greatly aggrieved and much surprised at the least interference. (emphasis added by author: Keynes, 1919: 10–12)

As Keynes notes, moving across national borders was easy if you were wealthy or white in the early twentieth century. Indeed, it was perhaps exponentially easier if you were both. Government regulation of "borders" and "immigration" was less intense in 1910 than today, and many settler-colonies actively sought out European migrants to boost their labour force and economies, including their real estate economies (see the discussion of emigration in Chapter 4). Ferguson (2008) hedges that relative to global population, international migration was "almost certainly" more pronounced in the first decade of the twentieth century when compared to the first decade of the twenty-first century. In the United States, for example, 14 per cent of the population was born overseas in 1910 compared with less than 12 per cent in 2003 (Ferguson, 2008: 287). Ferguson's claims do not stack up for the settler-society of Australia, where in 2011 "almost a quarter (24.6 per cent) of Australia's population was born overseas and 43.1 per cent of people have at least one overseas-born parent" (Australian Bureau of Statistics, 2011).

In any case, globalisation is a contested concept, and I certainly do not want to further essentialise the term or its many predecessors and derivatives (e.g., transnationalism, hyperglobalism, transformationalism, planetary urbanism) (Brenner, 2014; Bryane, 2003; Madden, 2012; Robertson, 2013; Shaw, 2015). In fact, I want to leave the term behind, save its usefulness for very loosely setting up the temporal scope of the vignette that follows: that is, the first wave of so-called globalisation that occurred roughly between 1850 and 1914, and the second from 1960 up until today (Baldwin and Martin, 1999: 1; Hatton and Williamson, 1998). I want to look at the intersection of two quite specific regulatory settings, to see how they have pulsated – tightening and loosening – over time, to look at the ebb and flow of these policies. The two regulatory settings are (1) migration (see this section) and (2) housing policy (see the next chapter). In terms of global trade and migration, capital flows and real estate markets, and the industrial age (trade in goods) and information age (trade in ideas), there is much that separates the period between 1870 and 1914 from the period between 1960 and 2015. As Baldwin and Martin (1999: 1) put it, the two periods "share many superficial similarities but are fundamentally different."

The industrial revolution brought with it a rise in the international trading of goods, which was underwritten by technological investment and innovation in the area of transport infrastructure. Between 1820 and 1920, about 55 million Europeans migrated to the settler-societies including the United States, Canada, and Australia (Hatton and Williamson, 1998: 3). It was a time that some social scientists, including Timothy Hatton and Jeffrey Williamson

(1998: 3), have called the "age of free mass migration." It is a phase that does not fully acknowledge the cultural limitations of the "freedom" to migrate during this time. Before the rapid reduction in transport costs that was associated with the industrial revolution, transport was prohibitively expensive, and, subsequently, there were three key methods that enabled mass transnational mobility from the fifteenth to the early nineteenth century (Hatton and Williamson, 2008; O'Rourke and Williamson, 1999). The first was the forced mass migration of slaves, largely from the African subcontinent to the Americas. The second was indentured servitude, a labour system whereby a person secured a "loan" for their transnational passage, which they "paid back" once they arrived through the provision of their labour to their loan-providing employer in the settler-society. The third was convict transportation from Europe to the settler-societies (Dowd and Timberlake, 1998: 7). The transport technologies of the nineteenth century have a long history, most immediately linking back to the transport practices of the joint-stock companies, such as the *Dutch East India Company* and *East India Company* from the seventeenth century (Stern, 2011: 9). Although the Dutch were not initially interested in colonisation as a project of emigration and settlement, but rather as a project of war and commerce (Weaver, 2003: 183).

The emigrants to the United States and Australia in the nineteenth century were different to those who arrived in the twentieth century because the underlying societal conditions – the geopolitics – were different. The early nineteenth-century emigrants were farmers and artisans who travelled in family groups; they were often poor and agrarian. They travelled from the rural areas of their homeland with the intention to acquiring land to allow them to settle on a frontier in the settler-societies (Crafts, 2000; Dowd and Timberlake, 1998; Weaver, 2003). By the end of the nineteenth century, the industrialisation of the workforce had pulled many Europeans into the cities in their home country before they migrated into the urban centres in the settler-societies (Hatton and Williamson, 1998: 10).

Similar to the transformation in transportation technologies, the agrarian relations between labour, capital, and land also have a much longer history. In 1690, William Petty argued – earlier than most and within a distinctly agrarian register – that population growth drives capital values in privately owned land. "If there were but one Man living in England," wrote Petty (1690: 286) in a frequently-cited passage from *Political Arithmetick*, "then the benefit of the whole Territory, could be but the livelihood of that one Man: But if another Man added, the rent [profit] of the same would be double. ... *And moreover, where the Rent [profit] of Land is advanced by reason of Multitude of People*" (emphasis added by author: Petty, 1690: 286). With the benefit of hindsight, it was perhaps an obvious supply versus demand observation to make. It was a powerful argument, most significantly for Petty himself. He even contemplated a programme to repatriate the British colonists in America back to their homeland so that "the Rents of Lands shall rise by this closer cohabitation of People" (Linklater, 2014: 61, citing Petty, 1690: 289). "The effect that a growing population had on increasing the value of land was to become the fundamental driving force that powered the expansion of private property economies," writes Linklater (2014: 61). It "would turn out to be the secret weapon that made exclusive, private property the most dynamic way of owning the earth," he added (p. 62).

In the early nineteenth century, the "capital gain" that could be made by "improving the land" had become both a cause and effect of increasing internal migration. de Tocqueville (1835) notes the violent practices that are required when taking the land from Indigenous peoples. It "is difficult to describe the rapacity with which the American rushes forward to secure the immense booty which fortune proffers to him. In the pursuit he fearlessly braves the arrow of the Indian …" He then observes two waves of internal migration:

> I have spoken of the emigration from the older States, but how shall I describe that which takes place from the more recent ones? Fifty years have scarcely elapsed since that of Ohio was founded; the greater part of its inhabitants were not born within its confines; its capital has only been built thirty years, and its territory is still covered by an immense extent of uncultivated fields; nevertheless the population of Ohio is already proceeding westward, and most of the settlers who descend to the fertile savannahs of Illinois are citizens of Ohio. These men left their first country to improve their condition; they quit their resting-place to ameliorate it still more; fortune awaits them everywhere, but happiness they cannot attain. The desire of prosperity is[sic] become an ardent and restless passion in their minds which grows by what it gains. They early broke the ties which bound them to their natal earth, and they have contracted no fresh ones on their way. *Emigration was at first necessary to them as a means of subsistence; and it soon becomes a sort of game of chance, which they pursue for the emotions it excites as much as for the gain it procures.* (de Tocqueville, 1835: emphasis added by author)

The land claiming and migration practices observed by de Tocqueville were built upon public land sales. Weaver (2003: 110) writes more explicitly about colonial migratory pathways: the "wagon road between the Blue Ridge and Allegheny mountains may once have been a buffalo track, and migrants and government surveyors used similar tracks in territory just east of the Mississippi." Linklater (2014: 220) shows that between May 1800 and June 1820 over 13.6 million acres of public land was sold in the United States. The average price per acre was less than $1.70. de Tocqueville's records show that the relationship between migration and land might have started as a means of subsistence or a dream for a new or better life, perhaps even survival, but it soon developed into a commercial, subjective experience. Claiming, buying, or working the land became a mentality. Linklater calls this subjective experience the "psychological experience of owning land" (Linklater, 2014: 230). To paraphrase de Tocqueville (1835), the financial gain the land can procure excited the emotions in the internal migrant, to which he added the subjective claim that the "passions which agitate the Americans most deeply are not their political but their commercial passions ..." It is a powerful and revealing statement when viewed from the early twenty-first century, and it pulls the mobility and mentality of the contemporary foreign real estate investor into stark relief. In the early nineteenth century, the passion for chasing capital gains in real estate – which is a founding feature of a real estate mentality – was regulated by the material increases in the value of land. As people moved into an area, and the land market was established, the value of the unimproved formerly public land rose from around $1.70 to over $8.50 between 1800 and 1820 (Linklater, 2014: 220). Different interests for investing in land and real estate motivated the diverse range of individual investors in each location. Weaver (2003: 21) calls these locationally specific conditions "self-generated dynamics." They included internal migrants who were motivated to improve their economic conditions, for example, some "parents acquired land reserves for children" (p. 21). Others wanted to improve their social conditions, and viewed "populist land reforms" as a way to escape from poverty (p. 21). Land speculators were constantly jumping ahead of government surveys to scout for the best land and livestock grazers were on the lookout for new pastures (p. 21). The agrarian relations between migrating labour, capital, and land were modified through this process, as the migrants realised that the price of "unimproved" land could be quickly doubled by "improving" the land (e.g., by removing trees and turning the soil). It was this "capital gain, estimated at more than two thirds of a farmer's total capital stock, that provided the economic impetus for the furious rush into newly released public lands" (Linklater, 2014: 220).

The internal migratory practices that were simultaneously driving and producing land and real estate investments were always pushed beyond the imaginary boundaries of the nation state. The British and the United States, and later the Australian and other settler-colonial powers were all pursuing the same three-part *labour–capital–land* immigration strategy. It involved: (1) competing for immigrants to access their labour and capital (if they had any), (2) to use this labour and/or capital to develop their economies, and (3) to deploy "land in that cause" (Weaver, 2003: 215). George Sutherland (1898: 115) wrote in his pro-colonisation and British emigration thesis in 1898, "South Australia was funded, inasmuch as, according to that statute, the funds raised by the sale of land were to be expended in promoting the emigration of

British subjects only" (Sutherland, 1898: 115). Thus, the relational difference between settler-colonial sites – for example, comparing one colonial site to another to determine which country to invest your (foreign) capital and labour in – became an important driver of immigration. The transportation technologies of the industrial revolution were put to work in the service of this trans-settler-society and then internal *labour-capital-land* immigration strategy. The early nineteenth-century marine steam engine-powered "steamers" transported the goods produced in the settler-colonies (e.g., cotton, wool, or wheat) in one direction, and immigrants in the other (Linklater, 2014: 275; Sutherland, 1898: 123; Weaver, 2003), making them trans-settler-society technologies of labour, capital, and land. In inter-settler-societies, as the railways were built they increasingly rattled to the familiar sound of incoming and outgoing immigrants and goods (Linklater, 2014: 274). Then the trans-settler-society and inter-settler-society transportation technologies were integrated. Companies such as the famous *Kansas Pacific Railroad* packaged streamer and railway tickets that allowed migrants to travel from Britain and Germany to Kansas and Nebraska by sea and rail (Linklater, 2014: 274; Petrowski, 1969).

James Belich's (2009: 265–267) history of the *Rise of the Anglo-World* is compelling in this respect, drawing explicit links over an extended period between migrating labour and capital to buy land. For example, when a convict was freed from their ownership by a colonial power they were, as Belich puts it, "boom-prone" (p. 266). He writes, "Land buying and selling was another major urban activity, Sydney suffered from 'land mania'. ... Melbourne was worst. One speculator bought a town lot for £150 in 1836, sold it for £9,280 in 1839" (p. 267). Collectively, the migrants (convicts and free settlers alike) were viewed by the colonial powers as a ready supply of labour for each new settlement, labour that would soon be translated into capital that could be used to boost the local economy. The settler-colonial government in Australia was, therefore, willing to pay the outstanding transport fees for the "landless labourers" who had secured an "assisted passage" from Scotland to Tasmania in the mid-nineteenth century and came ashore with only the belongings they could carry with them (Linklater, 2014: 275). Belich (2009: 58) estimates that between the 1815 and 1930 around twelve million English, Scots, and Welsh emigrated permanently to North America, Australia, and South Africa. Many of these arrivals were young, which, in terms of labour capacity and "supply," proved to be an advantage for a new colony. Linklater (2014: 275) cites a Melbourne newspaper article from 1845 as stating, "There are no old people, and not many even who are advanced enough to come within the denomination of middle-age."

Earlier, in 1888, Simpson Newland (1888: 3), an early South Australian land sales analyst, perhaps even a land sales *provocateur*, set about comparing the "Different Land Systems" of the Australian states of South Australia,

New South Wales, Queensland, Victoria, with those of Canada, New Zealand, and the United States. His aim was to encourage the local authorities to lower their land transaction costs and streamline their land allocation processes so as to better complete with other Australian states and foreign countries for the limited supply of globally mobile immigrant labour and capital (Weaver, 2003: 219). He writes humorously, "Having toasted ourselves drunk with elation and self-congratulation, let us digest a little of the bread of humiliation and mentally enquire the results lately of our attempts to utilise the public estate by permanent settlement and increase of population" (Newland, 1888: 4). George Sutherland (1898: 211) instructed soon after, in 1898, that the "working capital of the colonists" should be directed back into the "enterprises" and infrastructure of the settler-colonists' newly "adopted country." "About ten millions sterling has been raised in South Australia by the sale of land," proclaimed Sutherland (1898: 211), "and the great bulk of this capital … has been spent in making roads, bridges, and other public improvements, besides promoting emigration upon which, at one time, the prosperity of the colony depended." Newland (1888: 4) makes reference to the challenges of securing "title," before the government guaranteed Torrens Title (Butt, 2010), a technology that revolutionised the legality of land title that was somewhat ironically born in South Australia in 1849. Over 20 states in the United States would adopt the Torrens Title system by the early twentieth century (Weaver, 2003: 107).

The sale of land was a trans-settler-society practice long before Torrens Title was introduced. Soon after the founding of the colony in South Australia, and with disappointing investment in smallholdings (i.e., small plots of land), "aimed to attract people with capital," the government permitted investors to buy larger plots of 4,000 and 20,000 acres (Weaver, 2003: 220). These land sales were negotiated in metropolitan centres, close to trans-settler-society communication networks and often far removed from the land to which the sales activity referred. Indeed, as George Sutherland (1898: 211) noted in 1898, the urban centres were where the land auction happened; "City land booms have always been a snare of the people of the Australian colonies. Sydney, Melbourne, and Adelaide have been each in its turn badly smitten by the mania for gambling in building allotments." Land orders were sold in London by supporters of the "South Australian scheme (1836) and the directors of the New Zealand Company (1839)" (Weaver, 2003: 220).

CITIZENSHIP: CULTIVATING THE REAL ESTATE CITIZEN

The vignettes in this chapter demonstrate the foundational importance of the organising technic of the nation state. This form of politico-territorial organisation allowed the settler body and then the citizen body to become a technology of colonial and then nation state power. If a colonial and then the nation state did not have the human or financial capital it desired, it simply migrated it in from Europe. Put in the service of the colony or nation state, these bodies were later assembled with banking practices and land and real estate mentalities to build the Great American and Great Australian Dreams. Free market, private property, and libertarianist mentalities, as we shall see in Chapters 6 and 7, would eventually be written into the textual and digital codes of the new print and digital technologies that increasingly enframe the citizenries of twenty- and twenty-first-century settler-societies.

Chapter 6

Technologies of Real Estate II
Policy, Books, Visas, Events

POLICY: CREATING THE HOUSING CONSUMER

Ruth Schwartz Cowan's (1976: 4) study of what happened to middle class American women, when the technologies with which they undertook their everyday household work changed, captures at the intimate level of the female body the rise of the industrial home during the twentieth century. "When we think about the interaction between technology and society, we tend to think in fairly grandiose terms," writes Schwartz Cowan (1976: 1). However, she concludes that "these grand visions have blinded us to an important and rather peculiar technological revolution which has been right under our noses: the technological revolution in the home" (p. 1). Mass-produced consumer goods for the industrial home to which she refers include hot water heaters, irons, washing machines, gas stoves, and later radios, automobiles and refrigerators, and then televisions. Advertisements for electric irons first started to appear in magazines targeting the "women market," such as the *Ladies' Home Journal*, after the First World War. In the decade between 1919 and 1929, the automobile industry employed over 425,000 workers, produced, and sold more than twenty-three million vehicles, and "sustained a distribution and service organisation with sales of almost five billion dollars" (Linklater, 2014: 248–249). Ford Motor Company employees are a well-known example of the industrial body (Galster, 2012), and a survey of workers indicated that in 1929, 98 per cent of these employees owned an electric iron and 49 per cent owned a mechanical washing machine (Schwartz Cowan, 1976: 5).

The industrial home, much like settler-colonial landed property before it and foreign real estate investment after it, was set to become an economic engine that governments could use to bolster (or prop up at times of crisis) their economy (Adam, 1931; Dufty-Jones and Rogers, 2015; Ley, 2015;

Weaver, 2003). The changing economy of hygiene in the 1920s' bathroom reveals how the human body is implicated in the rise of the property-owning democracy. Prior to the First World War, bathroom fixtures, such as bathtubs, sinks, and toilets, were custom- and hand-made out of porcelain for each dwelling (Pile, 2005; Schwartz Cowan, 1976). After the war, the bathroom industry was industrialised, and bathtubs, sinks, and toilets were mass-produced out of cast iron enamelware (Schwartz Cowan, 1976: 6). Schwartz Cowan (1976: 6) puts the dollar value of enamelled sanitary fixtures between 1915 and 1921 at US$2.4 million. However, as the industrial machinery kicked into gear, just 2 years later that figure had doubled US$4.8 million and had increased again to US$5.1 million by 1925. Soon after, the "discovery" of the "household germ led to almost fetishist concern about cleanliness of the home," and a new suite of industrial products and technologies were developed to keeping the home free of germs (Schwartz Cowan, 1976: 14). Surprisingly – or not – introducing new technologies into the home, such as the misleadingly named "labour-saving devices," did not mean women would do less work, contrary to popular belief (Watson, 1988). The time spent on some jobs did decrease, but new technologies and tasks were created to take their place (Schwartz Cowan, 1976: 14).

The significance of these "labour-saving devices" for the economics of the industrial *home* and *body* is not located in their intrinsic value as labour-saving technological objects, but rather as a suite of consumer goods that could be mobilised within the new housing-focused consumer economy. The industrial-scale manufacture of furniture, automobiles, refrigerators, washing machines, and vacuum cleaners honed in on the increasing buying power of the new real estate citizens (Ferguson, 2008; Schwartz Cowan, 1976; Watson, 1988). The production of refrigerators grew from 315,000 units in 1919 to 1.7 million in 1929, and in the same period, the number of radios in use increased to seven million (Linklater, 2014: 248–249). The economy that was created around the industrial home and the new industrial citizen on either side of the Great Depression shaped real estate and home-owning mentalities for the rest of the century.

The importance of the industrial body and home became evident when the Great Depression hit and the construction industry collapsed, revealing "the extent to which the wider US economy relied on residential investment as an engine of growth" (Ferguson, 2008: 243). The effects were inscribed deeply into the industrial *body* and *home* in cities such as Detroit (Galster, 2012), where in 1929 the automobile industry cut the workforce by half, and then cut the remaining employees' pay by half (Ferguson, 2008: 243). The US president Franklin D. Roosevelt responded with The New Deal (Olson, 1998). The mortgage and bank-lending changes (most significantly the creation of the new Federal National Mortgage Association, i.e., Fannie Mae) resulted in the government effectively underwriting the mortgage market from the 1930s (Shiller, 2008; Olson, 1998). These types of government programmes have subjective implications for the citizenry. After graduating from Yale University with an MBA degree at the turn of the twentieth century, James Truslow Adams (1931) went into investment banking before, in his 1931 classic *The Epic of America*, defining this historical moment with the aphorism "The American Dream." According to Ferguson's (2008: 250) analysis, the changes that are often attached to this aphorism would go on to become a major contributor to the significant increase in property ownership in the United States after the Second World War, pushing the home-ownership rate up from 40 per cent to 60 per cent by 1960 (also see Cohen, 2004; Linklater, 2014).

In Australia, the then Prime Minister Sir Robert Menzies (1942: 1) responded a short time after Roosevelt with a raft of economic and social policies that were firmly aimed at the subjectivity of middle class Australians, which he called "The Forgotten People" and "the backbone of this country." The implicit aim was to construct the Great Australian Dream mentality around home-ownership. Certainly, there are the much-discussed political drivers of the Great Australian and American Dreams, including the various housing and economic policy responses of successive governments in the United States and Australia (see: Adam, 1931; Cullen, 2004; Dufty-Jones and Rogers, 2015; Kemeny, 1983; Patterson Forrester, 1994; Paris, 1993). These included various public housing programmes, home-loan and thrift savings associations, national level financial loan and insurance schemes, and new taxation settings that encouraged and supported home ownership over other tenure forms (see, e.g.:Bourassa et al., 1995; Dufty-Jones and Rogers, 2015; Hulse and Burke, 2015; Kemeny, 1983; McCabe, 2016; Paris, 1993; Steele and Gleeson, 2011). There was also the discursive driver that was firmly aimed at the subjectivity of the Australian population, well at least a largely white colonial image of the Australian citizenry (Porter, 2010). Menzies' discursive work was aimed at the subjective bodies of "everyday" Australians:

> I do not believe that the real life of this nation ... is to be found in the homes of people who are nameless and unadvertised. ... The home is the foundation of sanity and sobriety; it is the indispensable condition of continuity; its health determines the health of society as a whole. ... The material home represents the concrete expression of the habits of frugality and saving "for a home of our own." Your advanced socialist may rage against private property even while he acquires it; but one of the best instincts in us is that which induces us to have one little piece of earth with a house and a garden which is ours: to which we can withdraw, in which we can be among our friends, into which no stranger may come against our will. (Menzies, 1942)

Earlier in the United States, President Warren Harding also laid out the importance of linking up the industrial *body* and *home*, a discursive tactic that would dominate political rhetoric about home-ownership in the last half of the twentieth century. In a letter to the chairperson of the Better Homes Campaign in 1922 written on behalf of Harding, the ghost-writer

> regards the campaign as of particular importance, because it places emphasis not only upon home ownership, which he regards as absolutely elemental in the development of the best citizenship, but upon furnishing, sanitation and equipment of the home … the home is their industrial centre as well as their place of abode, and it is felt that altogether too little attention has been paid to lightening the labours and bettering the working conditions of these women. (Harding, 1922, p. 1)

Susan Smith (2008: 521) conceptualises the home as a hybrid of mobile capital, physical materials, and subjective lived experiences, and this is a useful schema for conceptualising how "real estate dream" discourses entangle the flow of cash, the materiality of real estate, and the more subjective use values of home as a political strategy. In 1985, President Ronald Reagan (1985) invoked the "dream" metaphor again, proclaiming to the American citizenry that "the American dream belongs to you … deductions central to American values, will be maintained. The mortgage interest deduction on your home would be fully retained." It was a commitment that cost the US Treasury $76 billion (Ferguson, 2008: 253). According to consecutive Prime Ministers and Presidents in settler-societies, the home should be activated as the site of economic activity, which includes purchasing the home and then fitting it out, as Harding instructs, with "furnishings" and "equipment." On the surface, at least in the United States, this was a political strategy that was initially intended to attract the votes of newly enfranchised women (Linklater, 2014: 248–249). At a more subjective level, this collective enterprise of home making was constructed and promoted as an act of citizen- and nation-building in settler-societies across the Atlantic and Pacific oceans. After the Second World War, successive governments in Australia and the United States (as elsewhere) set about cultivating the real estate citizen to restart or augment their economies. The trans-settler-society migration of human and financial capital diversified from the colonial European migration patterns of the seventeenth and eighteenth centuries, as soldiers returned from war with little capital to spend on housing. Immigration continued, albeit often with a familiar colonial discriminatory thrust (see Chapter 5). Two interrelated post-war "booms" were about to hit – the baby boom and the property-owning boom. Biology drove the first (Kline, 2001). Post-war economic growth, public policy, and discourses about citizen- and nation-building drove the second (Mankiw and Weil, 1989).

In the United States, at the end of the Second World War, about half of all Americans owned their homes outright or were paying them off with bank-assisted finance (Ferguson, 2008: 231–282; Linklater, 2014: 359–360). By 1975, a short three decades later, that figure had increased to almost two thirds of all Americans. Australia's home-ownership rates also expanded rapidly after the Second World War, increasing from a little less than 50 per cent of all Australians owing their homes outright or paying them off in the late 1940s up to around 70 per cent in the 1960s (Bourassa et al., 1995). Compare this to, for example, the home-ownership rates for the Sydney metropolitan area that were recorded in the 1911 census, just before the First World War. The home-ownership rate was reported as being 31 per cent (Bourassa et al., 1995; Jackson, 1970). Jackson (1970; cited by Bourassa et al., 1995) estimates that this figure probably rose from 28 per cent in 1891 (see Table 6.1). In 1912, "the search for new ways of encouraging and spreading owner occupancy led the New South Wales government to amend the legislation governing its Savings Bank, allowing it to advance loans for house purchase. Similar legislation was also enacted in the other states. This initiative led to a rapid increase in the numbers buying their own homes in Sydney" (Bourassa et al., 1995: 85). Two World Wars and the Great Depression created shortages in not only human and financial capital, but also in the building materials and the labour supply needed to construct the new homes. These factors were compounded by the post-war "baby boom" that was driving high rates of new household formation and inadequate or substandard housing stock in Australian cities.

In his seminal work, *The Great Australian Nightmare: A Critique of the Home-Ownership Ideology*, Jim Kemeny (1983) argues that housing policy in Australia in the 20 years after the Second World War was "aggressively interventionist, and has been marked by extremely high levels of public expenditure on private housing" (p. 22). Kemeny (1983: 117) argues that there "is nothing 'natural' about Australia's high home-ownership rate." Instead, it was achieved "by means of heavily interventionist policies pursued by a supposedly laissez-faire conservative government" (p. 117) that was "aimed at subsidising the expansion of the owner-occupied market" (p. 16).

Table 6.1 Homeowners and Public Renters in Australia: As a Percentage of Occupied Dwellings during the Twentieth Century

Tenure Type	1911	1921	1933	1947	1954	1961
Owner/Purchaser	49.4	52.4	52.6	53.4	63.3	70.3
Government Tenant	n.a.	n.a.	n.a.	n.a.	4.3	4.2

Tenure Type	1971	1981	1991	2001	2006
Owner/Purchaser	68.8	70.1	68.9	69.5	68.8
Government Tenant	5.6	5.1	5.7	5.0	4.9

Sources: Bourassa (1995: 85); Hayden (2014); Jackson (1970); Australian Bureau of Statistics (2010; 2012).

There is disagreement about the significance of housing policy as a driver of the increasing home-ownership rates in the second half of the twentieth century, and many housing scholars do not share Kemeny's dystopian narrative about interventionist governments and the promotion of the property-owning citizenry as the principle driver for the rising home-ownership rates (Bourassa et al., 1995). Certainly there were other forces at play in Australia during this period, including a severe shortage of housing in the post-war period, the effects of rent control policies on the construction of new rental stock, limited housing tenure choice, and high rates of owner-building, among other factors (Bourassa et al., 1995; Dufty-Jones and Rogers, 2015). Economic growth, argues Chris Paris (1993: 46), was "driving ... improved housing provision in the 1950s and 60s," and it has been "overlooked in many discussions of Australian housing, which have emphasised the role of government policies." These statistics appear to show a relatively stable public housing population of between 4 and 6 per cent from the 1950s into the early twenty-first century. This was alongside a gradual increase in home-ownership from around 50 per cent in the early twentieth century up to around 70 per cent by mid-century, which then remained relatively stable well into the early twenty-first century. However, these statistics obscure some fundamental changes within the two housing tenure groups, namely the increasingly residualised nature of the public housing stock (Darcy, 2012; Darcy and Rogers, 2014, 2015; Rogers, 2014) and the steady decline of young first homebuyers from around the mid-1980s (Haylen, 2014; Taylor and Dalton, 2015). By 2012, the level of home-ownership was graduating by age. For example, close to 85 per cent of people who are aged 75 own their home outright, less than 3 per cent have a mortgage, and less than 10 per cent are renting (Australian Bureau of Statistics, 2012). About half of those aged between 25 and 34 are buying a home. Only 22 per cent own of those aged 15-24 are buying a home, with the remaining roughly 75 per cent renting (Australian Bureau of Statistics, 2012). Therefore, the children of so-called baby boomers are not purchasing housing at the same age as their parents, and they will not have the same housing fortunes (Dufty-Jones and Rogers, 2015).

In the state of New South Wales in Australia, Hayden (2014: 14) argues that there will be significant long-term wealth accumulation implications from the declining access to affordable housing in Australian cities. The proportion of Australian households that owned an investment property rose from 8 per cent in the 1990s up to 17 per cent in 2005 (Dufty-Jones and Rogers, 2015: 7 citing Kohler and Rossiter, 2005). The so-called baby boomer households, that is households that are headed by people who were born from 1945 to 1960 and entered middle age around the turn of the century, were able to become homeowners "most likely in the 1970s or 1980s and no later than the 1990s" and now "have the greatest holdings of all forms of wealth" (Haylen, 2014: 14). In other words, owner-occupiers in New South Wales "not only own all of the owner-occupied housing wealth, they also own most of the wealth in investment housing and most non-housing wealth," and the households that did not get into the home-ownership market during this period "have relatively little wealth of any sort," argues Hayden (2014: 14).

What is invisible in these statistics is the way that post-war housing and economic policy, economic growth, suburban consumerism through the industrial home, and capital growth in real estate worked on the body of the real estate citizen throughout the twentieth century. The citizen-building occurred, argues Lizabeth Cohen (2004), within what she calls the "Consumer Republic." And as if to confirm that the project of subjectification (Deleuze, 1986/2012, 1991; Deleuze and Guattari, 2004; Foucault, 2011; Simondon, 2006) was solidifying in the United States, President Bill Clinton (1995) proclaimed in 1995, first with a targeted statement aimed at the individual, "By the time your children start first grade, we want you to be able to own your own home" (p. 808), and then with a more universal statement about the collective mentality of the polity:

> All of our country will reap enormous benefits if we achieve this. ... Home-ownership encourages savings and investment. When a family buys a home, the ripple effect is enormous. It means new homeowner customers. They need more durable goods, like washers and dryers, refrigerators and water heaters. And if more families could buy new homes or older homes, more hammers will be pounding, more saws will be buzzing. Homebuilders and home fixers will be put to work. When we boost the number of homeowners in our country, we strengthen our economy, create jobs, build up the middle class, and build better citizens. (p. 808)

At the beginning of the twentieth century, when President Harding was dreaming up a consumer economy that could be built around the industrial *body* and *home*, he could hardly have imagined that by the end of the century the vast consumer economy would account for about 70 per cent of the gross domestic product of the United States (Linklater, 2014: 248–249). Of course, the economic machinery of mass production and consumption has a lineage back to Uncle Sam's factories that supplied the machinery and technologies of war, but these factories were repurposed to produce cars and appliances for sale to the new real estate citizenry (Cohen, 2004: 236). Cohen (2004: 236) shows that the discourse that developed towards the end of the war, which proclaimed that *mass consumption was a personal indulgence*, was quickly reformulated after the war into a discourse of *mass consumption being a matter of national civic responsibility* (i.e., an individual responsibility to the state and your fellow citizenry). A surprisingly diverse wide range of actors took up this utopian discourse, including business leaders, labour unions, government agencies, and the mass media, among others. The new post-war order within the Consumer Republic demanded, writes Cohen (2004: 237), "that the good customer devoted to 'more, newer, and better' was in fact the good citizen, responsible for making the United States a more desirable place for all its people," and it was built on the old rational idea that settler-societies move forward to "betterment" (Crabtree, 2013). In Australia and the United States, the utopian idea that private housing consumption would somehow lead to broader public benefits was misguided. Far from all of America *reaping enormous benefits* from the new real estate economy, as Clinton (1995: 808) announced in 1995, by the end of the century there were very clear winners and losers. If we permit Kemeny (1983) the poetic licence to label the Australian case of building the Great Australian Dream at the end of the twentieth century "The Great Australian Nightmare," then it would be comparatively appropriate to call the American case of building the property-owning democracy, at least in cultural terms, a real estate abomination. Take, for example, this statement by a neighbour of the first black family to move into Levittown, Pennsylvania, in 1957, as told here by a *Life Magazine* reporter, "He's probably a nice guy, but every time I look at him I see $2000 drop off the value of my house … the evening after Myers installed his family, an angry crowd gathered before their homes. Teen-agers began throwing stones and when they broke two windows police dispersed the crowd" (*Life Magazine*, 1957: 43). The twentieth-century white settler body was still claiming and defending land with violence in this settler-society (Porter, 2010).

This vignette demonstrates that the promise, that social and economic equality could be achieved through the real estate and consumer market in Australia and the United States, failed as a real estate consumer strategy in the twentieth century. By deploying the consumer home and body, so market-centric logic went, there was little need for progressive government intervention to redistribute existing wealth or to proactively address real estate, economic, and racial discrimination (Cohen, 2004: 237). As we now know, not everyone benefitted from the real estate technologies of the twentieth century, such as the increasing access to housing finance and mortgages, beneficial taxation settings, and the mass-produced housing consumer products (Dufty-Jones and Rogers, 2015; Ferguson, 2008). For example, men fared better than women, whites further subordinated blacks, and middle class Americans consolidated their position over the working class (Cohen, 2004: 237; Ferguson, 2008; Watson, 1988). Not only does government policy discriminate against some minority groups (Bennett et al., 2006), the intermediaries of real estate sales, bank loans and mortgages, and consumer goods also discriminate. The economic advantages that can be realised from real estate are stratifying, along racial and other lines. For example, the United States government policy setting of "red-lining" (Ferguson, 2008) segmented the real estate market into distinctive submarkets in pursuit of greater profits. After the 1960s, real estate intermediaries and government policy settings created distinct submarkets that were organised under categories such as race, ethnicity, gender, class, age, and lifestyle (Cohen, 2004: 238). "A metropolitan landscape emerged where whole communities were increasingly being stratified along class and racial lines. As home, particularly a new one, in the Consumers Republic became a commodity to be traded up, 'property values' became the new mantra" (Cohen, 2004: 237). Property values, neighbourhood prestige, and racial profiling combined – not least because white Americans more easily qualified for mortgages than African Americans – and along with it came the geographical profiling of suburbs and cities (Wacquant, 2008). Many white families took fright (i.e., white flight) from the cities with growing African American populations (Kruse, 2007). They felt, argues Cohen (2004: 237), that building white-only neighbourhoods was the best way to protect their investment, which in many cases represented their entire life savings, as settlers "they did everything within their means to restrict blacks' access to real estate."

BOOKS: REAL ESTATE TECHNOLOGY 1.0

James Kirby (2002) jokes in his financial self-help book *Investing for Dummies*, "In Australia … property is like a game and is followed like the footy." As a speech act, this is a profoundly revealing statement about Australians' obsession with real estate, linking the idea of real estate investment with a masculine and white notion of European-inspired sporting culture. Popular real estate investment books and the local and then global real estate magazines that followed from around the 2000s provide a good illustration of how a mediating technology might come to inculcate particular real estate mentalities across different class and generational boundaries. Of course, there are many other sociocultural, political, economic, and geopolitical processes that intersect, cross over, cut through, and bypass these real estate education manuscripts. However, the discursive tactics employed within these "wealth creation" manuscripts resemble the tactics that are being redeployed in the contemporary global real estate industry that I discuss in the next chapter, and so they are worth exploring in some detail here.

Kirby's book is part of a broader corpus of wealth creation books that began to emerge in the mid-twentieth century. By the end of the century, the publication of wealth creation books had become an industry in its own right. However, the timing of the rise of the wealth creation book is historically important, because their rise is located within particular post-war citizen and national-building exercises that framed the property-owning democracies discussed above. The home-owning or real estate investor baby boomers were born between 1945 and 1960 and were between 30 and 55 years old throughout the 1990s. This places many of them either in the midst of buying their first house or seeking to redeploy the capital that they had accrued from the purchase of their first home to buy a second (or more) investment property. They had also lived through a period of Australian history where the nation and what it meant to be an Australian was in a geopolitical state of cultural contention. Some geopolitical actors wanted desperately to pin the ideas about nationhood and citizenship down. The first Minister for Immigration, Arthur Calwell, famously coined the term "New Australians" to describe the European refugees who were travelling to Australia from their war-torn homelands in search of a new life. While Calwell argued that Australia needed to "populate or perish" (Calwell, 1947), his vision certainly did not include everyone (Robertson, 2013). Calwell was a staunch advocate of the White Australia Policy, and neither he nor the government of the time entertained the idea that the land might belong to Indigenous peoples. In 1947, he stated, "We have twenty-five years at most to populate this country before the yellow races are down on us" (Calwell, 1947). Calwell tapped into a long-standing cultural narrative about an Asian invasion that can be traced back to the hostility directed towards Chinese miners on the gold fields (see, e.g., the violence of the Lambing Flat riot in 1861 in Clarke, 2002: 67). Calwell even deported Malayan, Indochinese, and Chinese wartime refugees back to their "homelands," a problematic endeavour given that some of them had married Australian citizens and started families in Australia. Therefore, it seems a long way from this Calwellian era to a statement by Dominique Grubisa (2014a), the author of a 2015 global real estate investment self-help book, where she claims, "Having made her fortune in Australian real estate" (p. ii) – that is, "having bought, sold and held over $50M AUD worth of property over the last 10 years" (p. ii) – "she is passionate about enabling average Australians to become financially free and … bringing her knowledge, skills and teachings to the Asian market so that others can benefit from the enormous wealth to be made in the Australian property market" (Grubisa, 2014a: ii).

Indeed, a lot of geopolitical manoeuvring had taken place in the Asia-Pacific region in the 60 years between 1945 and 2015, but rarely did real estate become a prominent feature of the discussion. The rise in Japanese investment in Australian real estate in the 1980s (Hajdu, 2005) and the rise in Chinese investment from 2009 are two key exceptions (Rogers et al., 2015). Within the context of the changing geopolitical landscape in the Asia-Pacific, Kirby and Grubisa's narratives about real estate investment mentalities differ in one important respect for this discussion. Kirby's discourse is firmly bound by nation state discourses and links real estate investment mentalities to a perverse construction of Australian national identity. Grubisa's discourse lets go off Kirby's nation state–centrism and links Australian real estate investment mentalities to the new global real estate investor body; in this case, the Asian market she is referring to is largely the rapidly growing Chinese market. Notwithstanding these two "Asian" foreign real estate investment events noted above, within the long history of the geopolitics of real estate, the middle to latter part of the twentieth century was a period when the physical and cultural borders of settler-societies like Australia were closing in, firming up, and the flow of people was being more rigorously regulated by government policy (Robertson, 2013). We expect that the discursive construction of the narratives about "how to make money through real estate" in the self-help books to stick quite tightly to the social, cultural, and geopolitical historical contexts within which they were written. But what is fascinating about these books – and the global real estate investment magazines I discuss below – is that they deploy a common set of real estate investment discursive tactics from 1990 to 2015, despite the changing social, cultural, political, and geopolitical contexts. In other words, what real estate investment life-coaches teach people *to do* remain largely the same, the real estate mentality is similar, but the real estate and investors *they target* change according to the prevailing social, cultural, political, and geopolitical contexts. It is not a coincidence that a new collection of the real estate financial self-help manuscripts "appeared" on Australian bookshelves throughout the 1990s at the very moment the baby boomers were entering middle age. The books were produced at a time when building the Great Australian Dream seemed to be working. As noted above, creating an Australian real estate investor mentality, that is, the Great Australian Dream, was a central concern of the Australian government following the Second World War. The Australian government had assisted this real estate mentality to develop, in part, through their targeted taxation concessions and other housing subsidies (Dufty-Jones and Rogers, 2015; Hulse and Burke, 2015). However, the government was not the sole intermediary of these real estate ideals. Prior to the significant uptake of Internet systems by the real estate industries (Rogers, 2016b), these taxation and housing policy programmes were circulated and promoted through other diverse technological forms covering public policy, the media, and the mediating technology I am interested in here, the popular self-help financial books (Rogers, 2016a).

By the mid-1990s, books by Paul Clitheroe (1995; 1998) and Noel Whittaker (1995) were national bestsellers. Whittaker (1995: vii) writes with a financial hubris that continues throughout his book, "In March 1987 5,000 copies of *Making Money Made Simple* rolled off the printing press ... over 500,000 copies have now been sold and the local editions of the book are best-sellers in New Zealand and South Africa." Clitheroe (1995; 1998) and Whittaker's (1995)[1] books are two of the more popular real estate investment manuscripts from 1990s Australia, and they share a common discursive tactic that is directly aimed at the subjectivity of the reader. Clitheroe (1995: 163) opens his section on "Investing in property" by stating, "When Australians think investment, many think property, particularly residential property." Whittaker's (1995: 28) section on "The nature of real estate" opens with, "Real estate is one of the three major areas where the bulk of your money can be invested, so it follows that a sound working knowledge of real estate is ESSENTIAL for anybody who is serious about becoming wealthy" (Whittaker's emphasis). In terms of discursive content, both books focus on a now familiar set of real estate terminologies: (1) taxation rules (e.g., capital gains and sales taxes); (2) capital costs (e.g., buying costs including taxes); (3) growth (e.g., capital gain); (4) yield (e.g., rental income); (5) transaction costs (e.g., sales costs including taxes); (6) capital lending practices (e.g., bank loans); and (7) market profiling (e.g., location, growth, yield, taxation, and transaction cost matrices).

This discursive tactic has surprising similarities with the new suite of twenty-first-century embodied and digital mediating technologies discussed in the next chapter, with some important exceptions. The most important exception is the vastly different "scale" of the investment. In the second half of the twentieth century, a middle class Australian investor reading a self-help book was instructed to invest in "local" real estate, and the next suburb from where the investor lived was recommended by Clitheroe (1998). We see this tradition continue in the fascinating contemporary wealth creation books of the Australian real estate self-help educator Stuart Zadel (2014). His 2014 book, *The New Way to Make Money in Property Fast!* includes a chapter by Dominique Grubisa, the global real estate educator mentioned earlier. In a discursive move that would have Rene Descartes (1644) turning in his grave, Zadel switches the *body*, from the old philosophical mind-body dualism problem, with *money* to create the "mind-money connection" (Zadel, 2014: 11–30). And if you need more proof that his objective here is to put his book to work on the subjective body of the future real estate investor, he writes that to develop the "mind-money connection" you need to think about:

> What creates your mindset? ... The ultimate influence on your mindset, and therefore your behaviour and results – is your **conditioning**. Conditioning refers broadly to what you have been brought up to think and believe about the world you live in and yourself" (p. 21) ... "**Values** – Everyone has a hierarchy of Values. When it comes to finances, you will recognise your values by how you earn your money, how much of it you have and what you do with it. **Beliefs** ... some limiting beliefs might be: The money supply is limited. For me to get more, others have to go without; Money is the root of all evil ... Some empowering beliefs might be: money is abundant. The more I create the more there is to share; the *lack* of money is the root of all evil. (p. 22)

Zadel's (2014) project is explicitly directed towards creating a real estate mentality, and he has given away over 450,000 books for free. Within these books he seduces the would-be real estate investor with lines such as, "Does it surprise you to hear that the Tax Office can give *you* a refund for *creating wealth* through property?" (p. 6, emphasis added by the author). Therefore, the idea that middle class Australians in the second half of the twentieth century unilaterally discovered "how to get rich through real estate" wholly underplays the role of the intermediaries, such as government departments, various financial, taxation and real estate professionals, the media, and bestselling life-coach authors such as Clitheroe and Whittaker, and their contemporary protégés like Zadel and Grubisa. It grants too much agency to individual investors and gives too little credit to the other actors and technologies for inculcating investors with private property and real estate mentalities. Furthermore, Clitheroe, Whittaker, Zadel, and Grubisa seem to believe their own discourse, that, as Zadel (2014) puts it, they are the "masters" (p. 4) who have discovered, rather than being inculcated themselves, by the organising technics of real estate that makes up the information in their books (p. 4). "I encourage you to read it from cover to cover and to learn from the masters" (p. 4), instructs Zadel. More accurately, middle class Australians in the second half of the twentieth century had a set of real estate mentalities created for them when these intermediaries circulated specific real estate information through a range of pre-Internet technologies, such as housing and taxation policy, the media, self-help books and, in a more embodied process, as one Australian baby boomer real estate investor we interviewed for the *Global Real Estate Project* in 2014 put it, "talk'n about houses at dinner parties with friends." By the end of the twentieth century, five decades of continuous political, discursive, and financial debate about, and the practice of, domestic real estate investment in Australia had solidified the contemporary Australian aphorism – the Great Australian Dream. In the 1990s, this dream had become a collective mentality that was manifesting as an assumed right, perhaps even a duty to the settler-state, that Australians should own real estate. This mentality was implicitly underwritten by ideas around "improvement" and "betterment," and the assumption that life will be better if you own your own home. Indigenous notions of land were absent from the Great Australian Dream.

By comparison, the geopolitical landscape that frames the politics of Grubisa's book, which, as I noted earlier, is not insignificantly titled *Real Estate Riches Down Under: How to Make a Fortune Investing in the Australian Property Market* are varied. In terms of Australian political party politics and international relations, it can certainly be traced to a 1971 telegram from the then leader of the Australian opposition Labour party, Gough Whitlam, to the then Premier of the Republic of China, Zhou Enlai. The telegram reads,

"Australian Labour Party anxious to send delegation to Peoples Republic of China to discuss the terms on which your country is interested in having diplomatic and trade relations with Australia" (Freudenburg, 2013: 7). This telegram was sent at a turbulent geopolitical time. The next year, in 1972, Chairman Mao Tse-tung opened the door to United States president Richard Nixon and thereby signalled to the world a policy shift towards a more open China. Deng Xiaoping's 1978 Open Door policy was followed in the early 1980s with the Australian Hawke Labour government's *pro-Asia* geopolitical discourse (Hajdu, 2005), which coincided with the first twentieth-century wave of speculative Asian foreign real estate investment in Australia. That is, investment that was motivated by speculative real estate opportunities rather than being, for example, connected to more permanent migration practices, such as nineteenth-century Chinese migration during the gold rush (for a more detailed discussion about this geopolitics, see e.g., Hajdu [2005] for Australia and Ley [2011, 2015] for Canada today). In 1975, The Whitlam government established the Foreign Investment Advisory Committee, a predecessor to the FIRB, which Whitlam later reflected on by saying, "Real estate acquisitions would be disallowed unless made for the purpose of employee residence, use incidental to commercial ventures or for specific time period, after which they would be resold to Australian interests" (Whitlam, 1985: 220; cited by Hajdu, 2005: 175). Whitlam's cautious and targeted acceptance of foreign real estate acquisitions is vastly different to the more open acceptance of later Australian governments, and the subsequent foreign policy positions of the FIRB (Rogers et al., 2015). In the 1980s, the foreign investment practices of Japanese real estate investors gained considerable media attention. For example, in the early 1980s, one Australian media outlet was reporting, "Our Asianisation is gaining pace" (*The Sydney Morning Herald*, Robinson, 1983: 57) and by the late-1980s there were media reports about, "The new Asian invasion: how Australian property is being sold off" (*The Bulletin*, 29 September 1987, cited in Hajdu, 2005). In 1980s Australia, much like the early twenty-first century, some people believed that the rise in Asian investment in Australian real estate "was a prime cause of ... property inflation," which resulted in "increasing financial difficulties being faced by first home buyers" (Hajdu, 2005: 177). Hence, at several points between 1970s and the early twenty-first century, argues Hajdu (2005: 178), the "rise in anti-Asian sentiment was the last thing" the federal government wanted geopolitically when they were "trying to persuade the public that Australia's future lay with Asia."

This 1980s' geopolitical discourse was revived and referenced in the Australian Gillard government's 2012 *Australia in the Asian Century* white paper. In terms of geopolitics, a surprisingly consistent *pro-Asia* geopolitical discourse worked its way through the foreign policy positions of successive Australian federal governments, from both sides of politics, from the 1970s well into the early twenty-first century. Thus, it should not be surprising that one of the central tenets of the 2012 *Australia in the Asian Century* document was that "Asia is a changing world. ... The Asian Century is an Australian opportunity ... [and that] Within only a few years, Asia ... will also be home to the majority of the world's middle class" (Australian Government, 2012: 1). As the rise of the Four Asian Tigers and the BRICS countries demonstrates (Rogers et al., 2015; Rogers and Dufty-Jones, 2015), the expanding middle class from former, or even current, socialist states have strong commitments to private property real estate investments (Coase and Wang, 2013). What the Australian government failed to state in 2012, or indeed, perhaps even failed to comprehend, was that in many ways – and certainly with regard to housing – Australia was already in the Asian century and had been so for decades.

In July 2014, a broadsheet newspaper in Sydney captured the global up-scaling of the Great Australian Dream mentality with the headline, "In glamorous five star hotels across Singapore every weekend, property investors are lining up to buy a slice of the Australian dream" (Bagshaw, 2014: 1). As this headline shows, while the "dream" to invest in real estate is developing a degree of global universality, there has been a change in the geopolitics of the real estate transaction and the nationalities of those who are buying Australian real estate (Rogers et al., 2015). Similar to the second half of the twentieth century, real estate intermediaries were located right in the middle of these changing real estate practices and relations. In this case, they were global rather than trans-settler-society real estate professionals who were readily adapting their real estate practices. They added new discursive content to their established real estate discursive tactics in an attempt to target new markets and investor cohorts across different geographical and socio-economic scales. The practices of these global real estate professionals are captured in the pages of international foreign real estate investment magazines. In the Asia-Pacific this includes magazines such as: *Palace: Asia's Elite Property Showcase*; *Property Life: Asia's No1 Property & Lifestyle Guide*; and *Property Report: Luxury Real Estate, Architecture and Design*. These magazines assemble aspirational HNW consumer products and foreign investment data together in an attempt to shape, guide, and inform the foreign real estate mentalities and purchasing practices of HNW and UHNW individuals (Rogers, 2016a). For example, *Palace* magazine's Spring 2014 edition brought together advertisements for *Christofle* silver dinnerware and *Martell* cognac from France, *Zenith* watches from Switzerland, and *Jaguar* automobiles from the United Kingdom with a 16-page "Special Report" on "The allure of owning a property in one of Europe's major cities" (Kalkreuth, 2014: 45).

These Asian-based journalists and editors are using similar discursive tactics and real estate due diligence matrices to those used by Clitheroe and Whittaker in the 1990s, and Zidel in the 2000s. The difference is these new intermediaries are operating in a globalising real estate investment sphere and the publications are increasingly electronically networked into online media platforms to target different socio-economically stratified consumer groups (which I return to in Chapter 7). An Australian-Chinese sales agent working in Melbourne discussed this group as follows, "Several [of their] customers want to do this 188 immigration [Significant Investment Visa], but they're too scared that [the] Australian government will not approve their application, even though the application is quite up to the standard" (Interview: *Global Real Estate Project*). In terms of the foreign real estate investment magazines, the glossy Special Report in *Palace* magazine's Spring 2014 edition covers "foreign property ownership in Europe" by comparing Berlin, London, Madrid, Milan, Paris, and Rome (pp. 46–60). What is interesting about these magazines is the way the editors and journalists (i.e., the intermediaries) bring together the global real estate information. The discursive tactic in this Special Report creates a due diligence matrix to present the following discursive content: (1) foreign taxation rules (e.g., "Tax – Italy's property tax system, TASI, is prohibitive," p. 47); (2) capital costs (e.g., in London the "rate has slowed to 3.4 per cent for £10 million-plus homes," p. 46); (3) growth (e.g., "Since 2004 property prices have increased 58 per cent in Berlin," p. 50); (4) yield (e.g., "Parisian rental returns are still on the downside," p. 46); (5) transaction costs (e.g., in Italy, "40–50 per cent deposit of the property's purchase price is required upfront," p. 47); (6) liquidity (e.g., "more buyers are seeking a long-term lifestyle purchase rather than a short-term investment gain," p. 60); and (7) residency status (e.g., "Spain's new Golden Visa Scheme is also anticipated to boost demand from foreign nationals," p. 48).

On the latter point an emerging cohort of scholars are keen to shine an illuminating light on the intersection between foreign investment visas and real estate purchases (Johnson, 2014; Ley, 2015; Moos, 2010; Rogers, 2016a). Kit Johnson's (2014: 829) analysis of debates about immigration reform in the United States – including several proposals that would have granted residency status to foreign nationals on the condition that they purchase real estate in the United States – highlights what is at stake in these debates. While Johnson's analysis is too nation state–centric, he insightfully reflects that, "The 'American Dream' has long been used as a label for two different phenomena: owning one's own home and immigrating to the United States to seek freedom and opportunity. Intriguingly, the homebuyer visa implicates both" (Johnson, 2014: 830), and I turn to so-called real estate visas in the next section.

VISAS: GLOBAL REAL ESTATE CITIZENSHIP

Maurice LeFrak was a property developer in France throughout the second half of the nineteenth century, and he founded the LeFrak Organisation in 1883. His son, Aaron LeFrak, founded an American division of the organisation in

New York when he emigrated around 1901 (Strobel, 2008). In 1948, Maurice LeFrak's great-grandson, Samuel LeFrak, became the president of the LeFrak Organisation. Today, the LeFrak Organisation owns, develops, and manages residential and commercial real estate properties in numerous United States and United Kingdom cities. Samuel LeFrak's father, Harry, was a builder, and Samuel followed in his footsteps to become a builder, urban planner, and architect (Kelder, 1998; Strobel, 2008). In 1975, Samuel LeFrak's son, Richard LeFrak became the chairperson and CEO of the LeFrak Organisation, and by 2015 he was ranked 76 on the Forbes 400 rich list (Forbes, 2015). Clearly, the *body as real estate technology* is a central motif in the LeFrak family biography. However, in terms of the migratory *body*, there is much that separates Maurice from his great-great-grandson Richard.

Aaron LeFrak migrated to the United States just before 1907, when European immigration peaked at 1,285,349 persons entering the country. The borders had been porous for Europeans, but they would soon firm up with a suite of immigration changes, such as the *Emergency Quota Act* in 1921 and the *Immigration Act of 1924*. In 2009, a little over a century after Aaron immigrated to the United States, and at the tail end of the Global Financial Crisis, Richard LeFrak and market analyst Gary Shilling redeployed a familiar narrative about migration and real estate in a *Wall Street Journal* opinion editorial (op-ed) titled *Immigrants can help fix the housing bubble* (LeFrak and Shilling, 2009). Kit Johnson interviewed Gary Shelling in 2014 (Johnson, 2014: see fn. 36 on p. 837), who reported that LeFrak "had the initial idea. Shilling, for his part, researched the concept, compiled a white paper, and drafted their op-ed" (Johnson, 2014: 838). LeFrak's idea was simple; he wanted to "solve" the housing crisis that induced the Global Financial Crisis by drawing foreign capital and immigrant bodies into the repossessed housing stock by granting residency status to foreign real estate investors. Despite several reconfigurations and failed attempts to keep the idea afloat (e.g., see Senate Bill 744), LeFrak and Shilling's "buy-a-house-get-a-visa" idea eventually failed in the United States – leaving only the EB5 investor visa for foreign investors (Johnson, 2014: 842 and 846). The seemingly sarcastic response to LeFrak and Shilling's idea, from Shekhar Gupta, editor of *The Indian Express* newspaper in India, was perhaps, on reflection, a delicately veiled provocation:

> All you need to do is grant visas to two million Indians, Chinese and Koreans. We will buy up all the subprime homes. We will work 18 hours a day to pay for them. We will immediately improve your savings rate – no Indian bank today has more than 2 per cent nonperforming loans because not paying your mortgage is considered shameful here. And we will start new companies to create our own jobs and jobs for more Americans. (Friedman, 2009: 1)

LeFrak and Shilling's (2009) thinking was short term and firmly bounded in nation state terms, as you can read in quotes such as "Granting permanent resident status to foreigners who buy houses in this country will curtail a primary driver of the deepening recession and financial crises" (p. 1). Gupta was looking long term, and he also had in mind a more complete geopolitical picture. Gupta understood that the terms of the human and financial capital exchange were changing, radically, according to the prevailing geopolitical climate. Nevertheless, LeFrak and Shilling discursively constructed in their *New York Times* op-ed a desired "course of action" that was surprisingly familiar: move human and financial capital, and along with it the capacity to produce capital through labour, around the world in pursuit of economic growth and power. Free market capitalists should have welcomed their proposal, which positioned land and real estate, like any other form of "property," as a commodity to be traded on an open "global" property market. The right to freely own and trade property, as we are told by advocates for classical liberalism (Hoppe, 1993 [2006]; von Mises, 1912), "is an indisputable valid, absolute principle of ethics and the basis for continual 'optimal' economic progress" (Hoppe, 1993 [2006]: xi). However, there was something different about this transaction. Under the proposed visa scheme, the terms of exchange in the globalising real estate market included using the foreign capital to secure real estate *and* citizenship-like status, not unlike the early colonial days. LeFrak and Shilling's proposed visa would have directly linked residential real estate investment to citizenship-like status in a way that no other visa programme has fully achieved as yet. Unlike the earlier colonial movements of human and financial capital through land and real estate, these new movements of human and financial capital through "global" real estate markets ran into a problem when they hit the now firmly established and culturally mediated regulatory borders of the settler-nation states. This is because nation states regulate immigration (i.e., the movement of people) and foreign real estate sales (i.e., the movement of capital) via government policy (Ley, 2011, 2015; Tseng, 2000). Furthermore, global real estate professionals interpret and mediate these visa regimes between foreign real estate buyers and sellers according to the prevailing cultural and geopolitical landscape (Robertson and Rogers, in-press).

Ong (2005: 627) notes, "Nation-states seeking wealth-bearing and entrepreneurial immigrants do not hesitate to adjust immigration laws to favour elite migrant subjects, especially professionals and investors." Butler and Lees' (2006: 470) longitudinal study of local super-rich gentrifying elites in the City of London in the early 2000s was an early precursor to the opening up of London real estate to foreign investors that would soon follow. There are now visa programmes in many countries that foreign investors can use, either directly or indirectly, to purchase real estate, each giving them various pathways to "citizen-like" status, or eventually even a pathway to nationalisation in many countries around the world. For detailed case studies of countries that have businesses visas, many of which allow real estate purchases, see, for example, Ley (2015; 2011) and Rod Crider (2013) for Canada and the United States; Ramola Ramthohul (2015) for Mauritius; Jenena Džankić (2010) for Montenegro; Tseng (2000) for Taiwan; Rogers et al. (2015, 2015, 2016a) for Australia; Choon-piew Pow (2013) for Singapore; or Van Fossen (2007) for Pacific Island countries including Tonga, Samoa, the Marshall Islands, Vanuatu, and Nauru. There is also a growing body of scholarship on the relational geopolitics of "citizenship for real estate investment" visas across different continental spheres, which take in Europe, the Americas, the Asia-Pacific, and Africa – see, for example, Chris Paris (2011; 2013), Madeleine Sumption and Kate Hooper (2014), Jenena Džankić (2012), and Ayelet Shachar and Rainer Bauböck's (2014) collection of questions relating specifically to the European Union.

Each visa regime is different, mapping closely to the contemporary and historical migratory, cultural, geopolitical, and other features of each location. They also go by many names. One of the more recent names that taps into the rise in Chinese foreign real estate investment is the "Golden Visa" (Sumption and Hooper, 2013) or the "Golden Ticket" visa (Rogers et al., 2015: 10). In Australia in 2013, the global real estate company Knight Frank "created a special sales team specifically targeting wealthy Chinese investors following the introduction of the significant investment visa … the 888 visa – colloquially called the "Golden Ticket" visa – favours Chinese investors. [sic] (Property Observer, 2013: 1). The changing geopolitical landscape was clearly writing itself into these visa regimes, even including the auspicious use (吉利) of the number "eight" (八), which has special meaning in Chinese numerology because it sounds similar to the words meaning "prosper and wealth" (發). But arguably, the *pièce de résistance* for foreign real estate investors is Canada's *Business Immigration Programme* (BIP) "citizenship-by-investment" visa category (Ley, 2015: 5). David Ley shows that the BIP has been the key regulatory mechanism for bringing globally mobile HNWIs to the Vancouver housing market. "Business immigration was in principle a masterstroke," he concludes, "transferring embodied capital to the receiving country, conveying not just financial capital but also its enterprising creator" (Ley, 2015: 5). Australia's *Significant Investment Visa* (SVI) is more restrictive. Investors cannot use the visa programme to purchase residential dwellings, but the visa has been reimagined by the private financial management sector, who create special purpose investment vehicles in an attempt to allow foreign investors to use property trust purchases to meet the requirements of these visas (Rogers and Dufty-Jones, 2015: 232).

When it comes to the geopolitics of these visas, physical geography and cultural politics is important. For example, Australia and Canada are both settler-societies with very large landmasses and sizeable populations. Australia has a total area of 7,692,024 km^2 with a population of around 24,000,000 people. Canada has a total area of 9,984,670 km^2 with a population of around 36,000,000 people. Their different visa schemes, and resistance to them, run on similar geopolitical and economic divers and culturally driven critiques, often about "invading" Asian investors (Rogers et al., 2015). By comparison, Mauritius's suite of visa schemes (including the *Real Estate Scheme, Property Development Scheme*, and *Integrated Resort Scheme*) is mapped onto a vastly different physical geography and cultural politics. Mauritius has a total area of 2,040 km^2 with a population of around 1,250,000 people, and physical geography is often used in criticisms about the visa programme, although a range of culturally driven critiques are never far from the surface. Ramthohul (2015) argues that significant cultural "friction" exists between "local and elite migrants [as they] compete for scarce resources, especially land, on unequal terms" (p. 22). For many Mauritians, continues Ramthohul (2015: 18), the current friction over the allocation and ownership, and even the claiming of land via real estate visas touches an open nerve that stretches deep into the history of this settler-society, and the various colonial governance periods – Dutch Mauritius (1638–1710), French Mauritius (1715–1810), and British Mauritius (1810–1968). Ramthohul's (2015: 25) research shows that between 2009 and 2012, the foreign investors who accessed the *Real Estate Scheme* were from: France (47 per cent), South Africa (36 per cent), Mauritius (10 per cent), India (3 per cent), Great Britain (4 per cent). The data also show that the majority of the foreign investors of luxurious beach properties in Mauritius were European, followed closely by white South Africans. Yen-Fen Tseng (2000: 143) noted, quite astutely, that it is an empirical trap to only focus on the movement of financial "capital or trade flows." Tseng's work calls for a focus on "the persons who migrate with the capital" (i.e., the bodies), and I would add to Tseng's epistemological recalibration the need to focus on the global mediators who lubricate the flow of human and financial capital (Robertson, 2013; Robertson and Rogers, in-press). Consider the differences between the globally mobile real estate investor bodies that are moving through Mauritius, which I noted above, with the globally mobile real estate investor bodies that are moving through Canada via the BIP investment visa. Ley's (2015: 6; 2011) historical analyses show that BIP arrivals into Canada have been consistently dominated by Greater China. Drawing on work by Ware, Fortin, and Paradis (2010), Ley shows that between 1986 and 2008, 74 per cent of all foreign investors were Chinese. The driver, according to Ley (2015: 5), was geopolitical economic diversification; it was about moving "embodied capital" around the Asia-Pacific:

The background political economy included the attempt by Canadian governments to reboot a troubled regional economy through an infusion of activity from the growth region of Asia-Pacific. An important investment tool was a BIP, which welcomed capital and invited capitalists to transfer their entrepreneurial skills to Canada (p. 1). ... Permanent residence and later citizenship would be the reward for the geographical relocation of their human and financial capital across the Pacific (p. 2). ... Business immigration was in principle a masterstroke, transferring embodied capital to the receiving country, conveying not just financial capital but also its enterprising creator. (p. 5)

In Canada and Australia alike, the human body is as central to the local real estate practices that work within the cultural, financial and institutional borders of the nation state, just like the human body is central to the foreign real estate investment practices that cross over these same cultural, financial, and institutional nation states borders. Similar to the mediation of the Australian government's Great Dream of home-ownership by wealth educators and the local real estate industry in the late twentieth century, ideas about foreign real estate investment and associated real estate investment visas do not circulate through the networks of foreign investors and potential migrants unassisted. The global real estate industry has become a key intermediary of these real estate ideals. The global real estate companies now span the Asia-Pacific and have quickly deployed the *embodied cultural capital* (e.g., Chinese-Canadian real estate agents) they need within their companies to educate and focus the *embodied financial capital* (e.g., foreign real estate investors) in a way that suits the interests of these companies. An Australian-Chinese sales agent based in Melbourne, but who we interviewed in China as a part of the *Global Real Estate Project*, stated: "My company, we have Chinese staff in China – both in China and Australia – and the solicitor we use for our customers is Chinese-Australian. He can speak both languages" (Interview: *Global Real Estate Project*). The discursive effects of the mainstream media in Australia add more depth to this comment, such as the newspaper headline noted above about Singaporeans lining up to buy a slice of the Great Australian Dream. Brian Eng, "a foreign real estate manager at Singapore real estate firm Jalin", reports that Singaporean bodies are well suited for investing in Australian real estate because they have

> a love for the Australian lifestyle. ... Singaporeans have a love affair with Australian properties, they've studied there before, worked in these cities. ... It reminds them of good times, it's not uncommon for them to stay and work in Australia for 10 years after they have finished their studies. (Bagshaw, 2014)

Settler-societies such as Australia, Canada, and the United States are underwritten by the intersection of two interrelated dreams, the immigration and the home-owning dreams. The two dreams have in common, at least by those who buy into the dream ideology, "a sense of aspiration to join the middle class. ... Yet the homebuyer visa noticeably lacks that ethos. As a pre-packaged American Dream bundle at a price few can afford, the homebuyer visa seems to have nothing to do with upward mobility and everything to do with upper-class privilege," argues Johnson (2014: 832). Therefore, the dream to invest in real estate is developing a degree of global universality, and there has been a change in the geopolitical location of the real estate transaction and the nationalities of those who are buying into the new dream of owning Australian and other settler-society real estate (Rogers et al., 2015). Who the dream is for and who is mediating the information about how the dream can be achieved is changing according to the prevailing geopolitical climate. Ley highlights the celebrity-like status of global real estate professionals such as Hong Kong's Li Kashing's, who heads Li Kashing's Cheung Kong Holdings (Ley, 2015: citing Olds, 2001). "The combined profits of Li's listed firms alone added up to more than US$1 billion in 1993," notes Olds (2001: 116). "Li financially directs or is involved with a complex web of companies active in property, banking, oil and gas, telecommunications, infrastructure." As if to confirm his firmly embedded real estate mentality Li's real estate success and wealth give him superhero rather than celebrity-like status. He is known as *Chui Yan Li* in Hong Kong, aka "Superman Li" (Olds, 2001: 116 and 279).

EVENTS: THE BODY AS TECHNOLOGY

The global real estate industry is championing the movement of human and financial capital into real estate around the world, not only in settler-societies but also into real estate in the former colonial powers. The foreign investor and global real estate professional body is an important technology within this geopolitical process. This is clear at the international real estate fairs and expos, where a diverse meeting of international real estate sales agents, developers, architects, interior designers, publishers, wealth educators/advisers, financial planners, home loan brokers, foreign investment lawyers, and immigration consultants come together to sell foreign real estate and promote international migration (The Luxury Properties Showcase, 2014).

In broad terms, there are two types of real estate events, each targeting a different investor cohort. For example, The SMART Investment & International Property Expo targets middle class investors across Asia. The Luxury Property Showcase (LPS) event, held in several Chinese cities each year, targets high-net-worth investors. The Shanghai LPS event reportedly attracts "over 5,000 Chinese VIPs" – HNW foreign real estate investors – and it hosts "over 100 exhibitors from 30 countries" (The Luxury Properties Showcase, 2014). The event organisers report across the 2010–2013 LPS events the "top 10 represented countries" were "US, China, Australia, Singapore, UK, France, Italy, Thailand, Canada and Malaysia" (The Luxury Properties Showcase, 2014). Professionals from across the Asia-Pacific region, North America, and Europe are deeply embedded within this foreign real estate investment network. Seminars at the 2014 LPS included: how to buy "waterfront properties in the USA, Australia, New Zealand, Italy"; "Foreign resident permits through property investment ... learn about the residency application requirements, lifestyle and investment trends of ... the most popular nations"; and a "focus on Australian & New Zealand real estate: the new trends and regulation for Chinese investors" (The Luxury Properties Showcase, 2014). At a seminar about investing in "global city" real estate, the first question from the audience was, "can you tell me the taxation and immigration rules in the UK?" (recorded by the author at a public seminar). When asked about the information Chinese buyers were seeking at these events, a Chinese-Australian sales agent from Melbourne stated, information about "The house, the rent, like if the area is good, the location, like any famous universities or colleges, like schools nearby, the price of course, and the environment. But most customers from China ask about the universities. And that's why the properties in Melbourne very easily sell" (Interview: *Global Real Estate Project*).

Through an integrated assemblage of embodied and techno-discursive technologies, global real estate professionals are redeploying the discursive tactics and real estate due diligence techniques that were used by local real estate professionals in Australia in the 1980s–1990s in an attempt to capture foreign real estate investors. An Australian "global wealth educator" stated in a seminar in Singapore, "... so know what you're buying, know the area, know the demand, know the competition and buy to suit the market. Buy what everybody wants" (recorded by the author at a public seminar). While the discursive tactics of real estate professionals displayed a degree of due diligence continuity over the last five decades, the mediating technologies, discursive codes, and the subjective implications are far from consistent. Not only is there spatial creep in the way local real estate is being globalised, there was also temporal creep in the way the foreign real estate investors are beginning to think about real estate investment across generational timelines. The global real estate digital technology company Juwai (2014) reported the following case from California on their social media site: "In Palo Alto, CA, a Chinese family bought 'a million-dollar-plus home for a 2-yr-old they anticipate getting into Stanford' [University]." The next chapter moves onto the new digital coding practices of the twenty-first century, and real estate technology companies like Juwai. It covers the role of Internet-enabled foreign real estate technologies and the ways these new technologies are reshaping foreign real estate investment mentalities.

NOTE

1. I first came in contact with these two books as a child, when my baby boomer parents purchased them in the 1990s.

Chapter 7

New Discursive Code: Internet, Libertarianism, Upload, Download

INTERNET: GLOBAL REAL ESTATE CYBORG

In 2010, two Australians in their early 40s dreamt up a global real estate tech (digital technological) company "over a couple of beers in Hong Kong" (Wilson, 2015: 1). Simon Henry and Andrew Taylor have worked in real estate since the early 2000s, and they have been working in Hong Kong and Macao since the mid-2000s (Henry, 2015; Wilson, 2015: 1). A "crisis," like much of the real estate events discussed in this book, was central to the creation of Simon Henry and Andrew Taylor's company, *Juwai.com* (Juwai, 2014). Henry and Taylor deployed the Global Financial Crisis as a discursive device in an attempt to reset the way investors think about real estate in the Asia-Pacific region on a regional, if not a global, scale. Henry states,

> The (2008) global financial crisis had come to its end. Thousands in the financial sector had lost their jobs and most countries in the Organisation for Economic Co-operation and Development were either in recession or starting to come out of it. But China showed little sign of slowing down. ... People had money and they wanted to spend it and spend it not only on luxury goods but property ... property overseas. ... We could see [Chinese] mainlanders were changing the Hong Kong and Macao property markets. But what about beyond? ... There was nothing, as far as we could see, that catered to this growing market of Chinese, especially the middle class, who wanted to purchase property overseas. (Grigg, 2015)

We are at the beginning of a digitally driven, global expansion of the residential real estate industry. Millions of local residential homes from at least a quarter of the countries around the world have been uploaded for sale onto the Internet as global commodities to be traded by a new stratum of global real estate professionals and investors (Rogers, 2016a). It is surprising, however, that the digital uploading of residential real estate onto Internet-enabled real estate technologies has not attracted more attention. This globalising and digitising real estate industry is increasingly comprised of national and international real estate sales agents, property developers, financial advisers, home loan brokers, foreign investment lawyers, immigration consultants, and information technology professionals (Baum and Hartzell, 2012; Rogers et al., 2015). The emergence of the global real estate industry along with their new digital technologies introduces a new set of conceptual problems relating to the digitisation of the real estate industry. Most significantly, these new practices and technologies create a problem for nation state-centric and culturally essentialist analyses that use, for example, concepts such as "Western" or "Eastern," or rely heavily on foreign investment capital flows data, or buy into narratives about "invading Chinese investors" to understand changes in foreign real estate investment. Henry and Taylor's Australian-backed but Asian-based real estate tech start-up is now one of the largest international real estate websites operating in the Asia-Pacific (Juwai, 2014), and their company and its practices completely undermine any essentialist assumption we might hold about global real estate investment. Juwai uses technological and human capital to blend the "West" and the "East" together, and by facilitating the flow of human and financial capital throughout the Asia-Pacific, the Juwai case shows that Chinese investors do not hold all the agency when it comes to their investment in international real estate markets.

Henry, a co-founder and co-CEO, stated that he "realised the potential for an international property portal for Chinese buyers. After a year of ... doing research and focus groups in China and building our website, we launched in 2011" (Millward, 2014: 1). The Mandarin word "Juwai" is a neologism, which roughly translates as "home overseas." On Baidu, effectively China's version of Google, the term Juwai is "now a more searched term ... than international property," according to Henry (Grigg, 2015: 2). The tech company's core business is to advertise foreign real estate and to procure real estate sales across nation state boundaries for real estate companies from around the world, at least for now. Henry says the long-term goal "is to stay involved in the consumer's life after they have purchased a property. That means helping them choose a school or university, move overseas or decide on a holiday destination, all the while keeping up to date with the latest lifestyle trends and luxury items" (Grigg, 2015).

The new geopolitics that underwrites the transmission of discursive real estate code in the Asia-Pacific requires analytical processes that turn the complex forms of real estate knowledge into easily digestible and transferable information for investors, such as maps, graphs, flowcharts, information sheets, investment calculators, and investor profiles. These processes are written into the subjective bodies of the global real estate agents themselves, and digital real estate technologies are increasingly blurring the boundary between the body, technology, and mentality, giving new conceptual utility to Michel Foucault's notion of the subjective *body as technology*. In terms of the geopolitics of real estate, the twenty-first century will be the century of the real estate cyborg. Simon Henry in particular is both the Asia-Pacific poster boy for the real estate tech industry and a pre-eminent example of the twenty-first-century real estate cyborg. I do not want to introduce what Wilson (2012: 173) has termed a "cyborg fantasy" into this study of digital real estate technologies, or to romanticise the term "cyborg." However, a rigorous conceptual tool is needed for separating out any *dependencies* on a technological real estate object and the data that flow through these objects (e.g., the materiality of the technology), from the *implications* of subjectivity-body-object real estate encounters "for the headier notions of the self, identity, and bodily integrity" (Wilson, 2012: 173). Investigating the different subjective bodies (e.g., global real estate professionals and investors), technological objects (e.g., books and smartphones), and discursive codes (e.g., real estate data) that are assembled within particular real estate encounters, even if the real estate cyborg is a fantasy, is a potentially rich way to frame the rise of global real estate technologies and the new global real estate technicians like Simon Henry. The real estate cyborg is a conceptual shorthand term, a metaphor that attempts to capture the complex assemblages of bodies, technologies, and events – in much the same way as Haraway's (1983) notion of the feminist cyborg is a conceptual metaphor (Haraway, 1983; also see: Mitchell, 2004; Tufeki, 2012).

Like the LeFrak family, the body as a real estate technology is a central motif in Simon Henry's biography. Henry was born in the Australian state of Queensland in 1969, in the first wave of baby boomers' *babies* (Wilson, 2015: 1), which the Australian Bureau of Statistics (2014) defines as Generation X (i.e., those born between 1965 and 1981). Henry understands, at the very intimate level of his own subjective body, the value and utility of embodied cultural capital for enabling global real estate practices to cross over the cultural, financial, and institutional borders of nation states. He completed a Bachelors of Arts at the Australian National University and majored in Thai language in 1990. He then received an MBA (Management) from Queensland University of Technology in 1998 (Henry, 2015; Wilson, 2015: 1). It is not a stretch to surmise that real estate and investment ideals were further inculcated into Henry's body as the General Manager of Technology and then Associate Director (Projects) at LJ Hooker, one of Australia's largest real estate companies, while he held the role between June 2000 and July 2005 (Henry, 2015; Wilson, 2015: 1). Between November 2004 and December 2006, Henry was Program Manager at Realestate.com.au, a real estate tech company that was involved in the first wave of Web 1.0 real estate data uploading in Australia. Henry became the Group Product Manager at REA Group, a global digital real estate advertising company headquartered in Melbourne in January 2007 (and the discussion returns to LJ Hooker, Realestate.com.au and REA Group below). From April 2008, Henry relocated to Asia, working with two large tech companies in quick succession. Henry was: CEO of vproperty Limited, a multi-language property portal in China's Pearl River Delta from April 2008 to November 2010; and CEO of QOOS Limited, which became one of the largest Chinese consumer Internet portals in Macau. According to journalist Angus Grigg (2015: 2), who interviewed Taylor and Henry at regular interviews during Juwai's quick expansion from 2011, "Taylor and Henry spotted this mega trend early [the growing middle class and super-rich in China with increasing levels of disposable income] having both worked at REA Group in Australia." In July 2011, Taylor and Henry co-founded Juwai.com and appointed themselves joint CEO to capitalise on the changing geopolitical landscape in the Asia-Pacific.

This trajectory depicts Simon Henry as a metaphorical real estate cyborg. Similarly, George Washington, William Charles Wentworth, and later Stuart Zadel and Dominique Grubisa might be thought of as real estate cyborgs. Their human-technology *integration* refers to the way the organising technics of a particular moment have worked on their subjective human bodies, allowing the body to readily *integrate* particular mentalities, technologies, and codes into their everyday real estate practices. A different assemblage of the subjective-body-object-event, at any given moment, will, of course, lead to a different real estate reality. For Washington and Wentworth, it is surveying technics and the tools of the surveyor that partly informed their actions. For Zadel and Grubisa, it is real estate education as an organising technic, and the wealth education book as a technology that partly informs their actions. In the case of Juwai, Henry's subjective body is a powerful foreign real estate technology, partly because of his educational and professional histories, but also because of his access to and knowledge of digital technologies. He has intercultural skills that relate directly to Asia, and he has an in-depth knowledge of real estate practices and data. He also understands the real estate sales "event"; and as a member of Generation X, he understands the current geopolitical moment, that is, the rise of China and Asia more generally. Without all of these organising technics, mediating technologies, and discursive codes coming together, and more no doubt, Henry might not have created Juwai, as "a hybrid model without peer ... a cross between a software company, known in the industry as software for a service (SaaS), a social media platform and luxury publication" (Grigg, 2015).

Susan Smith's (2008: 521) notion of the home that I noted earlier, as a hybrid of mobile capital, physical materials, and subjective lived experiences, takes on a new meaning when confronted by the digital real estate platforms that are increasingly playing a key role in regulating these relationships. Digital technologies not only shape, they can also rupture the entanglements between the flow of cash, the materiality of real estate, and the more subjective use values of home. The boundaries of real estate and nation state, money and materials, people and homes, are being rearticulated through Internet-enabled real estate technologies (Rogers, 2016a). Real estate technologies like Juwai and the real estate cyborgs who work within these organisations are central to the operation and interconnection of global real estate professionals and businesses across different legal, spatial, cultural, linguistic, and technological frontiers (Isin and Ruppert, 2015; Rogers et al., 2015). The emergence of these global real estate tech companies opens up a suite of new global housing research questions. For example, what will be the subjective effect, if any, on the users of Juwai's global real estate technology when they access the "most integrated platform connecting international agents and Chinese buyers" on their tablet or smartphone? Juwai (2014: 1) state their tech product has "2.4 million property listings from 58 countries, giving Chinese buyers the most comprehensive collection of overseas property to search from." What will be the long-term domestic and foreign housing market effects, if any, if the next generation of Chinese and other nationals power-up a real estate tech product on their smartphone to look for international real estate? I do not propose to answer these types of questions in this chapter. Rather, I pose these questions to clear a conceptual space to begin to think about how the globalising real estate tech products – which will increasingly frame how people from many countries around the world buy and sell residential real estate – might come to confirm, shape or remould different understandings about land, real estate, home, citizenship and property. Indeed, I set out here to ask a more fundamental question: what are the geopolitical implications of the digital commodification of real estate? This digital commodification involves detaching the material dwelling from the subjective lived experience of habitation and turning it into digital data that can be used to facilitate new types of capital circulation and accumulation.

Moreover, these are not just questions relating to the "global" real estate industry. These digital real estate platforms are also reshaping home at the "local" level. For example, BrickX is a small-scale real estate tech start-up in Sydney. Their promotional video, quoted verbatim below, strips the idea of fractional real estate investment from its complex financial industry moorings, leaving it in its most elementary form.

BrickX: The new way to enter the property market.
BrickX buys properties in prime locations.
Then divides each property into 10,000 "Bricks."

A "Brick" = A fraction of a property.
A $1 Million property = $100 per "Brick."
"Bricks" start at $66.
Invest in "Bricks" across a range of properties.
Earn monthly distributions from rental income.
Share the capital returns.
While we take care of the property management.
BrickX: The new way to enter the property market.
What are you waiting for?
(BrickX, 2015: how-it-works)

As discussed in Chapter 5, complex fractional financial practices underwrote the subprime mortgage implosion that resulted in a Global Financial Crisis (Ferguson 2008). The more primitive fractional "financial alchemy" (Ferguson 2008: 270) of BrickX breaks the dwelling down into a set of constituent parts that can be traded independently of the home itself. The use of fractional financial alchemy, argues Ferguson (2008: 254), "is not so much about real estate as about surreal estate" whereby the constituent parts of a dwelling are detached from the subjective use values of the home. These constituent parts can be commodified and sold to the highest bidder and there could be thousands of kilometres between those living in the dwelling, the mortgage borrower, and the fractional surreal estate investors. BrickX (2015: about) identifies strongly with the real estate tech industry, and particularly with the industry discourse of "disruptive technology." They claim that the unboundedness of their "innovative technology solutions to property investing" will "disrupt the [real estate] status quo" (BrickX, 2015: about). The digital functionality and globalising thrust of this new real estate industry forces us – conceptually, methodologically and empirically – to move beyond the nation state-centrism that frames much of the debate about domestic and foreign real estate investors (Baum and Hartzell, 2012; Tiwari and White, 2010). However, there are some familiar and resilient organising technics that frame the emergence of the real estate tech industry, and I cover these organising technics in the next section.

LIBERTARIANISM: REAL ESTATE TECH INDUSTRY

Isin and Ruppert (2015: 34) set up the context for the rise of the tech industry by noting that "power relations in contemporary societies are being increasingly mediated and constituted through computer networks that eventually came to be known as the Internet." There is a weighty theoretical corpus devoted to people, technology, and societal relationality (Burrows and

Savage, 2014; Ellul, 1954; Mitcham, 1994; Tufeki, 2014). However, the history of the World Wide Web and the Internet (Keen, 2015) and the developing real estate tech industry (Rogers, 2016b) are rarely cited contextual frames for thinking through twenty-first-century real estate relations, and there is a clear ideological landscape that broadly enframes the tech industry. In 1996, 7 years after Tim Berners-Lee invented the World Wide Web, Robert Franks and Philip Cook (1996) argued that information technologies were poised to exacerbate global economic inequality. In the same year, John Perry Barlow (1996) published *A Declaration of the Independence of Cyberspace* to discursively frame the rise of the Internet. The opening of Barlow's declaration was ideologically instructive:

> Governments of the Industrial World. ... I come from Cyberspace, the new home of Mind. ... You are not welcome among us ... Governments derive their just powers from the consent of the governed. You have neither solicited nor received ours. ... Cyberspace does not lie within your borders. Do not think that you can build it, as though it were a public construction project. You cannot ... You have not engaged in our great and gathering conversation, nor did you create the wealth of our marketplaces. You do not know our culture, our ethics, or the unwritten codes that already provide our society more order than could be obtained by any of your impositions. (Barlow, 1996: 1)

Barlow's libertarian proclamation provides revealing insights into the early thinking of information technologists. At the end of the twentieth century, these technologists were interested in moving from the "industrial" into the "information" age, and thereby denounced geographically bounded notions of governance and citizenship (Isin and Ruppert, 2015). They proclaimed the independence of cyberspace in an attempt to reconstitute it as an emerging marketplace *space* that could be decoupled from government regulation and taxation. Cyberspace, occurring to Barlow and his contemporary tech followers, should be self-regulated through a set of independent tech industry cultural and ethical norms. This type of libertarian enframing of technology was not unexpected. Carl Mitcham (1994) was writing about it in his *magnum opus* on technology in 1994. He argued in "the background of virtually all science and technology studies there lurks an uneasiness regarding the popular belief in the unqualified moral probity and clarity of the modern technological project" (Mitcham 1994, 1). Twenty years later, Andrew Keen (2015: 211), one of Silicon Valley's most vocal contemporary critical insiders, is still uneasy. Kean argues (2015: 189) a "disruptive libertarianism," which he describes as a free market liberalism that is bolstered by a "disdain for hierarchy and authority, especially the traditional role of government," persists as one of the central ideological reference points in the tech industry. This free market libertarianist thinking is the guiding ideology at tech conferences and large tech companies in the United States, and has been built into the paywalls of the tech industry's products and into bodies of the real estate cyborgs (Isin and Ruppert, 2015; Keen, 2015).

Keen (2015, 228) redeploys Silicon Valley's own lexicon back onto itself to conclude that the Internet-enabled tech industry is an "epic fucking failure." In the tech and venture capital industries the failure of your first tech start-up is celebrated as an entrepreneurial milestone. The tech industry is, however, not an entrepreneurial failure but rather a democratic failure. Keen's history of the Internet demonstrates that the utopian dreams for an open access and decentralised, but state-funded, World Wide Web of the mid-twentieth century were subsumed into the hegemonic, hierarchical, and monopolistic private tech sector of the twenty-first century. Isin and Ruppert (2015: 28) describe cyberspace as "a space of relations between and among bodies acting through the Internet," and the early phase of cyberspace development was "primarily a story of how the Internet was invented for national security and civic goals. It's a story about how public money ... paid to build a global electronic network," argues Kean (2015, 38). The economist Mariana Mazzucato (2013) points out that the most successful tech companies received public sector start-up funding (e.g., Apple) or university scholarship funding for the founding CEOs (e.g., Google). Before 1991, the United States government maintained legal control of the World Wide Web and companies that sought access to it were required to limit their use to "research and education," albeit, as Friedrich Kittler (1995) has shown, this often meant military research and development.

Reflecting on the rise of the World Wide Web and Internet, and the free market liberalism and disdain for government that information technologists deployed to frame its emergence, it is perhaps not surprising that real estate was so readily uploaded into this technological system. According to some real estate industry sources (Movoto, 2014), real estate listings periodically appeared on the Internet from about 1994. At the turn of the century, and only a decade after the creation of the World Wide Web, one of the first Web 1.0 real estate companies "was founded on the belief that selling or buying a home could be faster, easier and more efficient" (Zipreality, 2014). In the same year, Move (formally HomeStore) became one of the first Internet real estate companies to be publicly listed. Web 1.0 was one of the initial large-scale software paradigms on the Internet. This platform is typified by businesses that upload their core business functions onto the Internet in a fairly straightforward manner. The assumption behind Web 1.0 technologies is that a company's non-virtual technics will operate in the virtual spaces of the Internet in much the same way as they operated before the Internet. Uploading the practice of mailing letters onto an Internet platform as email, through a service provider such as Yahoo!, is a good example of this type of

Web 1.0 uploading practice. Throughout the first decade of the twentieth-first century, the Web 1.0 uploading of real estate practices, or taking the old real estate technics online, increased significantly. A tech developer from a real estate tech start-up I interviewed in Asia in 2014 stated, "Everything is going mobile of course, and we've benefitted tremendously ... within our first year the smartphone came out. And then we jumped on that. And so we really became an app builder concentrating on property, so managing the information that's there" (Interview: *Global Real Estate Project*). Large sections of the real estate industry are still operating in the Web 1.0 space. Real estate companies are contracting tech companies to help them upload their core business technics onto the Internet, as their first venture into cyberspace. In 2015, most real estate companies in Australia had an online presence of one form or another. These online platforms also allow the real estate companies to expand into regional and global real estate markets (Rogers, 2016a). Juwai (2014) is a good regional example. Within four years of establishment they became one of the largest international real estate websites in the world.

The rise of big real estate data in the early 2000s expanded the scope for uploading real estate, and it was accompanied by the emergence of a suite of big real estate data companies. The Real Estate Transaction Standard (RETS), a real estate data exchange protocol for real estate professionals, was launched in the United States in 1999. This was followed in the early 2000s with the Internet Data Exchange (IDX), a real estate property search site that allowed the public to conduct real estate searches. These types of data companies are beginning to trade in real estate data. In the Asia-Pacific, in 2006, the Korean government introduced the Real Estate Trade Management System to collect real estate transaction data. In 2011, the North American big real estate data analytics company CoreLogic (2014) acquired RP Data, which provides real estate analytical services in Australia and New Zealand. CoreLogic's stated intent was to further expand in the Asia-Pacific region. In 2014, to take a trans-Pacific case, REA Group (2014: 2), which is majority owned by News Corp Australia, a subsidiary of News Corp, announced their "intention to acquire a 20% stake in Move" (i.e., the first publicly listed Internet real estate company mentioned above). According to the REA Group (2014: 2), "News Corp, parent of our majority shareholder, intends to hold the remaining 80%."

The emergence of digital real estate platforms over several decades shows that these technologies have been increasingly up-scaled in three key ways: "(1) geographically, at first regionally and then globally; (2) electronically, to include more third-party big data analysis; and (3) socio-economically, to increasingly target, and at times exclusively, HNW individuals and global real estate investment" (see Rogers, 2016a: 9). The long-term empirical question that remains for housing scholars with an interest in information technologies is: are these real estate industries shifting their digital technics onto the newer Web 2.0 software paradigms? The move from Web 1.0 to Web 2.0 represents a paradigmatic shift towards big data and big "data factories" (Burrows and Savage, 2014; Keen, 2015). Technology writers have grouped the companies in this category under the technological neologism, Googlenomics (Keen, 2015). These companies give away their software tools and services for free or close to free but simultaneously become big data companies that "target their users'" behaviour and taste through the collection of their "data exhaust" (Keen, 2015: 60). The "laws" of Googlenomics proclaim that tech companies can create their own markets by operating in the space between "the browser," "search engine and destination content server, as an enabler or middleman between the user and his or her online experience" (Keen, 2015: 59).

The history of the Internet shows the danger of Web 2.0 technologies is that they foster business monopoly and social inequality. Indeed, the biggest Web 2.0 tech companies are banding together to lobby governments, citizenries, and even themselves for increasing "freedom" from government regulation across various digital, economic, and socio-political spheres (see The Internet Association, 2015). Zeynep Tufeki (2014: 1) even argues that Web 2.0 big data companies "now have new tools and *stealth* methods to quietly model our personality, our vulnerabilities, identify our networks, and effectively nudge and shape our ideas, desires and dreams" (Tufekci's emphasis). Their digital practices, according to Tufekci (2014), Isin and Ruppert (2015), and Keen (2015), can be designed to change the way the users of the technologies think about the world and themselves. Tech industry libertarians, following Barlow's (1996: 1) declaration, go further still to argue that cyberspace is the new "home of mind," and these are not idle threats. The Web 2.0 giant Facebook has conducted secretive online experiments with users' data in an attempt to control their mood, leaving Tufeki (2014: 1) to ask: the "question is not whether people are trying to manipulate your experience and behaviour, but whether they're trying to manipulate you in a way that aligns with or contradicts your own best interests." There is some evidence that the larger, more globally focused, real estate tech companies are moving towards quasi-Web 2.0 technologies (Rogers, 2016b). Unlike the Web 1.0 technologies, these Web 2.0 style companies manage and own the real estate tech products they build. Their tech products include real-time real estate data user interfaces that are typical of the Web 2.0 software paradigm. Some of the real estate tech start-ups have Australian, European, and North American interests, such as the two Australians that founded Juwai (www.juwai.com) and the Singaporean real estate start-up StreetSine Technology Group (www.srx.com.sg). By focusing on these two examples, the next section discusses these types of real estate tech start-ups to expose the real estate technics and data that are being uploaded onto the Internet.

UPLOAD: REAL ESTATE AS A GLOBAL COMMODITY

The simplest Internet-enabled technology for uploading real estate data is a Web 1.0 investor-focused real estate sales interface. These interfaces place the investor at the centre of a relatively closed network of small data about real estate at a particular site (Rogers, 2016b). Perhaps the most common are the website platforms that are built for and then managed by existing real estate companies. These companies upload sales information about individual properties onto their own website with limited analysis or technological manipulation. An Australian example is the real estate company LJ Hooker, who initially commissioned a tech company to upload their local newspaper and real estate shopfront window advertisements onto a web-based platform (ljhooker.com.au). From the early 2000s, these Web 1.0 real estate technologies have diversified into third-party real estate websites. In Australia, several large news media companies commissioned or secured an ownership stake in the most popular sites, including domain.com.au (Fairfax Media) and realestate.com.au (News Corp, 60 per cent ownership). These real estate technologies allow independent real estate companies and professionals to upload their sales information to a third-party website. It is the technological interface, the "embodied" and "situated" experience of the real estate investor in cyberspace, which represents "a complex interplay between real [i.e., material] and digital geographies" (Isin and Ruppert, 2015: 32), that I want to focus on here.

For analytical purposes, I have called the digital act of targeting a real estate investor with a piece of technological hardware and software an *investor-focused* digital act. By using this term I mean to demarcate the technological act that has been intentionally designed to target a specific population group. The concept of the digital act equally applies, therefore, to real estate professionals (i.e., *professional-focused* digital act) and those who are looking for a rental property (i.e., *tenant-focused* digital act). A good example of a *professional-focused* real estate tech platform in Australia is onthehouse.com.au, which is owned by the Console Group. This real estate tech company, who argue that their "software has been supporting the Australian real estate industry since 1992," states their "Console suite" tech product "is designed to help [real estate professionals] build better relationships, talk to more prospects, increase leads, close more deals, operate with greater efficiency, and monetise your data and website traffic" (Console Group, 2015: 1). The *investor-focused* capabilities of the national real estate websites noted above have more recently been regionally and globally "upscaled." Juwai argue that their geopolitical location is important – that is, Hong Kong – allowing them to get beyond China's "Great Firewall," which can block or slow down sites hosted elsewhere (Juwai, 2014). The sale of Australian, Canadian, and United States real estate to Chinese nationals through the Internet is a key business strategy for this real estate tech company. Juwai (2014) state, "For Chinese Consumers Juwai.com is an international Chinese platform – hosted in China, entirely in Chinese. Chinese consumers get instant access to international property listings, language and search tools, as well as relevant research and information they need to make informed decisions about overseas property purchasing." In terms of the small real estate data that is flowing through their tech platform to target Chinese investors, for a fee Juwai translates local Australian (and other country's) dwelling specific real estate data from English to Mandarin, tapping into Henry's intercultural knowledge. They provide in-house cross-cultural and language translations and Chinese social media compatibility: "Our professional editorial team translates in a style and tone that resonates with Chinese buyers", and Juwai's "Mobile App with Chinese social channel integration [is] combined with online Chinese social media features" (Juwai, 2014: 1). It is a mistake to assume that Juwai is a digital real estate company that solely operates in the "virtual" world of cyberspace. Juwai is very much operating in the material world, with offices in Shanghai and Hong Kong. Juwai utilises culturally dependent relational technologies, such as translating real estate advertisements from English into Mandarin, in an explicit effort to make their website "Asia ready" to attract Australian, Canadian, and United States and other real estate companies to advertise through their website. The human body is central to the process, for both decoding and recoding the real estate information, and as a target for the new digital discursive code.

In terms of the bodies that are used to decode and recode the real estate information, the global real estate industry is increasingly employing globally mobile real estate professionals who have complicated cultural identities and nation state allegiances. Some professionals we interviewed for the *Global Real Estate Project* said they were Chinese, others said they were Australian-Chinese, and others Canadian-Chinese. These professionals are bridging the cultural and linguistic gaps between the many countries and cultural groups. One agent we interviewed stated, "I'm originally from China, and completed my formal education in Australia. I'm bilingual. So there is no obstacle for me to communicate across cultures and languages" (Interview: *Global Real Estate Project*). Another stated, "I completed my college education in Australia. So my personal experience allows me to communicate across with Chinese clients" (Interview: *Global Real Estate Project*). These Australian-Chinese and Chinese-Australian agents are communicating information not only about Australia's demography and geography, but also about Australia's visa, foreign investment, home loan, real estate, and education systems. One agent talks about their clients by saying, "Firstly, they want to immigrate to Australia. Except this group, there are some clients who will not qualify to immigrate to Australia" (Interview: *Global Real Estate Project*). Another stated, "It can be clarified into three major motivations: (1) immigration, (2) study overseas, and (3) investment. Seventy per cent of my clients are purchasing houses for investment" (Interview: *Global Real Estate Project*).

Juwai, being based in Hong Kong, decodes and recodes information in terms of its own internal content (news, research data, and advertising), external content (policy, news, and research), and translation of foreign agents' data into Mandarin. The discursive code running through *Juwai* is frequently decoded and subsequently recoded for their different target groups, which includes potential Chinese investors and foreign-based real estate sales agents. For example, China is the largest single nation contributor to Australia's international student population, and about 27 per cent of all international student enrolments in Australia are Chinese (Department of Education, 2014). This information was used to market the services provided by Juwai to Australian real estate sales agents with the advertising slogan, "His parents are looking to buy … now. 85% of high net worth Chinese send their children to study abroad. List your properties on the #1 property portal for Chinese buyers" (Juwai, 2013). Juwai translates and mediates, through their own industry-organising technics, a range of internally and externally produced data, news and nation state technical constraints, but always with the end goal in mind, which is to facilitate the sale of international real estate. For example, the firm foregrounds educational mobilities as being deeply embedded within investor mobilities and long-term migration prospects. In one case, they created simple graphics by decoding and recoding the data in the Hurun Wealth Report, which show that 60 per cent of wealthy Chinese are seriously considering emigrating overseas, and 85 per cent want to educate their children overseas. It is important to note, however, that some of the data produced by companies such as Juwai.com are collated from their own web-based databases, which, at a minimum, could have a built-in sampling bias (Robertson and Rogers, in-press).

The Australian-based global real estate agent Ivy Xiao (2013) coaches her colleagues by arguing that understanding and communicating local real estate, political, visa, financial, and legal information across cultures is central to securing international sales. Xiao draws attention to the need to integrate the digital technologies into the body of the bilingual real estate agent in an educational opinion editorial (op-ed) entitled, *Tips for getting the most from Chinese property expos: Ivy Xiao*. Xiao's op-ed shows that digital technologies are wholly integrated with older mediating technologies, such as "print" media and interpersonal sales. She writes about the embodied practices of real estate professionals at global real estate events by saying,

> More than 40,000 visitors turned up to the recent Shanghai Overseas Property & Investment Immigration Expo, which was attended by ACproperty.com.au to promote Australian properties in China. An investment booklet, co-published by Property Observer and ACproperty.com.au, *Australia's allure for Asian residential property investment*, was distributed [for free] to visitors. (Xiao, 2013: 1)

In comparison with these *investor-focused* digital acts, the more sophisticated Web 2.0 style *professional-focused* real estate sales technologies place real estate and other professionals at the centre of a diffuse network of big and small data about investors, property developers, immigration agents, financial institutions, and other real estate information (Rogers 2016a). Within the real estate tech industry, Web 1.0 and quasi-Web 2.0 platforms can operate independently or they can sit happily alongside each other within a broader tech platform. Juwai's portable online analytical tool for real estate professionals is a good example, and it operates alongside their Chinese *investor-focused* digital acts. Their *professional-focused* real estate platform networks real estate professionals from around the world into "Juwai's exclusive audience of 1.5 million high-net-worth Chinese consumers" (Juwai, 2014). The global real estate company Engel and Völkers (2014) also developed an online real estate *professional-focused* product called "my life," which they describe as "Practical Knowledge for Sales Advisors." Again, these digital acts are wholly integrated with older mediating technologies and the embodied practices of real estate professionals operating at the global level. Juwai has an "Event Services" division of the company, which explicitly brings together the digital and embodied technologies. They advertise the service to foreign real estate sales agents as follows:

> Attending the right events can be key to your integrated Chinese marketing strategy. Face-to-face interaction not only builds trust with Chinese buyers, it gives you vital insight into their purchasing habits too. China's event landscape, however, is ridden with barriers – from language and culture to standard business practices. We leverage our local market expertise to give you even greater access to Chinese buyers through event services, helping you extend your global reach and achieve brand exposure at the best events and expos across China. (Juwai, 2014)

StreetSine (2014), in Singapore, also "integrate big data sets with mobile workflow applications to help real estate-related organisations and professionals employ real-time, relevant, proprietary information in the marketing of their products and services." Their tablet-friendly platforms "provide the property market with computer-generated pricing," which is a tech product they have trademarked as Home Report™. StreetSine (2014) market their Singapore Real Estate Exchange platform, trademarked as SRX™, to "property-related professionals," including real estate agents, bankers, and lawyers. Similar to Juwai, their *professional-focused* digital acts operate alongside a suite of *investor-* and *tenant-focused* digital acts, with their tech products also targeting real estate buyers, sellers, landlords, and rental tenants. StreetSine's big real estate data set can provide extremely fine-grained information about Singaporean real estate, all the way down to a "computer-generated price" for an individual dwelling. They call this computer-generated price an X-Value™. As the real estate professionals use SRX™, the technology captures their real estate data exhaust, thereby growing the company's data set. However, the real estate data set that produces the X-Value™ is only available because of the government's historic role in the provision of public housing in Singapore (Chua, 1997). The government collects the bulk of the real estate data that this technology is built upon. Thus, the role of the government as a real estate data collector and provider is central to StreetSine's Web 2.0 style real estate technology.

Isin and Ruppert (2015: 26) argue these new sociotechnical relationships enable a special class of digital speech act, and what is at stake in these digital technics and acts is "the production, dissemination, and legitimation of knowledge." More recently, the Web 1.0 and Web 2.0 style real estate platforms have had multimedia channels incorporated into the technologies to broadcast high-quality digital audio/visual discursive content about the private real estate market. StreetSine has a regular national radio interview and podcast slot on Singapore's ONE FM radio station. The podcast programme covers real estate topics such as real estate prices, home loans, and the local private property market. They have been critical of the Singaporean government's affordable housing interventions, such as the foreign investment "cooling measures" that attempted to mitigate house price increases (e.g., "Condo market hit hard by cooling measures" podcast on www.srx.com.sg/podcasts). A real estate tech start-up executive interviewed for the *Global Real Estate Project* stated: "now I'm a free-market capitalist-libertarian, ... I can see how information technology can help ... allow this asset class [residential real estate] to be a more frequently traded asset class." The discursive code within these types of multimedia tech products and the statement by the real estate tech executive show that a free market liberalism, which is built upon private property ideologies and underwritten by a disdain for government intervention, is deeply embedded within some of these new real estate technics and digital acts. It is also an embodied technical mentality within the body of the tech professional.

The recent formation of the political lobby group The Internet Association (2015) is a good pan-tech industry example of where this embodied technical mentality might lead. The Internet Association is an alliance of some of the largest and wealthiest Web 2.0 tech companies, including Facebook, Google, and Amazon. This lobby group argues that every tech company should be "uninhibited" by government taxation, regulation, and censorship. They also argue that they should not be held responsible for the user-generated digital acts they enable through their platforms. For example, they state, "Internet intermediaries must not be held liable for the speech and activity of Internet users" (The Internet Association, 2015: 1). The Internet Association is advocating for an instrumental computer science view of technology, which allows the lobby group to position the "freedom" to produce electronic code in cyberspace as more important than thinking about an appropriate regulatory environment that might be used to guide their digital acts, and the effect that their technologies have in the material world (Burrows and Savage, 2014; Isin and Ruppert, 2015; Keen, 2015).

The practice of uploading real estate onto the Internet is not developed in a political vacuum, and there are many examples of resident-led or researcher-led tech resistance to market-centric real estate practice. It is not my intention to explore these alternative forms of digital real estate technics here. However, The Anti-Eviction Mapping Project (United States) and Our House Swap (Australia) are two exemplary cases that are worthy of brief mention. The Anti-Eviction Mapping Project is a web-based "data analysis collective" that uses a crowd-sourcing platform to recruit geographic information system (GIS) specialists to document "the dispossession of San Francisco Bay Area residents in the wake of the Tech Boom [Web] 2.0" (Anti-Eviction Mapping Project 2015: 1). The public housing tenant managed Our House Swap website bypasses the state housing authorities' role in mediating tenants' residential mobility choices (Our House Swap, 2015: 1). These types of digital initiatives are enframed by anti-gentrification and collective ownership mentalities that represent counter mentalities to market-centric real estate technics. The Anti-Eviction Mapping Project, Our House Swap, StreetSine, and Juwai website technologies show that underneath these technological platforms are a set of organising real estate technics and housing and real estate mentalities, which have quite literally been uploaded as forms of real estate or housing power and/or resistance. The real estate technics that are now associated with buying and selling real estate as private property in the globalising digital real estate industry have a clear lineage back to pre-Internet real estate technics in countries such as Australia (Rogers, 2016a). Over the last century, the real estate industry has categorised their real estate technics and ascribed to their many real estate actions a set of linguistic referents, which are: (1) capital costs, (2) capital lending, (3) growth, (4) yield, (5) liquidity, (6) transaction costs, (7) taxation costs, and (8) ownership rules (Baum and Hartzell, 2012; Rogers, 2016a; Tiwari and White, 2010) (see Table 7.1). These technic referents signify the broader set of actions that the real estate professionals, investors, tenants, governments, financial institutions, and other actors come together to undertake.

The agonistic struggles that underwrite these types of performative technics, as Isin and Ruppert (2015: 33) point out, transcend the material world/ digital world divide – the digital acts are always *in the world*. The pre-Internet language acts and real estate technics of local real estate professionals, such as real estate advertisements in local newspapers and shopfronts, were readily uploaded into the Internet as regional and then global technics. Therefore, there is a larger historical context that frames the emergence of Internet-enabled real estate technologies, which includes the transfer of market-centric real estate mentalities from pre-Internet into Internet-enabled real estate technologies. The historical mapping of these real estate technics could go further to expose how these real estate technologies are mediated across different technological, generational, and geographical scales (Rogers, 2016b). To understand twenty-first-century digital real estate technologies, housing scholars need to know more about how real estate technics and mentalities are transferred from one mediating technology to another, from one generation of real estate professionals to another, and from one investor to another.

DOWNLOAD: REAL ESTATE 2.0

A global digital expansion of the residential real estate industry is underway. Millions of local residential homes from some of the wealthiest countries around the world are being uploaded for sale onto thousands of Internet-enabled real estate platforms. While critical housing scholars (Crabtree, 2013) and some digital citizenries (Our House Swap) are abandoning and thinking beyond the technics and mentalities of land and real estate as private property, the globalising real estate industry is digitising, uploading, and "up-scaling" the local real estate technics and mentalities of prior eras onto their new tech products. In the Asia-Pacific, the real estate tech industry has uploaded the real estate technics and mentalities that built the Great Australian Dream. The new real estate technologies are enframed by market-centric and libertarianist real estate technics that readily account for the legal frameworks of different nation states and the cultural and linguistic barriers that previously restricted trans-cultural and trans-national real estate sales. The real estate technology entrepreneurs are building tech products that have libertarianist, private property, and market-centric mentalities built into their very functionality. A further task for housing scholars is, therefore, to analyse the way the real

Table 7.1 The Digital Commodification of Real Estate

Time Period	Digitisation of Real Estate 1960s–2000s		Digital Real Estate as Commodity 2000s–2016	
	1960s–1990s	1990s–2000s	2000s–2016	2010–2016
Target group	Investor- and then tenant-focused	Investor- and tenant-focused	Investor-, tenant-, and professional-focused	Investor- and professional-focused
Embodied mediating technologies	Local real estate sales agents meeting with local buyers and sellers	Local real estate sales agents meeting with local buyers and sellers	Local real estate sales agents meeting with buyers and sellers	Global real estate sales agents meeting with foreign buyers and sellers, and other global real estate professionals at international events
Other mediating technologies	Advertisements in local newspapers and real estate shopfronts	Online local advertisements via www.ljhooker.com	Online local advertisements via www.srx.com.sg/	Online global advertisements via www.juwai.com
Discursive code	Local real estate technology. Very small non-digital discursive data.	Local real estate technology. Small data; Web 1.0 moving towards Web 2.0	National real estate technology. Small and big data; Web 1.0 and 2.0 assemblages	International real estate technology. Small and big data; Web 1.0 and 2.0 assemblages
1. Capital costs 2. Capital lending 3. Growth 4. Yield	Neighbourhood level data about real estate costs and bank loans; with comparative forecasts about growth, yield, and liquidity	Neighbourhood level data about real estate costs and bank loans; with comparative forecasts about growth, yield, and liquidity	Stratified neighbourhood to international level comparative data about real estate costs; with comparative forecasts about growth, yield, and liquidity	Comparative international data about real estate costs and bank loans; with comparative forecasts about growth, yield, and liquidity
5. Liquidity 6. Transaction costs	National level or below bank loan information; with comparative buying, selling, and renting cost data	National level or below bank loan information; with comparative buying, selling, and renting cost data	Stratified neighbourhood to international level information about bank loans; with comparative data about buying, selling, and renting costs	Comparative international data about bank loans; with buying, selling, and renting cost matrices for various countries
7. Taxation costs	National level or below data about taxation settings	National level or below data about taxation settings	Some information about national or international comparative taxation settings	Comparative international data about national taxation settings in various countries
8. Ownership rules	Little information about national level citizenship rights in relation to private property	Little information about national level citizenship rights in relation to private property	Little information about national level citizenship rights in relation to private property	Comparative international data about special foreign investor visa schemes for real estate

estate investors and professionals are "downloading" this information onto their smartphones and tablets, indeed, downloading these mentalities into their subjective bodies. Housing scholars need to think through the relationships between the user, the technological object, and the digital code that is flowing through a given embodied user and technological object assemblage. The conceptual framing of such a project must deal with the way the users interact with these new types of real estate platforms and digital code to ask whether we can record the change(s) in land, real estate, and housing mentalities, if any, that result from these new digital real estate technologies. Finally, the rise of Web 2.0 style real estate technologies, and the buying and selling of real estate tech companies, has made real estate data *itself* a sought after and tradable commodity. Government regulation should ensure that big real estate data become open source, publicly available, and free. Internet history shows that large tech companies are not committed to free open source big data capture, transparency, and social democracy, and the large Web 2.0 tech companies are driving towards technological oligarchy in their respective entrepreneurial fields. What might be lost if real estate tech companies follow suit is the ability to creatively innovate outside the sets of market-centric real estate technics and mentalities that framed twentieth-century real estate practice. In short, without government intervention, the online market-centric real estate technics and mentalities of the twenty-first century, much like the local offline technics of the twentieth century, could negatively affect global housing equity. Therefore, the final chapter returns to the central aim of the book, which was to explore how different assemblages of bodies, technologies, land, real estate, events, history, and territory have developed over time. The concluding chapter returns to the different historical and contemporary land and real estate crises that I have explored in this book, to reflect on how they took shape, how they assembled and dispersed, and to identify any common subterranean organising technics, mentalities, mediating technologies, or discursive codes that have accumulated over time.

Chapter 8

Global Real Estate Assemblages

REAL ESTATE: THE TWENTY-FIRST-CENTURY *PANEM ET CIRCENSES*

The geopolitics of property, capital, and rights that emerged after the Second World War enabled significant domestic real estate investment in settler-societies and the former colonial-power countries, including the United Kingdom, United States, Canada, and Australia. The war created a cultural and territorial crisis that motivated many settler-societies to reimagine their cultural identities and stabilise their political and territorial borders. It also allowed these countries to mobilise real estate consumption as a national project of economic recovery and citizen-building. The new post-war citizen – the baby boomer – lived through a period of history where the idea of the nation and what it meant to be a citizen was in a state of cultural contention. The settler-societies were busy reimagining their collective identities around nationhood and citizenship, but they also understood the importance of migration and real estate for rebuilding their national economies (Robertson, 2013). Creating a "Great Dream" of homeownership within a property-owning democracy was a central concern of many settler-societies following the Second World War. Today, baby boomers that became homeowners in Australia between 1970 and 1990 have, not surprisingly, greater holdings of wealth than any generation since (Dufty-Jones and Rogers, 2015). They also have greater holdings of wealth than the baby boomers that did not purchase real estate or become homeowners between 1970 and 1990 (Dufty-Jones and Rogers, 2015; Jacobs, 2015, in-press). Post-war housing and economic policy, ideas about nationhood and citizenship, and the responsibility to be a suburban consumer of the industrial home were worked deeply into the bodies of twentieth-century real estate citizens (Ferguson, 2008). Those who bought into the "Great Dreams" of homeownership between 1970 and 1990 were rewarded with economic growth at the level of the nation states as well as individual real estate capital growth at the level of the home.

During peacetime, however, the physical territorial borders of many settler-societies slowly started to loosen up, again, to allow new forms of human and financial capital to move more readily across their regulatory, physical, and later, cultural borders. As the memory of the Second World War faded, a different set of politico-territorial and economic conditions and policies started to emerge, which were based on new cultural ideas like multiculturalism, and economic ideas like reopening the nation state to international (free) trade. The changing cultural, economic, and regulatory conditions meant that real estate could be claimed in new ways, while some of the older ways of claiming real estate were becoming less viable. What emerged, then, at the end of the twentieth century, was a suite of old and new crises in land and real estate. The crisis of Indigenous land rights rose to the surface within several settler-societies as the settler geopolitics of claiming, regulating, and defending the land and real estate, which was originally stolen (in one way or another) from Indigenous people, was called into question (Porter, 2010, 2014). As the populations grew and the effects of the property-owning democracy took hold in major capital cities around the world, a crisis in housing affordability emerged in many so-called global cities (e.g., London, New York, Sydney, Vancouver, and Hong Kong). By the late 2000s and early twenty-first century, it was becoming increasingly harder, by a long measure, for the children of the baby boomers to buy into the real estate market in the settler-societies they lived in, especially when compared with the experience of their parents (Dufty-Jones and Rogers, 2015). Then the geopolitical rise of Asia at the end of the twentieth century, and the rise of China in particular, augmented the way human and financial capital would hereinto circulate around the world. As the baby boomers in settler-societies were busy buying real estate in the second half of the twentieth century, the land revolutions were underway in China. The collectivisation of land may have effectively removed the land from the private property market, for a time, but it would be radically reinserted a few decades later. Strong private property land and real estate mentalities emerged from the other side of the Cultural Revolution as the privatisation and commodification of land and real estate became a key technic for building wealth in China. The "surplus" Chinese capital would break free of the national borders by the end of the century. The newly enfranchised middle class and super-rich Chinese, along with their much discussed real estate mentalities, looked for foreign real estate opportunities. Thus, as the baby boomer real estate dream was coming to an end in the 1980s and 1990s, the Asian (and BRICS) local and foreign real estate dreams were still in their infancy. By 2015, Asian foreign real estate investment was the new real estate crisis in many global cities around the world, and it is easy to blame the baby boomers or Asian investors for the crisis of housing affordability in these cities. However, as argued in Chapter 1, this was just a semblance of a much larger geopolitical crisis in land and real estate.

Keith Jacobs (2015: 53–54) argues that housing scholars in settler-societies often develop arguments that attribute real estate crisis to a failure of government policy implementation; "policies fail – we are led to believe – because of factors such as bureaucratic inertia and mismanagement." Jacobs contends that "addressing the systemic causes" that will shape the next real estate crisis is only a priority for governments when the crisis will affect real estate owners and investors. Governments' main real estate objective is to protect "the wealth and opportunities for profit for homeowners and investors. In this regard, governments, while not operating as a monolithic agency, nonetheless have been largely successful in concealing the contradictions that are a salient feature of existing housing policy" (Jacobs, 2015: 53–54). Governments only act when it will affect their real estate *panem et circenses*.[1] Real estate consumption appears to be an activity that is undertaken by individual agents who have the capacity to act rationally and to think objectivity about that activity. However, as we have seen, this turns out to be a mere semblance of the agency and subjective capacities of the real estate investor. Governments and other historical actors have used the real estate investment practices of various populations as a tactic to build colonial or national economies. Real estate is the twenty-first-century *panem et circenses* because it keeps the citizenry occupied with mortgages and focused on capital gains. Meanwhile, the *real* land and real estate power and geopolitics is being mobilised underneath this semblance of individual freedom, consumption, and progress. It is an effective means of quieting public discontent about housing discrimination or political opposition to policy settings that largely benefit land and real estate owners, because the real estate mentality implicates large sways of the citizenry in the activity in question. It also implicates them in the negative social outcomes that stem from that activity and mentality. For example, one of the reasons why governments have failed to address the housing affordability "crises" in global cities is that they often fail to *try* to address the crisis. As if to confirm Jacobs's (2015) claim, the recent Australian Treasurer refused to acknowledge the broad public sentiment that Sydney had a housing affordability problem, saying that rising real estate prices were positive for the Australian economy and real estate owners. The Treasurer's comment reflected the Great Australian Dream of a prior era and a different geopolitical moment when he stated, "A lot of people would much rather have their homes go up in value rather than fall in value … if housing were unaffordable in Sydney, no-one would be buying it. … The starting point for a first home buyer is to get a good job that pays good money. … Then you can go to the bank and you can borrow money" (Clarke and Bennett, 2015: 1). Buying and selling real estate is a part of the national project of nation- and citizen-building, but it is also a part of the contemporary *panem et circenses* of settler-societies. We need to look beyond real estate crises in the contemporary nation state to the historical geopolitics of land and real estate more broadly if we are to address the land and real estate challenges that beset the contemporary and will beset the future city.

In this book, I set out to look beyond the semblances of the familiar and recognisable real estate crises in contemporary settler-society cities – two of the current being housing affordability and individual foreign real estate investment in residential real estate. There is, as we have seen, a long history of land and real estate crises. The vignettes in this book show how these crises took shape and how they were assembled from many different practices, mentalities, discourses, technologies, geographies and politics of land and real estate. The aim of the book was to create an anticipatory forward-looking analysis of the geopolitics of land and real estate, to identify, if possible, the subterranean technics, mentalities, technologies, and discourses that have accumulated within the practices of land and real estate claiming over an extended time period. There were certainly many synergies and intersections across the diverse vignette material presented in this book. In this final section, I look forward to the future city and outline just three of the more pressing subterranean themes that emerge from across the vignettes: (1) land and real estate mentalities, (2) crisis: as opportunity, and (3) real estate geopolitics.

MENTALITIES: LAND AND REAL ESTATE

The first consistent subterranean theme that is evident across the historical and contemporary vignettes is the observation that the geopolitical practices of land and real estate are heavily reliant on collective land and real estate mentalities. The body is an important technology that is involved in the transmission of subjective ideas (mentalities) about land and real estate, but it is also centrally involved in the material processes (materialities) of bringing different land and real estate realities into being. Changing a subjective real estate or land mentality is extremely hard, and it takes concerted and ongoing subjective work to develop the mentality as well as the cultural maintenance to enliven it. Simondon (2006: 17) was right to argue that the technical mentality must already be present in the cognitive schema of the actor before an event takes place. There are many examples of this in the vignettes, including the one noted above about developing the great dream of home-ownership as a real estate mentality.

The oral songlines and land-telling traditions of Indigenous people in Australia are also telling. The land mentalities of Indigenous peoples in Australia have a very long history. There are strict cultural rules and norms about how the subjective transmission of these ideas about land can be disclosed and transferred from one body to another. The cultural maintenance of these land mentalities involves ritual practices that are material too, such as those that define what might occur at a particular site. This was – is – and always will be – the *context of all contexts* when it comes to land and real estate mentalities in Australia. It is the subterranean theme that enframes every land-claiming or real estate activity in Australia and many other settler-societies. Of course, at different historical moments Indigenous peoples assemble their oral songlines in different ways. Their practices change with the prevailing geopolitical conditions, and that is why we see different subject(ive)-body-object-event assemblages at different points in time. At one point in history an Indigenous person might be performing an oral story about land in *country* using an object such as didgeridoo. At another moment in time an Indigenous person might be recalling an oral story about land in *a court of law* using an object such as legal text written on paper, as in the Mabo case. While the way the subjective-body, object, and event are assembled might be different, both contribute to the cultural maintenance of the same land mentality over time. That is why settlers have worked so hard to marginalise this deep reality about Indigenous land in Australia, because this land mentality radically and continually undermines their successive claims to the land. Australia's history is full of cases where colonial settlers (Adolphus Elkin and William Stanner) or contemporary settlers (John Howard and Keith Windschutte) attempted to use Cartesian-inspired and European-framed narratives about land to produce counter narratives about land claiming in Australia. These attempts to recode Indigenous land mentalities are an attempt to "displace subjectivity" and, therefore, expose the land biases, norms, values, and mentalities of the recoding settlers (Berry and Pawlik, 2005: 2).

By comparison, the land revolution in China is revealing because it shows how the Communist Party sought to recode a collective land mentality over the top of a long-standing feudal land mentality. The Communist Party understood that changing the land mentality of poor peasants would take a broad, ongoing, and fiercely focused social programme of subjective recoding and maintenance through land occupation and use. Considering it took thousands of years for the Indigenous land mentalities to develop, the Communist Party had set itself a very short timeline to re-educate the population. As outlined in the vignette, the peasant body was used as the technology and the site through which the land revolution would be mobilised, and the party used a recoding technology that already held a central place in the collective coding of subjectivities in Chinese villages – the village acting group. The problem for the

Communist Party was that the peasants had no knowledge of alternative land systems. Therefore, they used the peasants' social experiences at the hands of the landowners to manipulate their thoughts about the landed gentry. These dramatic performances and storytelling at the village level presented stories about despot landlordism and land reform, with landlords portrayed as land oppressors and the peasantry as exploited and landless. These events were focused on changing the land mentalities of the audience, and reconfiguring land and body as a technological tool that could be mobilised in the land revolution. However, when the revolution did take place, and the peasants claimed the land from the landlords, some peasants' actions demonstrated how hard it was to recode the old feudal land mentality in the bodies of the peasants. Some peasants, still clearly operating under a feudal land mentality, reverted to the behaviour that they had been taught to rally against in the village dramas, such as using physical and sexual violence, extortion, and bribery. This reminds us how difficult it is to recode a land or real estate mentality.

The Juwai case shows how the prevailing real estate mentalities are integrated into a far more complex subjectivity-body-object-event assemblage. In this case, the global real estate professionals and foreign investors were assembled with books, smartphones, and global real estate data within an increasingly diverse array of real estate encounters. These events and technologies have been purposely designed to work across the legal frameworks and the cultural and linguistic frontiers of different nation states; the very boundaries and barriers that restricted trans-cultural and transnational real estate sales after the Second World War. The real estate technology entrepreneurs are building tech products that have libertarianist, private property, and market-centric mentalities built into the software of their tech products. This is significant, because we are at the beginning of a global digital expansion of the residential real estate industry, and millions of residential homes are being uploaded for sale onto thousands of Internet-enabled real estate platforms around the world.

The lessons about land and real estate mentalities for contemporary and future land and real estate practices are, therefore, threefold. First, changing a subjective real estate or land mentality is an extremely difficult task, and one that takes a lot of cultural and/or political will, in addition to a very long time to build it into a collective mentality that might endure over time. Second, land and real estate mentalities stick closely to the prevailing geopolitics, and it is hard to work outside the prevailing land or real estate mentality. Third, land and real estate mentalities are shaped by culture, but essentialised notions of culture do not bind them. This is important empirically, because a *culture of* private property in a society is a good indicator that many citizens will have private property mentalities. The implication of the latter point is that we should investigate the cultures and mentalities of land and property that transcend any essentialised cultural identities, such as being "Chinese," "Australian," "British," or "American." These essentialised cultural identities turn out to be unproductive as analytical categories for understanding the importance of the collective land and real estate mentalities of a particular political community. For example, twenty-first-century "Eastern" and "Western" foreign real estate investors are better analysed as a political community that have *converging* real estate mentalities. Furthermore, it is not enough to challenge the dominant land or real estate mentality of a given epoch with another land or real estate mentality. Rather, the new land or real estate mentality needs to be written into the bodies of the subjects involved; it needs to be recoded over the top of the dominant land or real estate mentality for it to have any material effects. For example, a real estate owner might say they want to address housing affordability in their city, so long as it does not affect the price of their real estate investment. To move beyond this unresolvable tension, a new way of conceiving of housing is needed. If real estate "value" is the operative term in the discussion, there is little room to implement a material change in the urban landscape. However, the vignettes demonstrate that introducing an alternative real estate mentality, say land as common property, is no easy task. In the contemporary climate it would take, at the very least, a significant commitment from government and a mass public education programme to recode the real estate mentalities of the population.

CRISIS: AS OPPORTUNITY

The second consistent subterranean theme that runs across the historical and contemporary vignettes is that land or real estate crises further embed the prevailing organising technics of land or real estate into society, rather than reworking the technic to address the failings or switching to another technic. This is important because the prevailing organising technics of land or real estate in the vignettes often contributed to crises in land or real estate. Furthermore, when the crisis is over, some of the organisations and sectors that were directly implicated in the crisis emerge to benefit from the reconfiguring of technics, technologies, and practices that the crisis produced.

In the case of Indigenous oral land-storying practices, and the material land practices that sit alongside it, the settler-colonists brought with them a new set of rationalist-legal land mentalities, practices, technologies, and discourses that created a land catastrophe for Indigenous peoples. It was the introduction of a new set of legal land mentalities and technologies for measuring and dividing up the land, and law courts within which new legal stories about the land as individual property could be told and enforced, that initially created the binary tension between settler-colonial and Indigenous notions of land. However, after a long struggle to have the claiming of Indigenous land by settlers acknowledged by some of the settlers themselves, the logical next course of action should have been, at a minimum, to review the land-claiming event and to make sure that it never happens again. Indeed, a more morally focused course of action might have allowed Indigenous peoples to decide how they would like to use the land moving forward. What happened in the past, much like what happens today, is that the settlers press forward with their own land mentalities, practices, technologies, and discourses, and in a perverse move, they even present their organising technics of land as the solution to the land crisis they created. The Australian government is still intervening in the land and cultural practices of Indigenous peoples today (Porter, 2010, 2014; Stringer, 2007).

Banks are not benevolent organisations and they have a long history of contributing to real estate crises only to be reimagined after the crisis as one of few organisations that is capable of providing a solution. In the United States, banks have a particularly disturbing history of evicting poor citizens from their land and homes. Consider the mass eviction of the tenant farmers from the land during the Great Depression. In this case, the new land mentalities of the United States came together with new farming machinery from the industrial revolution, unfavourable weather over a number of years, and a banking sector that was actively foreclosing on failing loans. The crisis in land and failing loans had been created in part by the banking sector itself, and in this case, many of the banks failed along with the landowners. The Global Financial Crisis was a different story. The banking sector used their newly created banking practice of "securitisation," whereby a bank is allowed to originate loans and then repackage and sell them on to another lender, to create a whole suite of loans that explicitly targeted low-income Americans. The banking practice was, of course, implicitly underwritten by the government as a strategy to bring the Great American Dream of home-ownership to poor Americans. Mortgage brokers hit the streets and targeted low-income, poor, and often black neighbourhoods with low-documentation and NINJA (no-income–no–job–or–asset) home loans. Families with poor credit histories were explicitly targeted. The crisis now known as Subprimia, when it did hit, was nowhere near as devastating for the people who believed in the land mentalities, banking technologies, and fractional accounting algorithms, as it was for the people who were holding the loans.

The real tragedy of the Subprimia crisis is that, in time, the real estate and other sectors reimagined the Global Financial Crisis as an opportunity. Many of the poor families that took out these loans never should have been given home loans in the first place. They were sold a scaled down version of the Great American property-owning dream that was, perhaps, always doomed to fail. Some of their repossessed homes, in the neighbourhoods where real estate markets survived, were marketed as "distressed" real estate and a "bargain" in the new post-Global Financial Crisis economy. While the Great American Dream of home-ownership was fracturing from the bottom-up in the United States, over in the Asia-Pacific the CEO of one of the world's largest international real estate sales websites was talking about another opportunity to come out of the Global Financial Crisis. While people were losing their jobs and homes in Europe and the United States, the Chinese had money to spend on international real estate. So again, the banking and the real estate sectors shifted their focus in search of a new source of real estate capital and investors.

The lessons about reimagining land and real estate crises as an opportunity for contemporary and future land and real estate practices speak directly to the way complex assemblages of material, embodied, and discursive technologies form and function. The globalising real estate and banking sectors create complex financial tools and technical practices that can go on to produce amazingly simple real estate "brutalities" (Sassen, 2014: 220), such as evicting poor Americans from their homes *en masse*. While these sectors are built from complex assemblages of material, embodied, and discursive technologies, they can be guided by a simpler set of mentalities about private property, improvement, speculation, minimal government, and capital accumulation.

REAL ESTATE GEOPOLITICS

The third consistent subterranean theme that runs across the historical and contemporary vignettes is that real estate and land claiming is shaped by the geopolitical moment. The Feudal period, Colonial period, the First World War, the Second World War, and the post-war period were all implicated in land and real estate practices. The new geopolitical moment is being defined by the rise of China. We are already seeing major changes in the real estate practices that will come to be associated with this geopolitical moment. I want to conclude with some reflections on the rise of the global real estate industry, because individual foreign real estate investment is at the forefront of public and policy debate in global cities around the world. However, little attention has been paid to the mediating role of the global real estate industry. As the vignette on Juwai showed, what is often conceptualised as occurring at the "global-level," such as the global real estate sales events that Juwai runs, is very much an event that involves embodied actors and actions within particular sites. There is a productive utility in letting go of rigid notions of scale in an analysis of the geopolitics of foreign real estate investment. This industry is made up of transnational sales agents, international property developers, international real estate publishers, foreign home loan brokers, global investment lawyers, and immigration and visa consultants. In one sense, these diverse actors are working in the spaces between nation states. In another sense, they are very much locally emplaced, people who are a part of a much broader assemblage of different mentalities, technologies, bodies, localities, regions, nation states, and global flows of human and financial capital. Those who work in this industry are, nonetheless, engaged in embodied everyday actions in different locations in the world economy. It is true that these global real estate professionals are partly networked together through a suite of transnational real estate practices and new electronic real estate technologies. However, it is their everyday life, and the different topologies of power that they work within, the power structures that are constantly changing, that makes this industry an important sector to research.

The border, understood as a physical territorial frontier that can be secured with physical force, as it was understood by the actors in many of the vignettes presented within this book, is no longer a useful notion for investigating the global real estate industry. Neither is the political border, which can no longer be completely secured by political legitimacy or government regulation. The global real estate industry is actively assisting investors to exploit visa, taxation, and investment loopholes in foreign countries. This means that we must be critical of conceptualisations of foreign investors as invasive, as occasionally occurs in media discourse and public debate in western settler-societies. More correctly, foreign investors are being drawn into complex geopolitical assemblages, which are "constituted by" real estate and financial professionals and given authority by governments within the translocal spaces within many nation states.

Foreign real estate investment occurs not only as the latest example of settler-societies moving human and financial capital around to underwrite their real estate consumer economies, but more precisely because completely securing the physical and political borders of modern settler-societies is now impossible. Settler-societies are involved in an ongoing negotiation between the cultural, territorial, political, and economic configurations of their borders, and this negotiation is being directed by what is happening "on the ground." But not only what is happening on the ground in one settler-society, but what is happening on the ground across many nation states. The emergence of this translocal polity of foreign real estate investors and professionals has also coincided with the rise of the Internet as the new platform for buying and selling real estate. By utilising new digital media technologies to link settler-society real estate with foreign buyers, the global real estate professionals are implicated in producing a new type of foreign investor. Real estate investors and professionals are also implicated in the complex assemblages of embodied, linguistic, textual, numerical, and electronic interactions. There is a need to understand the incremental reconfiguration of local real estate as property, the increasing mobility of Asian (and other BRICS) capital, the movement of human bodies, and the increasing tensions between domestic and foreign investment property rights, not to mention questions of Indigenous land. These global real estate intermediaries are using their newly developed real estate practices and technologies (Rogers, 2016a) to link different real estate, immigration, education and financial actors and systems together in new ways (Rogers et al., 2015). Middle class global real estate professionals are even eulogising global super-rich investors and capital (also see Dorling, 2014; Paris, 2013) to promote a global real estate mentality through their practice (Rogers, 2016a).

Looking forward, therefore, the new global real estate industry is building a translocal network that draws on many of the organising technics, real estate mentalities, knowledge systems, and real estate practices that created significant housing inequity over a long timeline. These globalising real estate technicians are not presently spurring on creative innovation for more democratic technics of housing and land. They are not testing new technics that might address the increasingly unaffordable housing landscapes in many global cities around the world. They are not using technology to imagine or discover innovative ways to retool real estate and housing so that it is more equitable and freedom creating, which are the ideals that the Internet was supposedly built upon. The real estate tech entrepreneurs are uploading the local real estate technics and mentalities, which created significant housing inequity and exacerbated housing disadvantage in the second half of the twentieth century, as international real estate technics for the twenty-first century. The market-centric, libertarian real estate technicians of the twenty-first century, much like technicians of earlier periods, could negatively affect global housing equity.

NOTE

1. The metonymy "Bread and Circuses" (*panem et circenses*) is attributed to the Ancient Roman practice of appeasing the citizenry. It refers to the political practice of keeping the citizenry busy and entertained – and seemingly content – by providing expensive food and entertainment as a means of quieting public discontent and, therefore, political opposition. Juvenal (circa 100AD) *Satire X*. Available at: http://www.thelatinlibrary.com/juvenal/10.shtml.

References

"A". (1835) Real estate as an investment (author unknown but listed as "A"). In: Buel J. (ed.) *The Cultivator, a Monthly Publication Designed to Improve the Soil and the Mind.* New York: The New York Agricultural Society.

Acuto M. and Curtis S. (2013) Assemblage thinking and international relations. In: Acuto M. and Curtis S. (eds.) *Reassembling International Theory.* New York: Palgrave MacMillan.

Acuto M. and Curtis S. (2013) Reassembling International Theory. In: Acuto M. and Curtis S. (eds.) *Reassembling International Theory: Assemblage Thinking and International Relations.* New York: Palgrave MacMillan.

Adam J. T. (1931) *The Epic of America,* New Brunswick: Translation Publishers.

Adams M. (2015) *Land: A New Paradigm for a Thriving World,* Berkeley: North Atlantic Books.

Adelman J. and Aron S. (1999) From Borderlands to Borders: Empires, Nation-States, and the Peoples in between in North American History. *The American Historical Review* 104: 814–841.

Anderson B. (2014) *Encountering Affect: Capacities, Apparatuses, Conditions,* Surrey: Ashgate.

Anderson B., M. Kearnes, C. McFarlane and D. Swanton (2012). "On assemblages and geography." *Dialogues in Human Geography* 2(2): 171–189.

Anderson F. (2006) *The War That Made America: A Short History of the French and Indian War,* New York: Penguin Books.

Anderson K. (1987) The Idea of Chinatown: The Power of Place and Institutional Practice in the Making of a Racial Category. *Annals of the Association of American Geographers* 77: 580–598.

Anderson K. (1990) "Chinatown Re-orientated": A Crical Analysis of Recent Redevelopment Schemes in a Melbourne and Sydney Enclave. *Australian Geographical Studies* 28: 137–154.

Anderson K. (1995) *Vancouver's Chinatown: Racial Discourse in Canada, 1875–1980,* Kingston: McGill-Queen University Press.

Ang I., Tambiah Y. and Mar P. (2015) *Smart Engagement with Asia: Leveraging Language, Research and Culture*. Melbourne: ACOLA.

Ashcraft A., Bech M. L., and Frame W. S. (2010) The Federal Home Loan Bank System: The Lender of Next-to-Last Resort? *Journal of Money, Credit and Banking* 42: 551–583.

Australia-China Council. (2012) *Submission to the Australian in the Asian Century White Paper*. Barton: Australia-China Council.

Australian Bureau of Statistics. (2010) *Level of Homeownership*. Available at: http://www.abs.gov.au/ausstats/abs@.nsf/Lookup/bySubject/1370.0~2010~Chapter~Levels of home ownership (5.4.3).

Australian Bureau of Statistics. (2011) *2011 Census Reveals One in Four Australians is Born Overseas*. Available at: http://abs.gov.au/websitedbs/censushome.nsf/home/CO-59.

Australian Bureau of Statistics. (2012) *Homeowners and Renters*. Available at: http://www.abs.gov.au/ausstats/abs@.nsf/Lookup/bySubject/1301.0~2012~Main Features~Home Owners and Renters~129.

Australian Bureau of Statistics. (2014) *TALKIN' 'BOUT OUR GENERATIONS: Where are Australia's Baby Boomers, Generation X & Y and iGeneration?* Available at: http://www.abs.gov.au/ausstats/abs@.nsf/Latestproducts/3235.0FeatureArticle12014?opendocument&tabname=Summary&prodno=3235.0&issue=2014&num=&view=Australian Gov. (2012) Australia in the Asian Century. Canberra: Commonwealth of Australia.

Australian Government. (2012) *Significant Investor Visa*. Canberra: Department of Immigration and Citizenship.

Australian Government. (2012, 2013, 2014, 2015) *Foreign Investment Review Board – Annual Report*. Canberra: Foreign Investment Review Board.

Bachelard G. (1969) *The Poetics of Space*, Boston: Beacon.

Bagshaw E. (2014) Singaporean Investors Hungry for a Piece of the Australian Housing Market. *The Sydney Morning Herald*. Sydney: Fairfax.

Bailyn B. (1995) *History in Context*, Melbourne: La Trobe University.

Baldwin R. and Martin P. (1999) *Two Waves of Globalisation: Superficial Similarities, Fundamental Differences*. Tubingen: Institute of World Economics.

Barlow J. P. (1996) *A Declaration of the Independence of Cyberspace*. Available at: https://projects.eff.org/~barlow/Declaration-Final.html.

Baum A. and Hartzell D. (2012) *Global Property Investment: Strategies, Structures, Decisions*, Oxford: Wiley & Sons.

Belich J. (2009) *Replenishing the Earth: The Settler Revolution and the Rise of the Anglo-World, 1783–1939*, Oxford: Oxford University Press.

Bennett J. (1988) *Divided Circle: A History of Instruments for Astronomy, Navigation and Surveying*, Hachette: Phaidon.

Bennett L., Smith J., and Wright P. (2006) *Where are Poor People to Live?: Transforming Public Housing Communities*, New York: M. E. Sharpe.

Benston G. and Harland J. (1990) *Separation of Commercial and Investment Banking*, Hampshire: Palgrave Macmillan.

Bermingham A. (1986) *Landscape and Ideology: The English Rustic Tradition, 1740–1860*, Berkeley: University of California Press.

Berry D. and Pawlik J. (2005) What is Code? A Conversation with Deleuze, Guattari and Code. *Kritikos: An International and Interdisciplinary Journal of Postmodern Cultural Sound, Text and Image* 2: 1–17.

Berry J., McGreal S., and Scales P. (1999) Pacific Rim cities: the relationship between planning systems, property markets and real estate investment. In: Berry J. and McGreal S. (eds.) *Pacific Rim: Planning Systems and Property Markets*. London: E & FN Spon.

Blainey G. (1993) The Black Armband epithet, Sir John Latham Memorial Lecture (appeared as "Drawing up a balance sheet of our history"). *Quadrant* 37: 10–15.

Boldrewood R. (1890) *The Squatter's Dream: A Story of Australian Life*, London: MacMillan.

Bourassa S., Greig A., and Troy P. (1995) The Limits of Housing Policy: Home Ownership in Australia. *Housing Studies* 10: 83–104.

Bowra C. (1937) The Proem of Parmenides. *Classical Philology* 32: 97–112.

Braidotti R. (2013) *Posthuman*, Cambridge: Polity.

Brenner N. (2014) *Implosions/Explosions: Towards a Study of Planetary Urbanization*, Berlin: Jovis.

Brick X. (2015) *BrickX*. Available at: http://www.brickx.com.

Bryane M. (2003) Theorising the Politics of Globalisation: A Critique of Held et al.'s "Transformationalism". *Journal of Economic & Social Research* 5: 3–17.

Buchan B. and Heath M. (2006) Savagery and Civilization: From Terra Nullius to the "Tide of History". *Ethnicities* 6: 5–26.

Buchanan I. (2012) Symptomatology and Racial Politics in Australia. *Rivista Internazionale di Filosofia e Psicologia* 3: 110–124.

Burrows R. and Savage M. (2014) After the Crisis? Big Data and the Methodological Challenges of Empirical Sociology. *Big Data & Society* 1.

Butler J. (1997) *Excitable Speech: A Politics of the Performative*, New York: Routledge.

Butler T. and Lees L. (2006) Super-gentrification in Barnsbury, London: Globalization and Gentrifying Global Elites at the Neighbourhood Level. *Transactions of the Institute of British Geographers* 31: 467–487.

Butlin N. (1994) *Forming a Colonial Economy: Australia 1810–1850*, Cambridge: Cambridge University Press.

Brumby J. (2011) Chinese investment an opportunity, not a threat. *Australia-China Business Week*.

Buckley, P., J. Clegg, A. Cross, X. Liu, H. Voss and P. Zheng (2010). The determinants of Chinese outward foreign direct investment. *Foreign Direct Investment, China and the World Economy*. P. Buckley. Basingstoke, Palgrave Macmillan: 81–118.

Buckley P., Cross A., Tan H., et al. (2010b) Historic and emergent trends in Chinese outward direct investment. In: Buckley P (ed.) *Foreign Direct Investment, China and the World Economy*. Basingstoke: Palgrave Macmillan.

Büdenbender M. and Golubchikov O. (2016) The Geopolitics of Real Estate: Performing State Power via Property Markets? *International Journal of Housing Policy*, In-Press.

Burrows R. and Savage M. (2014) After the Crisis? Big Data and the Methodological Challenges of Empirical Sociology. *Big Data & Society* 1.

Butt P. (2010) *Land Law*, Sydney: Thomson Reuters.
Cain P. and Hopkins A. (1993) *British Imperialism, 1688–2000*, London: Longman.
Calvert L. (2015) *Chinese Investors Drive Up Property Prices In Major World Cities*. Available at: http://www.homesabroad.co.uk/news-story/chinese_investors_drive_up_property_prices_in_major_world_cities-29/.
Calwell A. (1947) *How Many Australians Tomorrow?* Available at: http://www.multiculturalaustralia.edu.au/doc/calwell_2.pdf.
Cassirer E. (1930) *Form und Technik*, Hamburg: Felix Meiner Verlag.
Castells M. (1996) *The Rise of the Network Society, The Information Age: Economy, Society and Culture Vol. I*, Oxford: Blackwell.
Castells M. (1997) *The Power of Identity, The Information Age: Economy, Society and Culture Vol. II*, Oxford: Blackwell.
Castells M. (1998) *End of Millennium, The Information Age: Economy, Society and Culture Vol. III*, Oxford: Blackwell.
Cavanagh E. and Veracini L. (2013) Editors Statement. *Settler Colonial Studies* 3.
Chan A. (2009) *Orientalism in Sinology*, Palo Alto: Academic Press.
Chancellor J. (2012) Property Portal The homepage Now Offers Chinese Language Listings. *Property Observer*, Melbourne: Property Observer.
Chancellor J. (2013) *Pressing the Right Chinese Button for Australian Real Estate Sales*. Melbourne: Property Observer.
Chua B-H. (1997) *Political Legitimacy and Housing: Singapore's Stakeholder Society*, Abingdon: Routledge.
Clark P. (2008) *The Chinese Cultural Revolution: A History*, Cambridge: Cambridge University Press.
Clarke F. (2002) *The History of Australia*, London: Greenwood Press.
Clarke M. and Bennett J. (2015) "Get a good job": Joe Hockey accused of insensitivity over advice to first-home buyers. *ABC NEWS*. Canberra: ABC NEWS.
Clinton W. (1995) Public Papers of the Presidents of the United States: William J. Clinton 1995. Washington: United States Government Priniting Offfice.
Clitheroe P. (1995) *Making Money: The Keys to Financial Success (ed.1)*, Ringwood: Penguin.
Clitheroe P. (1998) *Making Money: The Keys to Financial Success (ed.3)*, Ringwood: Penguin.
Clune D. and Turner K. (2009) *The Governors of New South Wales 1788–2010*. Annandale: The Federation Press.
Coase R. and Wang N. (2013) *How China Became Capitalst,* Basingstoke: Palgrave Macmillan.
Cohen L. (2004) A Consumers' Republic: The Politics of Mass Consumption in Postwar America. *Journal of Consumer Research.* Oxford University Press/USA, 236–239.
Collins D. (1798). An Account of the English Colony in New South Wales. *Digital Text, University of Sydney Library*. Volume 1 - Complied by Permission, From the Mss. of Lieutenant-Governor King. p. i - 489.
Connor J. (2002) *The Frontier Wars, 1788–1838*, Sydney: University of New South Wales.
Console Group. (2015) *Solutions for Real Estate Agents*. Available at: http://www.onthehousegroup.com.au/.

Corry O. (2013) Global assembalges and structural models of international relations. In: Acuto M. and Curtis S. (eds.) *Reassembling International Theory: Assemblage Thinking and International Relations*. New York: Palgrave MacMillan.

Corelogic. (2014) *Corelogic Announces Completeion of RP Data Acquisition*. Available at: http://www.corelogic.com/about-us/news/corelogic-announces-completion-of-rp-data-acquisition.aspx.

Coulthard G. (2014) *Red Skin, White Masks: Rejecting the Colonial Politics of Recognition*, Minneapolis: Minnesota Press.

Cowen D. and Smith N. (2009) After Geopolitics? From the Geopolitical Social to Geoeconomics. *Antipode* 41: 22–48.

Crabtree L. (2013) Decolonising Property: Exploring Ethics, Land and Time through Housing Interventions in Contemporary Australia. *Environment and Planning D: Society and Space* 31: 99–115.

Crafts N. (2000) *Globalisation and Growth in the Twentieth Century*. New York: International Monetary Fund.

Crider R. (2013) Promoting Economic: Development Through Foreign Investment. *Economic Development Journal* 12: 23–29.

Croxton D. (1999) The Peace of Westphalia of 1648 and the Origins of Sovereignty. *The International History Review* 21: 569–591.

Cullen J. (2004) *The American Dream: A Short History of an Idea that Shaped a Nation*, Oxford: Oxford University Press.

Darcy M. (2012) From high-rise projects to suburban estates: Public tenants and the globalised discourse of deconcentration. *Cities*, 35, 365–372.

Darcy M. and Rogers D. (2014) Inhabitance, Place-making and the Right to the City: Public Housing Redevelopment in Sydney. *International Journal of Housing Policy* 14: 236–256.

Darcy M. and Rogers D. (2015) Place, Political Culture and Post-Green Ban Resistance: Public Housing in Millers Point, Sydney. *Cities* iFirst.

Davis J. (1905) *Corporations: A Study of the Origin and Development of Great Business Combinations and of their Realtion to the Authority of the State*, G. P. Putnam's sons: London.

de Tocqueville A. (1835) Democracy in America. London: Saunders and Otley.

DeLanda M. (2000) *A Thousand Years of Nonlinear History*, Massachusetts: The MIT Press.

DeLanda M. (2006) *A New Philosophy of Society: Assemblage Theory and Social Complexity*, New York: Continuum.

Deleuze G. (1971) *Lecture: Capitalism, Flows, the Decoding of Flows, Capitalism and Schizophrenia, Psychoanalysis, Spinoza*. Available at: http://deleuzelectures.blogspot.com.au/2007/02/capitalism-flows-decoding-of-flows.html.

Deleuze G. (1986/2012) *Foucault*, Minneapolis: University of Minneapolis Press.

Deleuze G. (1991) *Empiricism and Subjectivity: An Essay on Hume's Theory of Human Nature*, New York: Columbia University Press.

Deleuze G. and Guattari F. (1987) *A Thousand Plateaus: Capitalism and Schizophrenia*, London: University of Minnesota Press.

Deleuze G. and Guattari F. (2004) *Anti-Oedipus: Capitalism and Schizophrenia*, London: Bloomsbury Academic.

DeMare B. (2007) *Turning Bodies and Turning Minds: Land Reform and Chinese Political Culture, 1946–1952* (unpublished thesis). Los Angeles: University of California.

DeMare B. (2015) *Mao's Cultural Army: Drama Troupes in China's Rural Revolution*, Cambridge: Cambridge University Press.

Descartes R. (1644) *Principia philosophiae (Principles of Philosophy)*. Translation with explanatory notes by Valentine Rodger and Reese P. Miller (Reprint ed. 1991). Dordrecht: Reidel.

Dirlik A. (2003) Global Modernity?: Modernity in an Age of Global Capitalism. *European Journal of Social Theory* 6: 275–292.

Dittmer J. (2013) Geopolitical Assemblages and Complexity. *Progress in Human Geography* 38: 385–401

Dittmer J. and Gray N. (2010) Popular Geopolitics 2.0: Towards New Methodologies of the Everyday. *Geography Compass* 4: 1664–1677.

Dittmer, J. and J. Sharp (2014). General Introduction. In: J. Dittmer and J. Sharp (eds.) *Geopolitics: An introdcutory Reader*. London: Routledge.

Dorling D. (2014) *Inequality and the 1%*, London: Verso.

Douglas D. and Dybvig P. (1983) Bank Runs, Deposit Insurance, and Liquidity. *Journal of Political Economy* 9: 401–419.

Dowd K. and Timberlake R. (1998) *Money and the Nation State: The Financial Revolution, Governement and the World Monetary System*. London: Transaction Publishers.

Dufty-Jones R. (2016) Housing and home: objects and technologies of neoliberal governmentalities. In: Springer S., Birch K. and MacLeavy J. (eds.) *Handbook of Neoliberalism*. London: Routledge.

Dufty-Jones R. and Rogers D. (2015) Housing in Australia: A new century. In: Dufty-Jones R. and Rogers D. (eds.) *Housing in 21st-century Australia: People, Practices and Policies*. London: Routledge, 1–20.

Džankić J. (2010) "Transformation of citizenship in Montenegro: a context-generated evolution of citizenship policies" (working paper). Edinburgh: School of Law, University of Edinburgh.

Džankić J. (2012) *The Pros and Cons of ius Pecuniae: Investor Citizenship in Comparative Perspective*. St. Louis: Federal Reserve Bank of St Louis.

Easley R. (2009) *The Emancipation of the Serfs in Russia: Peace Arbitrators and the Develpment of Civil Society*, London: Routledge.

Edgington D. W. (1996) Japanese Real Estate Investment in Canadian Cities and Regions, 1985–1993. *Le Géographe canadien* 40: 292–305.

Elden S. (2013) *The Birth of Territory*, Chicago: University of Chicago Press.

Elkin A. (1932) Social Organization in the Kimberley Division, north-western Australia. *Oceania* 2: 296–333.

Ellul J. (1954) *The Technological Society*, Toronto: Vintage Books.

Ellul J. (1981) *A temps et à contretemps*, Paris: Centurion.

Engel & Völkers. (2014) *Practical Knowledge for Sales Advisors*. Available at: http://www.engelvoelkers.com/company/academy-further-training-education/academy-video-my-life.

Ermarth, E. (2010). "What If Time Is a Dimension of Events, Not an Envelope for Them?" *Time & Society* 19(1): 133–150.
Ermarth, E. (2011). *History in the Discursive Condition: Reconsidering the Tools of Thought*. London: Routledge.
Fairclough N. (1992) *Discourse and Social Change*, Cambridge: Policy Press.
Fairclough N. (2003) *Analysing Discourse*, London: Routledge.
Fairclough N. (2004) Critical discourse analysis in researching language in the new capitalism: Overdetermination, transdiciplinarity, and textual analysis. In: Young L. and Harrison C. (eds.) *Systemic Functional Linguistics and Critical Discourse Analysis: Studies in Social Change*. London: Continuum.
Featherstone D. (2011) On Assemblage and Articulation. *Area* 43: 139–142.
Feng L. (2009) *Landscape and Power in Early China: The Crisis and Fall of the Western Zhouu 1045–771 BC*, Cambridge: Cambridge University Press.
Ferguson N. (2008) *The Ascent of Money: A Financial History of the World*, London: Penguin Press.
Fitzgibbons A. (1995) *Adam Smith's System of Liberty, Wealth, and Virtue: The Moral and Political Foundations of The Wealth of Nations*, Oxford: Clarendon Press.
Forbes. (2015) *#205 Richard LeFrak & family*. Available at: http://www.forbes.com/profile/richard-lefrak/.
Foucault M. (1966) *The Order of Things*, London: Routledge.
Foucault M. (1969) *The Archaeology of Knowledge*, Oxon: Routledge.
Foucault M. (1975) *Discipline and Punish: The Birth of the Prison*, London: Penguin.
Foucault M. (1980) Power/knowledge: Selected interviews and other writings 1972–1977. Complied by Gordon C. (ed.). New York: Pantheon Books.
Foucault M. (1997) The birth of bio-politics. In: Radinow P. (ed.) *Michel Foucault*, New York: New York Press.
Foucault M. (2001) Michel Foucault: The hermeneutics of the subject - Lectures at the College de France 1981–1982. Complied by Gros F., Ewald F., and Fontana A. (eds.). New York: Picador.
Foucault M. (2011) The government of self and others - Lectures at the College de France 1982–1983. Complied by Gros F., Ewald F., and Fontana A. (eds.). New York: Picador.
Foucault M. and Miskowiec J. (1986) Of Other Spaces. *Diacritics* 16: 22–27.
Franks R. and Cook P. (1996) *The Winner-Take-All Society: Why the Few at the Top Get So Much More Than the Rest of Us*, New York: Penguin.
Freudenburg G. (2013) *For the Record: Gough Whitlam's Mission to China, 1971*, Sydney: Whitlam Institute.
Friedman T. (2009) The Open-Door Bailout. *Wall Street Journal*. New York: News Corp. Available at: http://www.nytimes.com/2009/02/11/opinion/11friedman.html?_r=0.
Friedman M. (1963) *A Monetary History of the United States, 1867–1960*. Princeton University Press.
Frost R. (1923) *The Gift Outright*. New York: Henry Holt and Company
Galster G. (2012) *Driving Detroit: The Quest for Respect in the Motor City*, Philadelphia: University of Pennsylvania Press.
Gauder M., Houssard C., and Orsmond D. (2014) *Foreign Investment in Residential Real Estate*, Sydney: Reserve Bank of Australia - Bulletin.

Geldard R. (2007) *Parmenides and the Way of the Truth*, Rhinebeck: Monkfish.
Giedion S. (1948) *Mechanization Takes Command: A Contribution to Anonymous History*, Oxford: Oxford University Press.
Glucksberg L. (2016) A view from the top. *City* 20: 238–255.
Goodman D. and Chant C. (1999) *European Cities & Technology: Industrial to Post-industrial City*, London: Routledge.
Gottliebsen R. (2012) Chinese buying Hits Unprecedented Levels in Sydney, Melbourne and Brisbane, Providing an Iron Hand under Housing. *Business Spectator*. Melbourne: Business Spectator. Available at: http://www.propertyobserver.com.au/forward-planning/investment-strategy/economy-and-demographics/16163-an-iron-hand-under-housing-as-chinese-buying-hits-unprecedented-levels-robert-gottliebsen.html.
Graziosi B. (2002) *Inventing Homer: The Early Reception of Epic*, Cambridge: Cambridge University Press.
Grigg A. (2015) How Aussie-born Juwai property portal beat its giant competitors in China. *Australian Financial Review*. Sydney: Fairfax. Available at: http://www.afr.com/brand/boss/how-aussieborn-juwai-property-portal-beat-its-giant-competitors-in-china-20150415-1mljxs.
Grubisa D. (2014a) Real estate rescues: How to profit in real estate in the new economy. In: Zadel S. (ed.) *The New Way to Make Money in Property Fast!*. Sutherland: Zadel Property.
Grubisa D. (2014b) *Real Estate Riches Down Under: How to Make a Fortune Investing in the Australian Property Market*, Belrose: Global Property Education.
Hajdu J. (2005) *Samurai in the Surf: The Arrival of the Japanese on the Gold Coast in the 1980s*, Canberra: Pandanus Books.
Hamilton G. (1996) Overseas Chinese capitalism. In: Tu W. (ed.) *Confucian Traditions in East Asian Modernity: Moral Education and Economic Culture in Japan and the Four Mini-dragons*. Harvard: Harvard University Press, 328–342.
Haraway D. (1983) A Cyborg Manifesto: Science, Technology, and Socialist-Feminism in the Late Twentieth Century. *(1991) Simians, Cyborgs and Women: The Reinvention of Nature*. New York: Routledge, 149–181.
Harding W. (1922) *Better Homes in America*. Available at: http://www.encyclopaedia.com/ebooks/17/59.pdf.
Harman G. (2013) Conclusions: Assemblage theory and its future. In: Acuto M. and Curtis S. (eds.) *Reassembling International Theory: Assemblage Thinking and International Relations*, New York: Palgrave MacMillan.
Harvey D. (2005) *A Brief History of Neoliberalism*, Oxford: Blackwell.
Hatton T. and Williamson J. (1998) *Age of Mass Migration*, Oxford: Oxford University Press.
Hatton T. and Williamson J. (2008) *Global Migration and the World Economy: Two Centuries of Policy and Performance*, London: MIT Press.
Hay I. (2013) *Geographies of the Super-rich*, Northampton: Edward Elgar Publishing.
Hayek F. (1944) *The Road to Serfdom*, London: Routledge.
Hayek F. (1948) *Individualism and Economic Order*, Chicago: University of Chicago.
Haylen A. (2014) *House Prices, Ownership and Affordability: Trends in New South Wales*, Sydney: NSW State Parliament.

Heidegger M. (1977) *(2013) The Question Concerning Technology and Other Essays*, London: Haper Perennial.

Henry S. (2015) *LinkedIn: Simon Henry 冼明*. Available at: https://www.linkedin.com/in/simonjhenry.

Hewitt R. (2010) *Map of a Nation: A Biography Of The Ordnance Survey*, London: Granta Books.

Hinton W. (1966) *Fanshen: A Documentary of Revolution in a Chinese Village*, New York: Monthly Review Press.

Hoel A. S. and Tuin I. (2012) The Ontological Force of Technicity: Reading Cassirer and Simondon Diffractively. *Philosophy & Technology* 26: 187–202.

Hoorn J. (2007) *Australian Pastoral: The Making of a White Landscape*, Fremantle: Fremantle Press.

Hoppe H-H. (1993 (2006)) *Economics and Ethics of Private Property*, Alabama: Ludwig von Mises Institute.

Hulse K. and Burke T. (2015) Private rental housing in Australia: Political inertia and market change. In: Dufty-Jones R. and Rogers D. (eds.) *Housing in Twenty-First Century Australia: People, Practices and Politics*, Aldershot: Ashgate.

Hyam R. and Janda M. (2014) Chinese property investment to be examined as House Economics Committee reviews foreign investment laws. *ABC NEWS*, Sydney: Australian Broadcasting Commission.

Hyatt D. (2005) Time for a change: A critical discoursal analysis of synchronic context with diachronic relevance. *Discourse & Society* 16: 515–534.

Isin E. and Ruppert E. (2015) *Being Digital Citizens*, London: Rowman & Littlefield.

Jackson R. (1970) Owner Occupation of Houses in Sydney 1871 to 1891. *Australian Economic History Review* 10: 138–154.

Jacobs J. (1996) *Edge of Empire: Postcolonialism and the City*, London: Routledge.

Jacobs K. (2015) A Reverse Form of Welfarism: Some Reflections on Australian Housing Policy. *Australian Journal of Social Issues* 50: 53–68.

Jacobs K. (in-press) *Housing: a Post War History*, London: Rougtledge.

Jacques M. (2012) *When China Rules the World: The End of the Western World and the Birth of a New Global Order*, New York: Penguin.

Javorcik B., Özden Ç., Spatareanu M., et al. (2011) Migrant Networks and Foreign Direct Investment. *Journal of Development Economics* 94: 231.

Jenkins K. (1991) *Re-thinking History*, Oxon: Routledge.

Jicai F. (1996) *Ten Years of Madness: Oral Histories of China's Cultural Revolution*, San Francisco: China books and periodicals.

Johnson K. (2014) Buying the American Dream: Using Immigration Law to Bolster the Housing Market. *Tennessee Law Review* 81: 829–876.

Jones Lang LaSalla. (2014a) *Investment Outlook, Global Amibitions: Los Angeles Becomes a New Focal Point for Chinese Capital and Development*, New York: Jones Lang LaSalla, 1–12.

Jones lang LaSalla. (2014b) *London proves to be the biggest magnet for Chinese commercial and residential investors in 1H 2014*. Available at: http://www.joneslanglasalle.com.cn/china/en-gb/news/438/london-proves-to-be-the-biggest-magnet-for-chinese-commercial-and-residential-investors-in-1h-2014.

Jones W. (2003) Trying to understand the current Chinese legal system. In: Hsu S. (ed.) *Understanding China's Legal System.* New York: New York University Press.
Juvenal. (circa 100AD) *Satire X.* Available at: http://www.thelatinlibrary.com/juvenal/10.shtml.
Juwai. (2014) *Juwai.* Available at: list.juwai.com.
Juwai. (2014) *Juwai.* Available at: list.juwai.com.
Kalkreuth S. (2014) Europe Calling. *Palace: Asia's Elite Property Showcase.* Singapore: Heart Media.
Kazanjian D. (1967) *The Colonizing Trick: National Culture and Imperial Citizenship in Early America,* Minneapolis: University of Minnesota Press.
Keen A. (2015) *The Internet is Not the Answer,* London: Atlantic Books.
Kelder D. (1998) *Masters of the Modern Tradition: Selections From the Collection of Samuel J. And Ethel Lefrak,* New York: LeFrak Organisation.
Kelly P. (2006) A critique of critical geopolitics. *Geopolitics* 11: 24–53.
Kemeny J. (1983) *The Great Australian Nightmare: a Critique of the Home-ownership Ideology,* Melbourne: Georgian House.
Kennedy, R., J. Zapasnik, H. McCann and M. Bruce (2013). "All Those Little Machines: Assemblage as Transformative Theory." *Australian Humanities Review* 55: 45–66.
Keynes JM. (1919) *The Economic Consequences of the Peace,* New York: Harcourt.
King George III. (1763) The Proclamation of 1763.
Kirby J. (2002) *Investing for Dummies: Identify and Manage the Best Investment for You,* Milton: Wiley Publishing Australia.
Kittler F. (1995) "Nachwort," in Aufschreibesysteme 1800/1900. In Metteer M. and Cullens C. (eds.) *English as Discourse Networks 1800/1900.* Munich. Stanford: Stanford University Press
Kittler F. (2002) *Optical Media,* Cambridge: Polity Press.
Kline W. (2001) *Building a Better Race: Gender, Sexuality, and Eugenics from the Turn of the Century to the Baby Boom,* Berkeley: University of California Press.
Knowles C. (2014) *Flip-Flop: A Journey Through Globalisation's Backroads,* New York: Pluto Press.
Kohler M. and Rossiter A. (2005) *Property Owners in Australia: A Snapshot,* Sydney: Reserve Bank of Australia.
KPMG. (2012) *Demystifying Chinese Investment.* KPMG and University of Sydney. Sydney
Krell A. (2002) *The Devil's Rope: A Culutral History of Barbed Wire,* London: Reaktion.
Kruse K. (2007) *White Flight: Atlanta and the Making of Modern Conservatism,* Princeton: Princeton University Press.
Kunt M. and Woodhead C. (1995) *Suleyman the Magnificent and His Age: The Ottoman Empire in the Early Modern World,* Oxon: Routledge.
Lanchester J. (2010) *Whoops! Why Everyone Owes Everyone and Noone,* New York: Simon & Schuster.
Lang C. (2011) Loosening Yuan Restrictions will Open Australia to Chinese Investors. *Property Observer.* Melbourne: Property Observer. Available at: http://www.

propertyobserver.com.au/finding/location/expat-and-international/13047-loosening-yuan-restrictions-will-open-australia-to-chinese-investors.html.

Langton M. (1999) Estate of mind: the growing cooperation between Indigenous and mainstream managers of North Australia landscapes and the challenge for educators and researchers. In: Havenman P. (ed.) *Indigenous Peoples' Rights in Australia, Canada and New Zealand*, Oxford: Oxford University Press, 71–87.

Langton M. (2000) Homeland, Sacred Visions and the Settler State. *Artlink* 20: 11–16.

Larner W. (2009) Neoliberalism. *International Encyclopedia of Human Geography*: 1: 374–378.

Latour B. (2005) *Reassembling the Social*, Oxford: Oxford University Press.

Latour B. (2007) Beware, Your Imagination Leaves Digital Traces. *Times Higher Literary Supplement* 6: 1–3.

Laurenceson J. (2008) Chinese Investment in Australia. *Economic Papers: A Journal of Applied Economics and Policy* 27: 87–94.

Lawson H. (1940) Settling on the land. In: Compiled by Angus and Robertson (eds.) *Prose Works of Henry Lawson*. Sydney: Halstead Press.

Lee A. (2001) *Picturing Chinatown: Art and Orientalism in San Francisco*, Berkeley: University of Calafornia Press.

Lefebvre H. (1991) *The Production of Space*, Oxford: Blackwell.

LeFrak R. and Shilling G. (2009) Immigrants Can Help Fix the Housing Bubble. *Wall Street Journal*. New York: News Corp. Available at: http://www.wsj.com/articles/SB123725421857750565

Lengel E. (2011) *Inventing George Washington: American's Founder, in Myth and Memory*, Sydney: Harper.

Ley D. (2011) *Millionaire Migrants: Trans-Pacific life Lines*, West Sussex: Wiley-Blackwell.

Ley D. (2015) Global China and the Making of Vancouver's Residential Property Market. *International Journal of Housing Policy* iFirst.

Life Magazine. (1957) *Integration troubles beset northern town: Its first Negros meet protests, then order, new friends prevail*.

Linklater A. (2014) *Owning the Earth: The Transforming History of Land Ownership*, London: Bloomsbury.

Locke J. (1689) *Two Treatises of Government*, London: Awnsham Churchill.

Lovekin D. (1991) *Technique, Discourse, and Consciousness*, Bethlehem: Lehigh University Press.

Lovitt W. (2013) Introduction. In: Heidegger M. (ed.) *The Question Concerning Technology and Other Essays*, London: Haper Perennial.

MacIntyre S. and Clarke A. (2004) *The History Wars*, Carlton: Melbourne University Press.

Macken L. (2014) Sydney expected to gain foreign buyers as Canada closes visa scheme. *Sydney Morning Herald*. Sydney: Fairfax.

Mackrell J. (2007) *The Attack on 'Feudalism' in Eighteenth Century France*, Toronto: University of Toronto Press.

MacMillan K. (2006) *Sovereignty and Possession in the English New World: The legal Foundations of Empire*, New York: Cambridge University Press.

Madden DJ. (2012) City Becoming World: Nancy, Lefebvre, and the Global—Urban Imagination. *Environment and Planning D: Society and Space* 30: 772–787.
Madrick J. (2012) *Age of Greed: The Triumph of Finance and the Decline of America, 1970 to the to the Present*, London: Penguin.
Magdoff F. (2008) Fanshen after forty years. In: Hinton W. (ed.) *1966, Fanshen: A Documentary of Revolution in a Chinese Village*. New York: Monthly Review Press.
Malabou C. (2015) Whither materialism? Althusser/Darwin. In: Bhandar B. and Goldberg-Hiller J. (eds.) *Plastic Materialities: Politics, Legality, and metamorphosis in the Work of Catherine Malabou*, Westchester: Duke University Press.
Malpas J. (2012) *Heidegger and the Thinking of Place: Explorations in the Topology of Being*, Cambridge: MIT Press.
Mankiw N. G., and Weil D. N. (1989) The Baby Boom, the Baby Bust, and the Housing Market. *Regional Science and Urban Economics* 19: 235–258.
Manne R. (2003) *Whitewash: On Keith Windschuttle's Fabrication of Aboriginal History*, Melbourne: Black Inc. Agenda.
Manyika, J., M. Chui, B. Brown, J. Bughin, R. Dobbs, C. Roxburgh and A. H. Byers (2011). Big data: The next frontier for innovation, competition, and productivity. New York: The McKinsey Global Institute.
Marx K. (1894) *Capital: A Critique of Political Economy (Volume I, Part III)*, New York: Cosimo Classics.
Marx K. (1983) Economico-philosophical manuscripts of 1844. In: Kamenka E. (ed.) *The Portable Karl Marx*. New York: Penguin.
Marx K. and Friedrich E. (1848) *The Communist Manifesto*, London: Penguin.
Mason M. (2014) Locals priced out by $24 billion Chinese property splurge. *The Sydney Morning Herald*. Sydney: Fairfax.
Massey D. (1992) Politics and space/time. *New Left Review* November–December: 65–84.
Massey D. (2005) *For Space*, London: SAGE Publications
Massumi B. (2009) "Technical mentality" revisited: Brian Massumi on Gilbert Simondon. *Parrhesia* 7.
Massumi B. (2011a) *Semblance and Event*, Cambridge: MIT Press.
Massumi B. (2011b) Tranalator's forward: Pleasures of Philosophy. In: Deleuze G. and Guattari F. (eds.) *A Thousand Plateaus: Capitalism and Schizophrenia (1987)*. Minnesota: University of Minnesota Press, ix–xv.
Mazzucato M. (2013) *The Entrepreneurial State: Debunking Public vs. Private Sector Myths*, New York: Anthem Press.
McCabe B. (2016) *No Place Like Home: Wealth, Community and the Politics of Homeownership*, Oxford: Oxford University Press.
McFarlane C. (2009) Translocal Assemblages: Space, Power and Social Movements. *Geoforum* 40: 561–567.
McLuhan M. (1967) *The Medium is the Massage: An Inventory of Effects*, New York: Bantam Books.
McNally L. (2015) *"Chinese invasion" leaflet campaign targeting foreign investors could fuel racism in Sydney, politicians fear*. Available at: http://www.abc.net.au/news/2015-05-29/chinese-invasion-leaflet-campaign-slammed-as-idiotic/6506412.

References

Menzies R. (1942) *The Forgotten People*. Available at: http://www.liberals.net/the-forgottenpeople.htm.

Mezzadra S. and Neilson B. (2013) *Border as Method, or, the Multiplication of Labor*, Durham: Duke Press.

Mills R. (1915) *The Colonisation of Australia (1829–42): The Wakefield Experiment in Empire Building*, Adelphi: Sidgwick & Jackson.

Millward S. (2014) *Right place at the right time: how two Australians created China's most perfect startup*. Available at: https://www.techinasia.com/story-juwai-overseas-property-portal-china/.

Mitcham C. (1994) *Thinking through Technology*, Chicago: University of Chicago Press.

Mitcham C. (2013) How the technological society became more important in the United States than in France. In: Jerónimo H., Garcia J. L., and Mitcham C. (eds.) *Jacques Ellul and the Technological Society in the 21st Century*. Dordrecht: Springer.

Mitchell W. (2004) *Me++ : The Cyborg Self and the Networked City*, Cambridge: MIT Press.

Mohr R. (2003) Law and Identity in Spatial Contests. *National Identities* 5: 53–66.

Morris C. (2014) *The Dawn of Innovation: The First American Industrial Revolution*, New York: PublicAffairs.

Moos M. (2010) The Globalization of Urban Housing Markets: Immigration and Changing Housing Demand in Vancouver. *Urban Geography* 31.

Movoto. (2014) *Real Estate through Time Infographic*. Available at: http://www.movoto.com/blog/infographic/real-estate-through-time-infographic/.

Mumford L. (1934) *Technics and Civilization*, Harcourt: Brace and Company.

Nayar P. (2004) ME++. *Journal for Cultural and Religious Theory* 5.

Newland S. (1888) *Our Waste Lands and our Productions*, Adelaide: Burden & Bonython, Advertiser Office.

Nicholls S. (2011) Chinese Millions - and a Loophole - Keep Luxury Home Market Buoyant. *Domain*. Melbourne: Fairfax. Available at: http://www.domain.com.au/news/chinese-millions-and-a-loophole-keep-luxury-home-market-buoyant-20110715-1hi4g/.

Nozeman E. and Van der Vlist A. (2014) *European Metropolitan Commercial Real Estate Markets*. Dordrecht: Springer.

Nozick R. (1974) *Anarchy, State, and Utopia*, London: Basic Books.

O'Farrell C. (2005) *Michel Foucault*, London: SAGE Publications.

Olds K. (2001) *Globalization and Urban Change: Capital, Culture and Pacific Rim Megaprojects*, Oxford: Oxford University Press.

Olson J. (1998) *Saving Capitalism: The Reconstruction Finance Corporation and the New Deal, 1933–1940*, Princeton: Princeton University Press.

Ong A. (2005) (Re)Articulations of Citizenship. *Political Science and Politics* 38: 697–699.

Ong A. (2006) *Neoliberalism as Exception: Mutations in Citizenship and Sovereignty*, London: Duke University Press.

Ong A. (2011) Worlding cities, or the art of being global. In: Roy A. and Ong A. (eds.) *Worlding Cities: Asian Experiments and the Art of Being Global*. Chichester: Wiley-Blackwell.

O'Rourke K. and Williamson J. (1999) *Globalization and History: The Evolution of a Nineteenth-century Atlantic Economy*, London: MIT PRess.

Olson J. (1977) *Herbert Hoover and the Reconstruction Finance Corporation, 1931–1933*, Iowa: Iowa State University Press.

Olson J. (1998) *Saving Capitalism: The Reconstruction Finance Corporation and the New Deal, 1933–1940*, Princeton: Princeton University Press.

Ortega JyG. (1939) Meditación de la técnica.

Ó Tuathail G. (1999) Understanding Critical Geopolitics: Geopolitics and Risk Society. *Journal of Strategic Studies* 22: 107–124.

Osborne P. (1995) *The Politics of Time: Modernity and Avant-Garde*, London: Verso.

Osiander A. (2001) Sovereignty, International Relations, and the Westphalian Myth. *International Organization* 55.

Our House Swap. (2015). "Our House Swap." Retrieved from https://ourhouseswap.com.au/.

Pain R. (2009) Globalized fear? Towards an Emotional Geopolitics. *Progress in Human Geography* 33: 466–486.

Paradies Y. C. (2006) Beyond Black and White: Essentialism, Hybridity and Indigeneity. *Journal of Sociology* 42: 355–367.

Paris C. (1993) *Housing Australia*, Melbourne: Macmillan Education Australia.

Paris C. (2011) *Affluence, Mobility and Second Home Ownership*, London: Routledge.

Paris C. (2013) The homes of the super-rich: multiple residences, hyper-mobility and decoupling of prime residential housing in global cities. In: Hay I. (ed.) *Geographies of the Super-rich*. Cheltenham: Edward Elgar.

Paterson B. (1902) *The Old Australian Ways*.

Patterson Forrester J. (1994) Mortgaging the American dream: A Critical Evaluation of the Federal Government's Promotion of the Home Equity Financing. *Tulane Law Review* 69: 373–456.

Peck J. (2010) *Constructions of Neoliberal Reason*, Oxford: Oxford University Press.

Peck J. and Tickell A. (2002) Neoliberalizing Space. *Antipode* 34: 380–404.

Pearce F. (2012) *The Landgrabbers: The New Fight Over who Owns the Earth*, London: Transworld Publishers.

Petrowski W. (1969) The Kansas Pacific Railroad in the Southwest. *Arizona and the West* 11: 129–146.

Petty G. (1967) Wakefield, Edward Gibbon (1796–1862). Australian Dictionary of Biography, National Centre of Biography, Australian National University.

Petty W. (1690) Political Arithmetick. In: Hull C. (ed.) *(1899) The Economics Writings of Sir William Petty Together with the Observations*. Cambridge: Cambridge at the University Press.

Piketty T. (2014) *Capital in the Twenty-First Century*, London: Harvard University Press.

Pile J. (2005) *A History of Interior Design*, London: Laurence King Publishing.

Porter L. (2010) *Unlearning the Colonial Cultures of Planning*, Farnham: Ashgate.

Porter L. (2014) Possessory Politics and the Conceit of Procedure: Exposing the Cost of Rights under Conditions of Dispossession. *Planning Theory* 13: 387–406.

Pow C-p. (2013) The world needs a second Switzerland: Onshoring Sinagpore as the liveable city for the super-rich. In: Hay I. (ed.) *Geographies of the Super-rich.* Cheltenham: Edward Elgar.

Property Observer. (2013) *Australia's Allure for Asian Residential propertyPInvestment*, Melbourne: Property Observer.

Ramthohul R. (2015) "High Net Worth" Migration in Mauritius: A Critial Analysis. *Migration Letter* 13: 17–33.

Ravina M. (1999) *Land and Lordship in Early Modern Japan*, Standford: Standford University Press.

Rawls J. (1971) *A Theory of Justice*, Cambridge: Harvard University Press.

Ray B., Halseth G., and Johnson B. (1997) The Changing "Face" of the Suburbs: Issues of Ethnicity and Residential Change in Suburban Vancouver. *International Journal of Urban and Regional Research* 21: 75–99.

REA. (2014) "Annual Report 2014". Melbourne: REA Group.

Reagan R. (1985) *Address to the Nation on Tax Reform*. Available at: http://www.presidency.ucsb.edu/ws/?pid=38697.

Ren X. (2013) *Urban China*, Cambridge: Politiy Press.

Reinhart C. and Rogoff K. (2008) Is the 2007 US Sub-prime Financial Crisis So Different? An International Historical Comparison. *American Economic Review* 98: 339–344.

Ricardo D. (1817) *On principles of Political Economy and Yaxation*, London: John Murry, Albemarle-Street.

Robbins P. and Marks B. (2010) Assemblage geographies. In: Smith S., Pain R., Marston S., et al. (eds.) *The SAGE Handbook of Social Geographies.* London: SAGE.

Robertson S. (2013) *Transnational Student-migrants and the State: The Education-migration Nexus*, Basingstoke: Palgrave Macmillian.

Robertson S. and Rogers D. (in-press) Education, Real Estate, Immigration: Brokerage Assemblages and Asian Mobilities. Journal of Ethnic and Migration Studies.

Robinson P. (1983) The Asianisation of Australia. *Sydney Morning Herald.* Sydney: Fairfax.

Rogers D. (2014) The Sydney Metropolitan Strategy as a Zoning Technology: Analyzing the Spatial and Temporal Dimensions of Obsolescence. *Environment and Planning D: Society and Space* 32: 108–127.

Rogers D. (2016a) Becoming a super-rich foreign real estate investor: globalising real estate data, publications and events. In: Forrest R., Wissink D., and Koh S. (eds.) *Cities and the super-rich: real estate, elite practices and urban political economies.* Basingstoke: Palgrave Macmillan.

Rogers D. (2016b) Uploading real estate: Home as a digital, global commodity. In: Cook N., Davison A. and Crabtree L. (eds.) *Housing and Home Unbound: Intersections in Economics, Enviroment and Politics in Australia.* London: Rougledge, 23–38.

Rogers D. and Darcy M. (2014) Global City Aspirations, Graduated Citizenship and Public Housing: Analysing the Consumer Citizenships of Neoliberalism. *Urban, Planning and Transport Research*, 2(1): 71–88.

Rogers D. and Dufty-Jones R. (2015) 21st Century Australian housing: New frontiers in the Asia-Pacific. In: Dufty-Jones R., and Rogers D. (eds.) *Housing* in *Twenty-First Century Australia: People, Practices and Policies.* Aldershot: Ashgate.

Rogers D., Lee C. L., and Yan D. (2015) The politics of foreign investment in Australian housing: Chinese investors, translocal sales agents and local resistance. *Housing Studies* i-First. Volume 30.

Rohrbough M. (1968) *The Land Office Business : The Settlement and Administration of American Public Lands, 1789–1837,* Volume 1, New York: Oxford University Press.

Rose-Redwood R. S. (2006) Governmentality, Geography, and the Geo-Coded World. *Progress in Human Geography* 30: 469–486.

Rosensweig J. (2010) *Winning the Global Game: A Strategy for Linking People and Profits,* New York: The Free Press.

Rousseau J-J. (1750) *Discourse on the Sciences and Arts,* Paris: Noël-Jacques Pissot.

Roy A. (2015) What is Urban About Critical Urban Theory? *Urban Geography* 1.

Ruming K. (2015) Reviewing the social housing initiative: Unpacking opportunities and challenges for community housing provision in Australia. In: Dufty-Jones R. and Rogers D. (eds.) *Housing in 21st-century Australia: People, Practices and Policies.* Farnham: Ashgate, 185–203.

Said E. (1978) *Orientalism,* London: Vintage Books.

Said E. (1993) *Culture and Imperialism,* London: Vintage.

Said E. (1999) *Out of place: A Memoir,* New York: Random House.

Said E. (2000) Invention, Memory, and Place. *Critical Inquiry* 26: 175–192.

Sassen S. (2006) *Territory, Authority, Rights: From Medieval to Global Assemblages,* Princeton: Princeton University Press.

Sassen S. (2014) *Expulsions: Brutality and Complexity in the Global Economy,* Cambridge: Belknap Press.

Schlesinger L. (2013) Chinese Online Searches for Australian Property up 61% as Macquarie Targets Significant Investor Visa Applicants. *Property Observer.* Melbourne: Property Observer. Available at: http://www.propertyobserver.com.au/forward-planning/investment-strategy/economy-and-demographics/22143-ytc-monday-april-29-news-chinese-searches-for-australian-property-up-61-juwai.html.

Schoolcraft H. (1854) *Information Respecting the History Conditon and Prospects of the Indian Tribes of the United States.* Bureau of Indian Affairs. Philadelphia: Lippincott, Grambo & Company.

Schumpeter J. (1927) The Explanation of Business Cycles. *Economica* 7: 286–311.

Schurmann F. (1968) *Ideology and Organisation in Communist China,* Los Angeles: University of California Press.

Schwartz Cowan R. (1976) The "Industrial Revolution" in the Home: Household Technology and Social Change in the 20th Century. *Technology and Culture* 17: 1–23.

Shachar A. and Bauböck R. (2014) *Should Citizenship be for Sale.* Italy: European University Institute.

Sharp J. (2007) Geography and Gender: Finding Feminist Political Geographies. *Progress in Human Geography* 31: 381–387.

Shaw K. (2015) Planetary Urbanisation: What Does It Matter for Politics or Practice? *Planning Theory & Practice* 16.

Shiller R. (2008) *The Subprime Solution: How today's Global Financial Crisis Happened, and What to Do About It*, Princeton: Princeton University Press.
Shook J. (2001) *The Chicago School of Functionalism*, 3. Bristol: Thoemmes Press.
Short J. (2013) Economic wealth and political power in the second Gilded Age. In: Hay I. (ed.) *Geographies of the Super-rich.* Northampton: Edward Elgar Publishing.
Simha R. K. (2012) *Colonialism 2.0.* Available at: http://in.rbth.com/articles/2012/03/11/colonialism_20_15086.
Simondon G. (2006) Mentalité Technique. *Revue philosophique de la France et de l'étranger* 131: 343–357.
Slavin M. (1986) *The Making of an Insurrection: Parisian Sections and the Gironde*, Cambridge: Harvard University Press.
Smith A. (1776) *The Wealth of Nations: An Inquiry into the Nature and Causes of the Wealth of Nations*, London: Methuen & Co.
Smith SJ. (2008) Owner-occupation: At Home with a Hybrid of Money and Materials. *Environment and Planning A* 40: 520–535.
Smyth W. (1919) Technocracy–Ways and Means to Gain Industrial Democracy. *Industrial Management.* 57 (March 1919): 208–212
Sobel D. (1995) *Longitude: The True Story of a Lone Genius Who Solved the Greatest Scientific Problem of His Time*, New York: Bloomsbury Publishing.
Spenglek O. (1931) *Man and Technics: A Contribution to a Philosophy of Life*, Munich: CH Beck Verlag.
Standing Committee on Economics. (2014) "Report on Foreign Investment in Residential Real Estate". Canberra: Commonwealth of Australia.
Stanley K. (2013) Eight reasons Chinese residential developers have emerged as a major force in the Australian market. *Property Observer.* Melbourne: Property Observer.
Stanner W. (1965) Aboriginal Territorial Organization: Estate, Range, Domain and Regime. *Oceania* 36: 1–26.
Steinbeck J. (1939) *The Grapes of Wrath,* New York: The Viking Press.
Stearns P. (1993) *The Industrial Revolution in World History*, Boulder: Westview Press.
Steele W. and Gleeson B. (2011) The Great Risk Shift: The Securitisation of Australian Housing. *Housing Studies* 26: 281–295.
Stern P. (2011) *The Comany-State: Corporate Sovereignty & the Early Modern Foundations of the British Empire in India*, Oxford: Oxford University Press.
Stier O. (2012) Understanding Chinese property buyers and sellers. *Property Observer.* Melbourne: Property Observer. Available at: http://www.propertyobserver.com.au/finding/residential-investment/15066-understanding-chinese-property-buyers-and-sellers.html
Storey K. (2016) *Settler Anxiety at the Outposts of Empire: Colonial Relations, Humanitarian Discourses and the Imperial Press*, Vancouver: UBC Press.
StreetSine Technology Group. (2014) *StreetSine Technology Group.* Available at: http://www.streetsine.com/.
Stringer R. (2007) A Nightmare of the Neocolonial Kind: Politics of Suffering in Howard's Northern Territory Intervention. *Borderlands.* November 19th: online.

Strobel H. (2008) *LeFrak, Samuel J.* Available at: http://www.anb.org/articles/20/20-01900.html.
Sumption M. and Hooper K. (2013) *Top 10 of 2013 – Issue #3: The Golden Visa: "Selling Citizenship" to Investors.* Available at: http://www.migrationpolicy.org/article/issue-no-3-golden-visa-selling-citizenship-investors.
Sumption M. and Hooper K. (2014) "Selling Visas and Citizenship: Policy Questions from the Global Boom in Investor Immigration". Washington, DC: Migration Policy Institute.
Supreme Court of New South Wales. (1833) MacDonald v Levy [8th March 1833]. Sydney: Sydney Herald (11th Macrh 1833).
Sutherland G. (1898) *South Australian Company: A Study in Colonisation*, London: Longmans, Green and Co.
Swanson J. and Williamson S. (1972) Estimates of National Product and income for the United States Economy, 1919–1941. *Explorations in Economic History* 10: 53–73.
Taylor A. (2012a) Four Tips to help You Sell Australian Property to Chinese Buyers. *Property Observer.* Melbourne: Property Observer. Available at: http://www.propertyobserver.com.au/forward-planning/investment-strategy/economy-and-demographics/19869-thursday-observer-how-to-sell-to-the-chinese-buyer-part-2.html.
Taylor A. (2012b) How to Sell Australian Property to the Savvy Chinese Investor: Juwai's Andrew Taylor. *Property Observer.* Melbourne: Property Observer. Available at: http://www.propertyobserver.com.au/forward-planning/investment-strategy/economy-and-demographics/19868-tuesday-observer-selling-to-chinese-buyers-part-1.html?start=1.
Taylor E. and Dalton T. (2015) Keynes in the Antipodes: The housing industry, first home owner grnats and the global financial crisis. In: Dufty-Jones R and Rogers D (eds.) *Housing in 21st-century Australia: People, Practices and Policies.* London: Routledge, 153–172.
Temple P. (2002) *A Sort of Conscience: The Wakefields,* Auckland: Auckland University Press.
The Anti-Eviction Mapping Project. (2015). "The Anti-Eviction Mapping Project." Retrieved from http://www.antievictionmap.com/about/.
The Internet Association. (2015) *We are the united voice of the Internet economy.* Available at: http://internetassociation.org/.
The Luxury Properties Showcase. (2014) *The Luxury properties Sshowcase.* Available at: http://shanghai.lps-china.com/.
Thrift N. (2008) *Non-Representational Theory: Space, Politics, Affect*, London: Routledge.
Tilley E. (2012) *White Vanishing: Rethinking Australia'sLlost-in-the-bush myth*, New York: Rodopi.
Tiwari P. and White M. (2010) *International Real Estate Economics,* Basingstoke: Palgrave Macmillan.
Tolstoy L. (1886) *How much land does a man need?* Available at: http://www.gutenberg.org/cache/epub/6157/pg6157.txt.
Trotman N. (2013) Schools Draw Chinese Buyers to Melbourne's Southeast. *Property Observer.* Melbourne: Property Observer.

Tseng Y-F. (2000) The Mobility of Entrepreneurs and Capital: Taiwanese Capital-Linked Migration. *International Migration* 38: 143–168.

Tufeki Z. (2012) We were always human. In: Whitehead N. and Wesch M. (eds.) *Human No More: Digital Subjectivities, Unhuman Subjects, and the End of Anthropology.* Colorado: University Press of Colorado, 33–48.

Tufeki Z. (2014) *Facebook and engineering the public.* Available at: https://medium.com/message/engineering-the-public-289c91390225.

Van Den Berg R. (2002) *Nyoongar People of Australia: Perspectives on Racism and Multiculturalism*, Leiden: Brill.

Van Fossen A. (2007) Citizenship for Sale: Passports of Convenience from Pacific Island Tax Havens. *Commonwealth & Comparative Politics* 45: 138–163.

Veracini L. (2013) "Settler Colonialism": Career of a Concept. *The Journal of Imperial and Commonwealth History* 41: 313–333.

Veracini L. (2015) Introduction: The Settler Colonial Present. *The Settler Colonial Present.* London: Palgrave Macmillan, UK, 1–12.

Virillio P. (2008) *Negative Horizon: An Essay in Dromoscopy*, London: Continuum.

Virillio P. (2009) *The Aesthetics of Disappearance*, Los Angeles: Semiotext(e).

Vlastos G. (1946) Parmenides' Theory of Knowledge. *Transactions and Proceedings of the American Philological Association* 77: 66–77.

von Mises L. (1912) *The theory of money and credit (Theorie des Geldes und der Umlaufsmittel),* Vienna: Jonathan Cape.

Tse-tung M. (1927) *Report on an investigation of the peasant movment in Hunan.* Available at: https://www.marxists.org/reference/archive/mao/selected-works/volume-1/mswv1_2.htm.

Wacquant L. (2008) *Urban Outcasts: A Comparative Sociology of Advanced Marginality,* Cambridge: Polity.

Wakefield E. (1829a) A Letter from Sydney, the Principal Town of Australasia.

Wakefield E. (1829b) Sketch of a proposal for colonizing Australasia.

Ware R., Fortin P., and Paradis P. (2010) *The Economic Impact of the Immigrant Investor Program in Canada.* Montreal: Analysis Group.

Washington, G., W. Crawford, V. Crawford and C. W. Butterfield (1877). *The Washington-Crawford letters. Being the correspondence between George Washington and William Crawford, from 1767 to 1781, Concerning Western Lands.*: Cincinnati: R. Clarke & Co.

Watson S. (1988) *Accommodating Inequality,* London: Allen and Unwin.

Weaver J. (2003) *The Great LandRush and the Making of the Modern World, 1650–1900,* London: McGill-Queen's University Press.

Webber R. and Burrows R. (2015) Life in an Alpha Territory: Discontinuity and conflict in an elite London "village". *Urban Studies.* pp. 1–21.

Whitlam G. (1985) *The Whitlam Government,* Melbourne: Penguin.

Whittaker N. (1995) *More Money with Noel Whittaker (ed.5),* East Roseville: Simon & Schuster.

Wicker E. (1996) *The Banking Panics of the Great Depression,* Cambridge: Cambridge University Press.

Williams J. and Williams E. (1940) New Techniques in Federal Aid. *American Political Science Review* 34: 947–954.

Wilson K. (2015) *First-mover Advantage.* Hong Kong: China Daily Asia.

Wilson R. (2012) Meaning making and the mind of the externalist. In: Menary R. (ed.) *The Extended Mind.* Cambridge: MIT, 167–188.
Windschuttle K. (2002) *The Fabrication of Aboriginal History*, Paddington: Macleay Press.
Winthrop-Young G. (2011) *Kittler and the Media,* Cambridge: Polity Press.
Wittgenstein L. (1922) *(1995) Tractatus Logico-Philosophicus*, London: Routledge.
Wolfe P. (2006) Settler Colonialism and the Elimination of the Native. *Journal of Genocide Research* 8: 387–409.
Wu F., Xu J., and Gar-On Yeh A. (2007) *Urban Development in Post-reform China: State, Market, and Space*, Abingdon: Routledge.
Xiao I. (2013) Tips for getting the most from Chinese property expos. *Property Observer.* Melbourne: Property Observer. Available at: http://www.propertyobserver.com.au/finding/location/expat-and-international/23217-wednesday-june-5-observer-esther-yong.html.
Zadel S. (2014) *The New Way to Make Money in Property Fast!*, Sutherland: Zadel Property.
Zhou C. (2013) "Chinese investors developing appetite for Sydney real estate". *ABC NEWS.* Sydney: ABC NEWS.
Zipreality. (2014) *About.* Available at: http://www.ziprealty.com/about_zip/index.jsp.
Žižek S. (2014) *Event: Philosophy in Transit,* London: Penguin.

Index

Aboriginal sacred, 42, 45
Adam, John, 81
Adams, James Truslow, 111
Adams, Martin, 5
Adelman, Jeremy, 77
agencement, 20
agricultural productive capacity, 79
alcheringa, 42
Alpha Territories, 4
Amazon, 148
The American Dream, 111
American Revolution, 70
Anarchy, State, and Utopia (Nozick), 89
Ancien Régime, 55
Anderson B., 21, 28, 31
The Anti-Eviction Mapping Project, 148
Anti-Traitor Movement, 58–60
Arara Abadi, 37
Aron, Stephen, 77
arpenteur-géomètre, 79
Arrente people, 42
Articles of Confederation, 86
Asian Financial Crisis, 9
Asian foreign investors. *See* baby boomers
Australia in the Asian Century document, 122–23
The Australian Agricultural Company, 75

Australian Bureau of Statistics, 135

Babeuf, François-Noël, 4
baby boomers, 18, 114, 117, 153, 155
Bailyn, Bernard, 4
Baldwin, Richard, 101–2
banking, and real estate technology, 91–100, 160
Barlow, John Perry, 139
Belich, James, 106
Bermingham, Ann, 52
Bermuda Company, 82n2
Berners-Lee, Tim, 139
Berry, David, 32
Better Homes Campaign, 112
BIP. *See* Business Immigration Programme (BIP)
Blaxland, Gregory, 44–45
Blue Mountains, 44–45
bodily capacities, 31
body, as technology, 27–28, 51, 68, 130–31, 156–59
Boldrewood, Rolf, 77
books, real estate technology, 117–24
bottom up process, 13
Brazil, Russia, India, China, and South Africa (BRICS), 6, 8, 123, 154, 163
BrickX, 137–38
British Empire, 36, 38

Buchanan, Ian, 47
Büdenbender, Mirjam, 9
Burke, T., 98
Business Immigration Programme (BIP), 127–28
Butler, Judith, 16
Butler, Tim, 101, 126

Calwell, Arthur, 118
Capital: A critique of political economy (Marx), 75
capital, and labour, 4–11, 101–7
capital gains, 104–5
Catherine II (Russian Empress, 1762–1796), 35
Cavanagh, Edward, 3
censitaires, 73
César-François Cassini de Thury, 84
Chicago School of Economics, 89–90, 96
Chinatown fire, 37–38
Chinese revolution, and land, 53–61
Chippewa, 44
citational practices, 16
citizenship, and real estate technology, 107–8
Clinton, Bill, 115–16
Clitheroe, Paul, 119–21, 123
coding, 32–35
cognitive schema, 24
Cohen, Lizabeth, 115, 117
Collins, David, 67
Colonialism 2.0, 6
colonialism, and land, 65–71
Commission of Editors of Homer, 41
commodity:
  land as, 77–81;
  real estate as, 143–49
Communist Eighth Army, 58
Communist Eight Route Army, 58
The Communist Manifesto (Marx and Engels), 4
Company of Merchant Adventurers to New Lands, 71–72
conceptual subterranean trends, 11

Connor, John, 67
Console Group, 143
Consumer Republic, 115–17
Continental Army, 70
convict transportation, 103
Cook, Philip, 139
CoreLogic, 141
Coulthard, Glen, 6
The Country Survey Book, 80
Cowen, Deborah, 13–14
Crabtree, Louise, 12
Crawford, William, 70
creation storytelling, 41–44
critical geopolitical scholarship, 12–13
Cromwell, Oliver, 91
Cromwell, Thomas, 48–49
the Crown, 72–73
The Cultivator, a monthly publication designed to improve the soil and the mind, 94
Cultural Revolution, 56, 61
cyberspace, 139–41

Davis, John, 71
A Declaration of the Independence of Cyberspace (Barlow), 139
decoding, 32–35
DeLanda, Manuel, 19–21
Deleuze, Gilles, 19–21, 26, 28, 30, 32, 34, 70
Deleuze–Guattarian-inspired assemblage theory, 13, 20
Deng Xiaoping, 122
Descartes, Rene, 120
determinism, technological, 25–26
de Tocqueville, Alexis, 86, 88, 104–5
Different Land Systems, 106
Discourse Networks 1800/1900 (Kittler), 33
discursive act/encoded performance, 62–63
discursive codes, 32–35, 68
Dittmer, Jason, 13, 28
domain.com.au, 143
Domesday Book, 50

Douglas, Diamond, 93
Draft Agrarian Law, 54
Draft Agrarian Law (1947), 60
Dreamtime *(time out of time),* 42–43
Dufty-Jones, Rae, 98
Dust Bowl, 1, 97
Dutch East India Company, 103
Dybvig, Philip, 93

Earl of Durham, 75
East India Company, 72
East India Company, 103
Efficiency Movement, 96
egalitarian lines, 86
Elden, Stuart, 5, 15, 50
Elkin, Adolphus, 42
Ellul, Jacques, 23, 25–26
embodied cultural capital, 128–29
embodied financial capital, 129
Emergency Quota Act, 125
Emergency Relief and Construction Act, 97
emigration, and land, 71–77
encoded performance/discursive act, 62–63
Engel and Völkers company, 146
Engels, Frederick, 4, 65
English Reformation, 49
Enlightenment, 23
The Epic of America (Adams), 111
Ermath, Elizabeth, 12, 15, 33–34
ethnographies, and real estate, 101–7
Euro-centrism, 7
events, real estate, 130–31
The Exact Surveyor, 80

Facebook, 148
Fairclough N., 16, 32
The Faithful Surveyor, 80
Fannie Mae, 98, 110–11
Fanshen: Documentary of the revolution in a Chinese Village (Hinton), 53
The Fanshen of Li Lanying, 54
FDI. *See* foreign direct investment (FDI)

Featherstone D., 31
Federal Home Loan Bank Act, 97
Federal National Mortgage Association. *See* Fannie Mae
Ferguson, Niall, 91, 98–99, 102, 111, 138
feudalism, and land, 48–53, 55, 71, 161
feudal landlord-tenant system, 57
FIRB. *See* Foreign Investment Review Board (FIRB)
first wave, 101
First World War, 101, 109, 110, 113
Flip-Flop. *See* rubber sandal
Folkes, Nick, 3–5
forced mass migration, 103
Ford Motor Company, 109
foreign direct investment (FDI), 7, 9–10, 17, 118–19, 162
Foreign Investment Advisory Committee, 122
Foreign Investment Review Board, 122
Foreign Investment Review Board (FIRB), 10
foreign land claiming, 13–14
The Forgotten People, 111
Foucault, Michel, 5, 12, 15, 18, 26–27, 29–30, 33–34, 135
Four Asian Tigers, 6, 123
Franks, Robert, 139
Freddie Mac, 98
French and Indian War, 70
French Revolution, 55
Friedman, Milton, 50, 90
Frost, Robert, 66

The Gate, 58, 61
Generation X, 136
geodesic triangulation, 84
geographic information system (GIS), 148
geopolitics:
history and silence, 35–39;
of real estate, 11–14, 161–63.
See also land; real estate
Georges III, King, 69

The Gift Outright (Frost), 66
GIS. *See* geographic information system (GIS)
Glass-Steagall Act, 98
Glaster, George, 98
global commodity, real estate as, 143–49
Global Financial Crisis, 7, 92, 96, 98–100, 125, 133, 160–61
globalisation, 2, 4–7, 9–12, 15–16, 18–19, 30, 101–2
glo-baloney, 101
Global Real Estate Project, 9, 121, 129, 144, 147
Goderich II, Viscount, 74
Golden Visa/Golden Ticket, 127
Golubchikov, Oleg, 9
Google, 148
Googlenomics, 142
Gorbachev, Mikhail, 86
Gouger, Robert, 74
grants, land, 73–74.
  See also Royal Charters
The Grapes of Wrath (Steinbeck), 1, 91
Great American Dream, 1, 99–100, 107, 111, 130, 153–54, 160–61
Great Australian Dream, 100, 107, 111, 116, 119, 121, 123, 129, 149, 155
The Great Australian Nightmare, 116
The Great Australian Nightmare (Kemeny), 113
Great Depression, 1, 92–93, 96–97, 110, 113, 160
Great Fire of London, 37
Great Firewall, 144
Greenspan, Alan, 90
Grigg, Angus, 136
Grubisa, Dominique, 100, 118, 120–21, 136
Guattari, Felix, 19–21, 30, 32, 34, 70
Guevara, Che, 37
Gupta, Shekhar, 125–26

Hamilton, G., 56
Haraway, D., 135

Harding, Warren, 112, 115
Harrington, James, 81
Harvey, David, 89
The Hatred of the Poor, 54
Hatton, Timothy, 102
Hayek, Friedrich von, 4, 89–90
Heidegger, Martin, 24, 28
Henry, Simon, 133–36, 144
Henry VIII, King, 48–50, 52
Hiawatha, 44
high-net-worth (HNW), 4, 8, 127
Hinton, William, 53, 56, 57, 59, 60
HNW. *See* high-net-worth (HNW)
Home Report™, 147
Hoover, Herbert, 96–97
Hoovervilles, 97
House of Commons, 52
housing policy, and real estate technology, 109–17
How much Land Does a Man Need? (Tolstoy), 36
Hulse, K., 98
Human Rights Watch report, 37
Hurun Wealth Report, 145

IDX. *See* Internet Data Exchange (IDX)
Immigrant Investment Visa, 8
Immigrants can help fix the housing bubble, 125
immigration, and real estate, 101–7
Immigration Act of 1924, 125
in capite (tenants-in-chief) tenurial system, 49–50
Inclosure Act 1773, 51
Inclosure Acts, 27, 31, 38, 48–53
indentured servitude, 103
Indian Rebellion, 68
industrial body and home, 110, 112, 115
industrialisation, and real estate, 87–88
Industrial Revolution, 55, 66, 102
instrumental task, 83
internal migratory practices, 105
Internet, and real estate, 133–38.
  See also specific types
The Internet Association, 148

Internet Data Exchange (IDX), 141
Investing for Dummies (Kirby), 117
investor-focused digital act, 143, 146–47
The Invisible Militia, 54
Isin, E., 138, 140, 142, 147, 149

Jacobs, Jane, 42
Jacobs, Keith, 98, 100, 155
Jacques, Martin, 7
James I, King, 71
Jefferson, Thomas, 38, 87
John M'Arthur v. Henry Kable, 95
Johnson, Kit, 124, 125, 130
joint-stock company, 76
Jones, W., 58–61
Journey to the West, 42
Juwai.com, 131, 133–34, 136–37, 142, 144–45, 148, 158, 161

Kansas Pacific Railroad, 106
Keen, Andrew, 139–40
Kemeny, Jim, 113–14, 116
Keynes, John Maynard, 101–2
Kirby, James, 117–18
Kittler, Friedrich, 25–26, 29, 33, 140
Knight Frank, 127
Knowles, Caroline, 13
kolkhozi (collectives), 36

labour:
  and capital, 4–11;
  and land, 71–77, 101–7
labour-saving devices, 110
Ladejinsky, Wolf Isaac, 36
Ladies' Home Journal, 109
Lamb II, William, 75–76
Lambing Flat riot, 118
Lambton, John, 75
land:
  and Chinese revolution, 53–61;
  and colonialism, 65–71;
  as commodity, 77–81;
  discursive act/encoded performance, 62–63;
  and emigration, 71–77;
  and feudalism, 48–53, 71, 161;
  grants, 73–74 (*See also* Royal Charters);
  and labour, 71–77;
  labour and capital, 4–11, 101–7;
  measurement, 77–81;
  mentalities, 156–59;
  and orality, 41–48;
  and ownership, 81–82;
  selling, 71–77;
  settling on, 1–4;
  surveying instruments, 78–80.
  See also real estate
Land: A new paradigm for a thriving world (Adams), 5
The Landgrabbers: The new fight over who owns the earth (Pearce), 5
landlordism, 55–56
Langton, Marcia, 43
Latour, Bruno, 13, 20, 30
Lawson, Henry, 66
Lawson, William, 44–45, 70
Lees, Loretta, 101, 126
LeFrak, Aaron, 125
LeFrak, Maurice, 124
LeFrak, Richard, 125–26
LeFrak, Samuel, 125
LeFrak Organisation, 125, 135
A Letter from Sydney, the Principal Town of Australasia (Wakefield), 74
Lévy-Bruhl, Lucien, 42
lex terrae, 74
Ley, David, 127–28, 130
libertarianism, 89–90, 138–43
Li Kashing, 130
Li Kashing's Cheung Kong Holdings, 130
Linklater, Andro, 3, 5, 37, 47, 48, 50, 52, 65, 75, 78, 80, 81, 84, 87, 88, 93, 98, 104–6
liquidity, 97, 124
LJ Hooker, 135, 143
Locke, John, 65
London Company, 71–72

Lord Melbourne. *See* Lamb II, William
Louisiana Purchase, 93
Louis XV, King, 84
Lovekin D., 24
LPS. *See* The Luxury Property Showcase (LPS) event
The Luxury Property Showcase (LPS) event, 130–31

Mabo vs. Queensland, 46–47, 62, 157
MacDonald v. Levy, 95
Making Money Made Simple (Whittaker), 119
Malpas, Jeff, 13
Māoris, 68
Mao Tse-tung, 53, 58–60, 122
Martin, Philippe, 101–2
Martindale, Adam, 80
Marx, Karl, 4, 26, 35, 55–56, 61, 65, 75–76, 89
Marxism, 25, 55, 60
mass-produced communiser goods, 109–10, 116
Massumi, Brian, 18–19, 24
May 4 Directive on Land Reform, 58
Mazzucato, Mariana, 140
McFarlane C., 31
McLuhan, Marshall, 29
measurement, of land, 77–81
mediating technologies, 27–32, 76
Medici family, 91
Meditation on Technics (Gasset), 25
Mehmed li Pasha, 36
Meiji emperor, 36
Menzies, Robert, 111
Mills, Richard, 76
Ming Dynasty, 42
Mises, Ludwig von, 89
Mitcham, Carl, 139
Mitchell W., 29, 34
Mogul Empire, 36
moments of crisis, 15–18
Monroe, James, 93
Move company, 140, 141

National Credit Corporation, 96
National Native Title Tribunal, 47
nation states, 84, 86, 162
Native Title Act 1993, 47
neoliberalism, 89
New Australians, 118
New Deal, 110
Newfoundland Company, 82n2
Newland, Simpson, 106–7
A New Philosophy of Society: Assemblage Theory and Social Complexity (DeLanda), 21
News Corp Australia, 141
The new way to make money in property fast! (Zadel), 100, 120
New York Agricultural Society, 94
New Zealand Colonisation Company, 75
The New Zealand Company, 75–76, 107
New Zealand Land Company, 75
NINJA (no-income–no–job–or–asset), 98, 160
Nixon, Richard, 122
Norman Kings, 74
Nozick, Robert, 89

Obwandiyag (Pontiac), 69
Odyssey (Homer), 41
O'Farrell C., 33
The Office of Surveyor General of Ireland, 77
Ojibwe, 44, 69
The Old Australian Way (Paterson), 66
ONE FM radio station, 147
Ong, Aihwa, 20–22, 126
Open Door policy, 122
orality, and land, 41–48, 157, 159
organising technics, 23–27, 68
Orientalism, 55
Ortega, y Gasset José, 25–26
Ottoman Land Code, 36
Ó Tuathail, Gearóid, 12
Our House Swap, 148
ownership, and land, 81–82
Owning the Earth (Linklater), 3

Pacific Commercial Advertiser (Storey), 67
Palace: Asia's Elite Property Showcase magazine, 123–24
paper-based technologies, 78, 80–81
Paris, C., 17, 114, 127
Parmenides, 41
Party Rectification. *See* The Gate
Paterson, Banjo, 66
path dependencies, 27
Pawlik, Jo, 32
Peace of Westphalia, 83
Pearce, Fred, 5
Pearl River Delta, 136
Peck, J., 89
The People's Drama Troupe, 54
Perry, T. M., 45
Peter the Great (Tsar of Russia, 1682–1721), 35–36
Petty, William, 4, 50–51, 65–66, 70, 77, 81, 91, 103
physical geographical demarcation, 79
Plymouth Company, 71–72
Political Arithmetick (Petty), 103
populist land reforms, 105
Porter, Libby, 6, 46, 47, 66
post-war housing, 153
professional-focused digital act, 143, 146–47
Property Life: Asia's No1 Property & Lifestyle Guide magazine, 123
property-owning democracy, 70, 83, 85, 88, 91, 94, 98, 110, 116, 154
Property Report: Luxury Real Estate, Architecture and Design magazine, 123
Proudhon, Pierre-Joseph, 4
Public Land Survey of America, 88

QOOS Limited, 136

Radical Jack. *See* Lambton, John
Rawls, John, 89
Reagan, Ronald, 90, 112
Reaganomics, 90

REA Group, 136, 141
real estate:
 citational practices of, 16;
 crisis moments, 15–18, 159–61;
 events, 130–31;
 geopolitics of, 11–14, 161–63;
 global citizenship, 124–30;
 as global commodity, 143–49;
 and globalisation, 2, 4–7, 9–12, 15–16, 18–19, 30, 101–2;
 individual foreign investment, 16–17;
 and industrialisation, 87–88;
 investment practice, 7–9;
 and libertarianism, 89–90, 138–43;
 mentalities, 156–59;
 panem et circenses, 153–63;
 and property-owning democracy, 70, 83, 85, 88, 91, 94, 98, 110, 116, 154;
 and revenue approach, 84–86;
 semblances and assemblages, 18–35;
 tech industry, 138–43;
 and Web 2.0, 149–51.
 See also land
Real Estate As An Investment, 94
Realestate.com.au, 135, 143
Real estate riches down under, 100
real estate technology:
 and banking sector, 91–100, 160;
 body as technology, 27–28, 51, 68, 130–31, 156–59;
 books, 117–24;
 and citizenship, 107–8;
 and creating housing consumer, 109–17;
 and cyborg, 133–38;
 and ethnographies, 101–7;
 events, 130–31;
 global citizenship, 124–30;
 and housing policy, 109–17;
 and Internet, 133–38;
 and labour-capital-land, 101–7;
 paper-based technologies, 78, 80–81;
 and state governments, 83–91;
 visas, 124–30

Real Estate Trade Management System, 141
Real Estate Transaction Standard (RETS), 141
recoding, 32–35, 44, 145, 158
Reconstruction Finance Corporation, 97–98
Redgrave, Jack, 77
Red Skins, White Masks: Rejecting the colonial politics of recognition (Coulthard), 6
Reinhart, Carmen, 98
RETS. *See* Real Estate Transaction Standard (RETS)
Ricardo, David, 65
The Road the Serfdom (Hayek), 5
Robert Jenkins, Esquire, v. William Kelly, 95
Rogoff, Kenneth, 98
Rohrbough, M., 80
Roosevelt, Franklin D., 110–11
Rousseau, Jean-Jacques, 4, 24
Roux, Jacques, 55
Roy, Ananya, 22
Royal Charters, 71–73, 75–76, 81, 82n1
Royal Proclamation of 1763, 69
RP Data, 141
rubber sandal, 13, 14n3
Ruming, K., 98
Ruppert, E., 138, 140, 142, 147, 149

SaaS. *See* software for a service (SaaS)
Said, Edward, 5, 41
Sassen, Saskia, 11, 20–22, 26–27
Schoolcraft, Henry, 44
Schumpeter, Joseph, 89
Schwartz Cowan, Ruth, 109
Second Sino-Japanese War, 58
Second World War, 2, 38, 56, 101, 111–13, 119, 153–54, 158, 161
securitisation, 98
seigneurial tenure, 73
self-generated dynamics, 105
semblances and assemblages, 18–35; discursive code, 32–35, 68;
mediating technologies, 27–32, 76; organising technics, 23–27, 68
Semblances and Event (Massumi), 18
settler-societies/settler-colonialism, 3–8, 10, 12, 36, 62, 65, 67–68, 70–71, 73–74, 78, 81–82, 85–86, 91–92, 95–96, 102–3, 106–7, 112, 129, 153, 156, 162
Settling of Accounts Movement, 58–59
Settling on the Land (Lawson), 66
Seven Years War, 69
Sharp, Joanne, 13
Shilling, Gary, 125–26
Shogunate, 36
Significant Investment Visa (SVI), 127
Simha, Rakesh Krishnan, 6
Simondon G., 24–25, 156
Singapore Real Estate Exchange (SRX™), 147
Sketch of a Proposal for Colonizing Australasia (Wakefield), 74
The SMART Investment & International Property Expo, 130
Smith, Adam, 4, 89–91
Smith, Neil, 13–14
Smith, Susan, 112, 136
software for a service (SaaS), 136
The Squatter's Dream: A Story of Australian life (Boldrewood), 77
Stanner, William, 42
state governments, and real estate technology, 83–91
Steinbeck, John, 1–2, 91–93, 97
Stephen, James, 76
Stern, Philip, 10, 72
Storey, Kenton, 67–68
StreetSine, 146–48
StreetSine Technology Group, 142
subject(ive)-body-object-event assemblage, 30–32
subjective task, 83
subject–object technologies, 29
subprimia crisis, 98, 160
Süleyman the Magnificent, 36
Sultan of Siak, 37

surveying instruments, 78–80
Sutherland, George, 105, 107
SVI. *See* Significant Investment Visa (SVI)
systematic colonisation, 74

Táin Bó Cúailnge (Linkater), 42
Tanzimat, 36
Taylor, Andrew, 133–34, 136
technical consciousness, 23
technical intention, 23
Technical Mentality (Simondon), 24
technical state of mind, 23
technological determinism, 25–26, 29
technology, body as, 27–28, 51, 68, 130–31, 156–59
telos, 16, 26
tenant-focused digital act, 143, 147
terra nullius, 45, 47, 66, 73, 74
territorial storytelling, 41–43, 66–67, 77, 157
Thatcher, Margaret, 90
Thatcherism, 90
A Theory of Justice (Rawls), 89
A Thousand Plateaus: Capitalism and Schizophrenia (Deleuze and Guattari), 19
Tips for getting the most from Chinese property expos: Ivy Xiao (Xiao), 145
Tolstoy, Leo, 36
Torrens Title system, 107
transportation technologies, 103
Treaty of Paris, 69, 73, 86
Treaty of Waitangi, 68
Tudor resistance, 51–52
Tufeki, Zeynep, 142

UHNW. *See* ultra-high-net-worth (UHNW)
ultra-high-net-worth (UHNW), 4, 8
ungoverned territory, 22
usury laws, 95

Valor Ecclesiasticus (church valuation document), 49

Vancouver housing market, 127
Van Diemen's Land Company, 75
Veracini, Lorenzo, 3
Virginia Regiment, 70
Virillio, Paul, 26
visas, and real estate technology, 124–30
vproperty Limited, 136

Wakefield, Edward Gibbon, 74–76, 78
Wang Gui and Li Xiangxiang, 54
Ward, Henry George, 76
War of 1812, 86
Washington, George, 70, 136
Washington Consensus, 89
Weaver, John, 2, 44–45, 47, 68, 73, 77, 78, 80, 81, 85, 86, 88, 92, 95, 97, 104, 105
Web 1.0, 140–43, 147
Web 2.0, 142, 147, 149–51
Wentworth, William Charles, 44–45, 77, 136
Westphalian sovereignty, 83–84
When China Rules the World (Jacques), 7
The White-Haired Girl, 54
Whitlam, Gough, 121–22
Whittaker, Noel, 119–21, 123
Williamson, Jeffrey, 102
William the Conqueror, 50
Wilson, R., 135
Winthrop-Young G., 26
Wittgenstein L., 35
Wolfe, Patrick, 6
World Wide Web, 139–40

Xiao, Ivy, 145
X-Value™, 147

Yahoo, 141
Yen-Fen Tseng, 128

Zadel, Stuart, 100, 120–21, 136
Zhou Enlai, 121

About the Author

Dallas Rogers is a research member of the *Institute for Culture and Society* and teaches into the *Urban Research Program* within the School of Social Sciences and Psychology, Western Sydney University. Dallas established the *Global Real Estate Project* to investigate the relationships between globalising urban space, discourse and technology networks, and housing poverty and wealth. With *Global Real Estate Project* collaborators from the National University of Singapore, University of Technology Sydney and Western Sydney University, he has undertaken numerous studies on the geopolitics and globalisation of real estate in the Asia-Pacific. He publishes on urban and housing issues in academic and industry journals, has appeared in domestic and international media, participated in a parliamentary briefing, and is regularly invited to speak at academic and professional forums. Dallas is interested in using digital media techniques to communicate research findings to non-academic audiences. His 2015 radio documentary *Searching for the Mousetribe, in the Confucian City* – a story about the urban poor in Beijing who call underground air raid bunkers their homes – was a part of the 2015 Festival of Urbanism. Please connect with Dallas on social media to share your research or to find out more about the *Global Real Estate Project:*

Web   https://dallasrogers.live
Twitter   @dallasrogers101